SOCIAL POLICY AND SOCIAL WORK

The Context of Social Work Practice

Prepared for the Silver School of Social Work of New York University

Dr. Gerald Landsberg   •   Dr. Marjorie Rock

Second Edition

Learning Solutions

New York   Boston   San Francisco
London   Toronto   Sydney   Tokyo   Singapore   Madrid
Mexico City   Munich   Paris   Cape Town   Hong Kong   Montreal

Pearson Learning Solutions, 501 Boylston Street, Suite 900, Boston, MA 02116
A Pearson Education Company
www.pearsoned.com

Printed in the United States of America

1 2 3 4 5 6 7 8 9 10 V036 15 14 13 12 11 10

000200010270587435

NM/SC

ISBN 10: 0-558-80790-9
ISBN 13: 978-0-558-80790-0

Copyright Acknowledgments

Contents

Chapter 5 – The Policy-Making Process at the Federal, State and Agency Levels

Chapter 6 – Policy Analysis and Evaluation at the Federal, State and Agency Levels

PART III – Contemporary Social Welfare Programs and Policies

Chapter 7 – Children and Family Services

Chapter 8 – Services to the Aged

Chapter 9 – Mental Health

Chapter 10 – Poverty/Economic Insecurity

PART IV – Conclusion: Toward a Just Society: The Role of Social Workers

INTRODUCTION

This text has been designed to reinforce the importance of understanding the impact of policy on direct care. That understanding is essential to students who will engage in clinical practice and it is also crucial for students who intend to plan, administer or conduct research on social work programs and services. Social work is a profession that provides services to individuals, families, groups and communities in a variety of settings. The link between policy and service delivery is fundamentally necessary for all entry-level professionals to understand. That link will be emphasized throughout the text.

In Part I of this text we discuss social policy as the broader context of social work practice. We discuss the key concept of social justice and the fundamental connection between social justice and the profession of social work. We also review the role that social control plays in the development and implementation of social policies, and how social control in contemporary society functions in relation to social work practice. The ethical injunctions for social workers rely on striving toward a just society on an individual, community and global level, while agencies, communities and nations often engage in implementing mechanisms of social control, although not exclusively. Are these incompatible forces that impact on social work practice? How do social workers respond to these forces? What are the primary values and ethical dilemmas faced by social workers as they confront the need to promote social justice concerns while functioning within the stated policies designed to maintain societal norms? Throughout we will explore these issues and the relationship between social work and social welfare policies as they impact on practice. In this part we will also discuss the agency as a primary setting for social work practice. We will describe voluntary not-for-profit agencies, public agencies and private agencies, noting the differences and similarities among them, and discussing how social policies are implemented in the agency setting.

In Part II we examine the historical factors that have shaped contemporary social work and social welfare with reference to early conceptions of charity and the transition from church to state obligations. We provide an historical overview of the American social welfare system and the development of the profession of social work in the United States within the context of important historical, social, political, and economic trends. The connection between the economic, social and political trends and ideology of the times in relation to emerging social policies is a major issue discussed in this section. From this discussion the text moves to a review of the public policy-making process in the United States at the Federal, State, and local levels. Included is a discussion of policy making at the agency level and how social workers are both impacted by, and impact on, this process. Finally, we will describe methods of analyzing and evaluating social policies at the macro (Federal and State) as well as at the micro (agency) level. Analysis and evaluation of social policies are activities that help us to understand whether a policy is implemented as intended, and whether or not a policy is effectively providing what it was mandated to provide, to the population who is the intended recipient.

In Part III we examine four major contemporary social welfare policies and programs significant for social workers. Children and family service policies are an important sector in which social workers practice. The policies that guide the social worker in working with children and families are, as many social welfare policies, entwined with social problems of poverty, lack of housing, lack of opportunities for education and lack of access to appropriate health care. Further, there have been major shifts in norms that have shaped our policies with respect to children and families and which need to be understood within the context of a social justice framework. We next discuss services to the aged. Those over 60 years of age represent the fastest growing population in the United States today. This population group presents policy makers with issues of access to health care, and with the need for policies reflective of lifestyle changes as well as policies that address quality of life issues for those who are living longer than ever before. Then we examine policies related to mental health. The epidemiologic evidence indicates that mental illness is not a rare phenomenon. We will describe the development of mental health services and the current policies that affect those with mental illness, including issues related to co-morbidities, particularly policies that address substance abuse, AIDS, and mental illness. In addition we will describe the contemporary policies related to access to mental health care and accessing barriers. Finally, we discuss issues relating to poverty.

Part IV provides an in-depth discussion of the role of social workers in promoting a just society. As globalization of the market place proceeds rapidly, inequalities have grown exponentially. The role of government in the lives of the disenfranchised in the United States has changed significantly within the recent past. Moreover, social problems around the globe no longer exist in isolation. "Thinking globally, acting locally" is a phrase that has meaning for social workers. In the final chapter we will present opportunities as well as challenges for social workers in the important work of promoting a just society. We will provide a framework for advocacy at the agency, community and broader levels so that social workers understand that to advance social justice is an integral part of the social work profession's mission.

As the reader uses this text, it is essential to remind ourselves that *social work, unique among helping professions, seeks not only to aid the individual and family but seeks to address the broader social condition*. Social work is inherently a political process and social workers need to be aware of this process. A tradition of concern for social justice and empowerment is a hallmark for our profession that has existed since the inception of the profession of social work and should serve to guide students in their education. Many observers have "contended that the social justice mission of social work is a unique characteristic that separates it from other professions and that one of the responsibilities of social work is to serve as the 'altruistic conscience' of society: "It is the bringing together of altruism and social justice that distinguishes the social work profession" (Haynes, D. & White, B., July 1999). As Swenson (1998) notes: "Social justice is increasingly being seen as the organizing value of social work. . . Clinical social work should not be equated with a practice based on a medical model, a focus on pathology, 'blaming the victim' or 'social conservatism.' Clinical social workers (and non-clinical social workers) can consider what a social justice perspective means and how it can be enacted in clinical contexts. They can think about work with individuals, families and groups from a social justice perspective" It is this social justice perspective that provides the context in which policy and its implications for social work are discussed throughout this text.

***PART I – Introduction and Overview of Social Policy as the Framework for Social
Work Practice***

Chapter 1 – Social Policy, Social Justice and Social Control: The Praxis for Practice

> *Ms. P. is a single mother of a five-year-old epileptic boy who came into a
> mental health clinic indicating she was depressed. She had been out of work for the
> past eight months due to her son's disability. She had a job as a receptionist but had
> to take so many days off to go to various doctor appointments that she eventually lost
> the position. In addition, she couldn't find a day care center with special services to
> care for her son. Her only brother was in jail and her mother was dying in the family's
> 7native Central American country. She went to apply for Temporary Assistance for
> Needy Families but was told by an eligibility worker that she needed to work to
> receive assistance which would reduce the time available to meet the needs of her son.*

Increasingly social workers and social work students are confronted by complex
cases like that of Ms. P. In examining this case the social worker and the social work
student need to think beyond the term "depression" as a clinical entity and look at the
policies that are impacting on Ms. P. These include the lack of day care for her disabled
child, lack of "family leave" policies and the adoption of the 1996 "Welfare Reform Act"
that often forces individuals into difficulties or dilemmas regarding childcare.
Understanding these policy issues is crucial in developing effective interventions for
Ms. P. and her child. This case clearly illustrates the fact that social policies affect the
practice of social work. Policies shape the lives of clients, the behavior and actions of the
social worker and the ability of the agency to serve clients.

For students entering the profession the questions, "Why study social policy?" and "What does it have to do with providing services to individuals and families?" can be perplexing. Too often the student finds himself caught in the "myth of the autonomous practitioner." Autonomous practice implies the social work practitioner works for and by himself and is not subject to outside authority or bureaucratic requirements. Autonomous practice implies that the social worker is in control, setting forth the policies that guide his or her practice based solely on professional knowledge, skills and values. While social workers might like to believe that it is only professional skills, knowledge and values that guide their own practice, this is far from reality. Whether you work with children, adolescents or adults; whether you work in foster care, mental health, a hospital or the criminal justice system; whether you work with senior citizens in a senior center or children in a psychiatric setting; whether you work in a hospice or a nursing home, or yes, even if you work in your own private practice, social policies will dictate who you can serve, how long you can provide services to your clients, how intensively you can provide services, how you will be reimbursed or your agency will be funded, how you will demonstrate accountability, and so on. You will become aware, as you enter your field placement, that your agency has its own policies and procedures which dictate how many clients workers will see, how often clients may be seen, where clients will be seen and how fees will be collected. Other agency policies will involve accountability procedures, that is, how the agency accounts to the funding agencies for the work that is done, how many units of service are provided, how effectiveness of service is evaluated, how client satisfaction is monitored and so forth. Your agency's policies, in turn, are part of a process that involves a Board of Directors if you are working in a voluntary agency, and the agency's funding sources. As you become more aware of how the agency functions, you will come to realize that multiple sources of funding further complicate policy directions.

What is Social Policy?

Social policies, especially public social welfare policies, are attempts to find answers to identified social problems at a local, state or national level. Social welfare policies can be addressed at the local, state and/or national level and, ultimately, affect the agencies in which social workers practice. Public social welfare policies are developed by governmental bodies, including the executive, legislative and judicial branches of government. In turn, they affect social service organizations. Public social welfare policies recognize that many problems cannot be solved by the private sector so that governmental intervention is essential. Public issues come in many sizes and shapes and can involve diverse topics e.g. transportation, education, water supply, child welfare, crime. Public issues are different than private troubles. A private trouble usually represents a problem which may impact on single individuals or families. The death of a beloved family member may cause deep and prolonged grief; an individual living in a rural area with no transportation may not be able to find a suitable job; a worker who has lost his job by a company closing are examples of problems affecting persons on an individual and do not necessarily constitute a public issue. However, when seemingly private issues such as abuse of children in families, the inability of numbers of poor families to access reasonable housing, or when major layoffs of employees from manufacturing plants occur and impact on significant numbers of a population they then may become part of the "public agenda". In other cases a major disaster such as an epidemic or terrorist threat, or a severe economic recession may lead to the recognition that there is a social problem worthy of public action. When this occurs governmental bodies are forced to recognize the problem, discuss it and perhaps, ultimately begin to take corrective actions. These actions will result in a "social policy" that is meant to address the defined situation by providing some service or benefit to the target population addressed. So social welfare policies may be seen as guiding principles which are the basis for laws, rules, and regulations meant to impact a specific population facing a broad social problem. Social welfare policies are, moreover, an expression of the values of a society in dealing with specific social problems. In a democracy such as the United States, there are many competing values at play in the policy process. Moreover, there are always a greater number of social needs than there are resources. Thus there is a tension in deciding what the "best" social welfare policy will be to address a specific problem. Social policies are a response to financial need and dependency needs of large segments of the population. While it is usual for these policies to emanate from the governmental sector, they will have an impact on non-governmental sectors including the both the non-profit and for-profit sectors in which social workers practice. In further sections of the book, the process of identifying a social problem and beginning to develop a social policy to address the problem will be discussed more fully.

By now, the student should realize that social policy is an abstract construct that relates to a public issue that has a social dimension e.g. mental illness, child abuse, AIDS, poverty, and which requires a governmental action. Issues that become part of the social welfare policy agenda change over time. Often this change is a result of economic and demographic shifts but may also be a response to an increasing awareness and sensitivity of the public of a specific problem. Social welfare concerns are also culturally bound; cultures may define the same behavior in different terms. For example, spanking a child may be the expected mode of discipline in some cultures yet is often seen in a different light today in the United States. As a result of changing views concerning discipline of children, there are now social policies which provide rules and regulations for teachers, for example, about what they can and cannot do to discipline children in the classroom. Likewise there are policies in child welfare agencies about how social workers and child care workers must interact with the children they serve. Other issues come to attention as new voices are added to the public process. Three decades ago a husband beating his wife or his child was a private family matter with no governmental involvement. Through the work of feminist and child advocacy groups, research studies and often the media, the broad impact of these behaviors on women and children were identified. These former private family issues are now much on the agenda for public discussion, debate and action which have resulted in social policies governing theses concerns. In the past, caring for aging members of a family was the primary responsibility of the children; however, with dramatic demographic shifts and growing numbers of the elderly especially the "older old", care of the elderly has become a topic of public discussion and actions. Another example of a formerly "private" issue becoming a public concern was the emergence of HIV which ultimately created a social problem that didn't exist until 20 years ago. Today, the rapid transmission of certain diseases globally such as SARS; the re-emergence of diseases since thought conquered such as tuberculosis; and the threat of terror on a global scale, are becoming recognized as social problems which require that policies be made.

As the student notes, "social policy" is a somewhat broad term. We can define the process of making social policies, the implementation of social policies and the evaluation of social policies however, and this book will do that in future chapters. We will also seek to translate the somewhat vague terms into social work language that practitioners can relate to.

Social Work and Social Policy

Before introducing the specific relationship between social policy and social work, we want to provide some definitions of social work itself. We can note that social work is the primary profession that provides social services. As the National Association of Social Work notes, "The primary mission of the social work profession is to enhance human well-being and help meet the basic needs of all people, with particular attention to the needs and empowerment of people who are vulnerable, oppressed and living in poverty" (NASW, 1996). Why then, the social worker may ask, do we need to understand social policy, why can't we just see individuals, families and small groups in order to help them adjust to life's circumstances and to enhance their coping skills? It should become clear to the student that in order to accomplish the mission of social work, we must work to change social policies that oppress certain groups, as well as working with individuals in that group. The student must come to understand that social welfare policies are the parameters within which social workers function. Social welfare policies give rise to programs with rules and regulations that impact on who can receive social services, how much service can be rendered, where services can be provided, and who will pay for these services.

As social workers, we must understand that, even as we work with an individual client, a family, a group or a community, we need to be focused on the broad issues as well as on the psychological factors that have brought the client to the agency, or stimulated the community to band together. By restricting our view to a narrow one of "pathologizing" our client's problem, we can forget the larger view: why is this client suffering at this moment? What brings a family in to a family service agency? Why does a particular neighborhood want to address the issue of school violence at a particular time?

Initially many social workers want to get "straight to the practice" of social work, but part of the "practice" of social work is to understand the policies that affect our practice. Beyond this understanding is a more significant issue: social workers are held responsible by the profession to promote social and economic justice for our clients by actively promoting social policies that will promote and enhance our clients' life. This means that part of the practice of social work is to function as active advocates on behalf of our clients, not solely on an individual basis but on a broader societal basis. In fact, the Code of Ethics which guides the principles that all professional social workers must adhere to, notes that the "primary mission of the social work profession is to enhance human well-being and help meet the basic human needs of all people, with particular attention to the needs and empowerment of people who are vulnerable, oppressed, and living in poverty." (NASW Code of Ethics)

Failure to engage in efforts to change social policies may undercut the value of our potential direct service interventions. While social work students may be drawn to the profession because of their desire to help individuals and families cope with disabling situations, the student should understand that efforts to ameliorate broader social conditions that affect clients are also part of the practice of social work. Efforts to change policies may seem like a difficult challenge, and they are, indeed, a challenge. However it is our mandate as social work professionals to work for policy changes in order to empower disenfranchised groups, as well as to ameliorate conditions for the individual client.

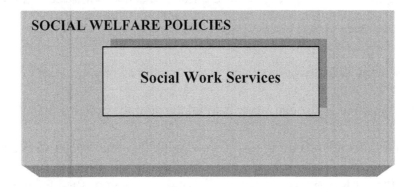

The relationship between social welfare and social work can be illustrated by an analysis of poverty and its relationship to social work services to children and families. Poverty is one social issue often encountered by social workers in working with clients. Social policies related to income and work greatly impact upon the lives of the poor and can help to ameliorate, but often, in practice, exacerbate problems in clients' lives. From the earliest recognition of the existence of poverty and the distinctions in social class to the present workfare program in the United States the lives of the poor have been directly shaped by policies of government officials.

Social workers in direct practice often pay more attention to the emotional lives of their clients, and less "tuned in" to the effect of poverty on clients' lives. It is important for direct practitioners to understand how social policies about income and work issues impact on clients and to become more sensitive to the need for advocacy actions on behalf of their clients. There are several key service issues in the area of poverty that must be considered. Some of these issues include:

1) Difficulty in finding jobs due to lack of education

2) Inadequate housing

3) High numbers of women and children living in poverty

4) Lack of access to and inadequate medical care and poor health

5) The pressures resulting from the current welfare laws with the poor being forced into workfare

These issues all may affect the inner life of the client: it is up to the social worker to address both the client's inner feelings as well as the impact of the external environment. We will more fully explore the effect of poverty in Chapter 4 in the discussion of the Personal Responsibility and Work Opportunity Reconciliation Act of 1996. Suffice it to note at this point that the emotional cost for a person who is struggling to find an "appropriate" workfare job while providing responsible day care for her young children can be daunting.

Mrs. L, a victim of domestic violence was constantly barraged with notices from the welfare department to begin to seek work. She had been receiving welfare benefits for herself and her children for several years however was now being forced to seek employment if she wished to maintain her benefits. Mrs. L. was the mother of two children, one of whom was developmentally disabled. Her first efforts were toward getting childcare for her children. She found a three day a week after school program for her 10 year old, Peter, but there was no care available for her younger son, Karl, age 6.

and developmentally disabled. Mrs. L. went from welfare worker to welfare worker explaining her inability to get childcare for her son who was difficult to manage. She was told to try harder. Her social worker and her son's therapist wrote letters and made telephone calls on her behalf, but the letters kept arriving at her home. Her treatment goals with her own social worker then became maintaining her benefits. The clinician was unable to work on underlying issues of sexual abuse in her childhood or stress related to caring for her son because the maintenance of benefits was the priority. She has not yet faced the possibility that her son's SSI benefits will be cut under the welfare reform changes.

It is important to stress that our clients are not only dealing with the individual problems for which we are counseling or assisting them, but are also affected by multiple issues in their environment. Thus, although a social worker may be treating a client for an anxiety disorder, it would also be important for the worker to consider social factors and policies that impact upon the client's mental health. Concerns such as poverty, communities in which there is a high degree of social disruption, communities that lack an adequate supply of decent housing, individuals who lack health insurance are all factors that may impact the client's emotional responses. These conditions that result from certain social policies are also the responsibilities of the social worker.

Social Justice and Social Work

One of the distinguishing characteristics of the social work profession is its emphasis on social justice. In fact, social justice concerns are fundamental to the profession as is noted in the NASW Code of Ethics, and social justice may be seen as an "organizing principle of the profession." As one of the fundamental principles of the social work profession we believe that we must work towards reducing inequities in the

distribution of basic resources. These include inequities in access to education, income,

housing, health care, decent employment and liberty. These inequities may also include

access to the political system; for example certain immigrants who have lived and

worked in the United States for decades but who have not become citizens lack access to

certain income benefits. This emphasis on social justice as an organizing principle is

what sets social work apart from other helping professionals. Students may well ask,

"but what is social justice?" How is it to be defined? And, most importantly for the

student, how do I put this principle into practice?

Before we present our definition of social justice let us present some background.

Van Soest (1995) identified three components of social justice: legal (what does a person

owe society), commutative (what people owe each other) and distributive (what society

owes a person) (Cited in Swenson, 1998). We will arbitrarily consider distributive justice

as the most important of the three components for social workers. In this regard, let us

note that social justice refers to a *fair distribution of a group or society's resources to its*

members. There are three terms that require further elaboration in the above. The first

term we wish to consider is the term "group." Who constitutes a "group"? A group may

refer to any size collection of individuals who consider themselves, and are considered by

the others in the group, as "members". Thus, a family (both nuclear and extended) may be

a group, a neighborhood may be a group, an agency may represent a group, a country

may represent a group and a people sharing an ethnicity and/or a religion may represent a

group. The second part of the statement concerns the word "resource." Resources may

refer to the use of the family's car or computer but usually refer to economic resources at the global level. In this context, the student may note that the words "social justice" and "social and economic justice" are often used interchangeably. This usually refers to the fact that the key is distribution of resources at a societal or global level, usually refers to access to economic resources. The next concern with the definition of social justice has to do with the word "distribute." Perhaps the word "redistribute" would clarify the meaning. While every group has resources, some members of a group have more resources, and some members have fewer resources. In a society in which there is wide variance between those who have many resources and those who have few resources, the key concept in the definition of social justice is to redistribute those resources more equitably or more fairly. Some have argued that "resources" include both economic and non-economic resources. Wakefield (1988) argued that these non-economic resources might include self-respect and other psychological attributes. In this sense, it is not difficult to see how a social worker engages in activities that promote social justice. We believe this is a key point. By including non-economic resources within a distributive justice framework, it becomes evident that social workers must be involved in activities that promote social justice for their clients. The question of "fairness" is more difficult to answer. In the social justice context, fairness refers to "equity", which has the same root as "equal". But "equal" and "equity" can be defined quite differently, depending on who is doing the defining. Thus, in a traditional patriarchal family, the females may get less of certain resources than the males (but in the family culture this distribution of resources would be considered fair). In a free market economy with a political system such as the United States, there will always be groups who are marginalized by the mainstream and thus may have less access to resources. For example, women who cannot support themselves and their children are often reliant on restrictive social welfare policies, victims of domestic violence may not have equal access to the criminal justice system as high paid executives of major corporations, those who work at jobs that tend to be devalued such as home attendants, janitors, and other such "piece workers" may not have equal access to health care and so on. In these cases, those in power are defining who gets "equal" treatment under the law. Thus, we may conclude that the concept of social justice which is socially constructed by those in power at a particular moment in time, is always relevant for social work practitioners. In our society, with unlimited human needs and limited resources, there will always be those who suffer at the margins of the society, those populations who are vulnerable due to oppressive policies and ideologies current at a specific period in time and those groups who lack access to the resources of the majority.

Now let us propose our definition of social justice. *Social justice means that every person in a society has an equal opportunity to access the necessary resources (including non-economic resources) to maintain a safe, healthy and productive life with opportunity to grow and develop to his/her maximum potential. In a socially just society, the distribution of resources would be equitable, without regard to race, culture, ethnicity, gender, religion or sexual preference.*

The key for social workers is that we are concerned that the way in which society's resources are distributed must be fair and that the gap between rich and poor, must be addressed in order to live in a just society. The corollary of this is that social workers, as part of the fundamental mission of the profession, must work to address social injustice as an integral part of their practice.

The philosophical underpinning of social justice may be seen in the writings of John Rawls. According to Rawls (1971), modern societies rest upon voluntary contracts by rational humans, which give rise to a set of moral principles by which we live. These ideas are rooted in the notion that human nature is essentially "good" and that rational beings can come together to form a social contract so that society can function without anarchy. While each individual in society should have an equal right to liberty without doing injustice to any other person's right to liberty, Rawls recognized that there is inherent inequality in society. Given this inequality the question of how resources should be allocated becomes significant. Should every person in society receive the same compensation, no matter what work is done? Should those who have suffered at the hands of oppressors for hundreds of years be entitled to a greater share of resources than those who have "only" been oppressed for a brief period? Questions such as these have implications for the direct social work practitioner. Policies such as "quota" systems for one group or another may be based on a variety of ways of defining "equal." Policies such as affirmative action are attempts to" equalize the playing field "for some groups; likewise controversies over policies such as gay marriage may be seen as denying equal resources to some groups based on their sexual orientation.

In the following case history we note that some might consider the "problem" to be the children fighting amongst themselves. The child welfare worker might have removed a child and placed the child in foster care to "ensure safety." As we shall see in the Chapter on Social Control, even social service agencies are not necessarily set up to ensure that resources are distributed equitably. Social service agencies are, after all, subject to the social policies that emanate from the majority and are subject to political ideology. Nevertheless, it is one of the underlying missions of social work to address these concerns in a systematic manner. The tasks may seem daunting and you, the student, may feel that you "have no time" to address these issues. Or you may feel powerless to address broad concerns. However we all must find ways to engage these issues for if we do not, we are not practicing social work in its entirety.

The following case example illustrates the ways that social workers act on their belief in social justice, even though the reality of social policies makes it difficult.

Case History

M is a 23-year-old Hispanic mother with three children. The family was living in a two-bedroom apartment where eleven people resided. Because of the overcrowded conditions, the children began fighting, and one of the neighbors called child welfare. Consequently, one of M's daughters was placed in foster care because of the overcrowded conditions. More than 1.5 persons per room is considered a severely crowded household. M felt hopeless to change her situation. The social worker at the foster care agency with responsibility for M's daughter contacted administrators with responsibility for Section 8 housing, but was told that the waiting list was closed. The worker explored the option of public assistance rent subsidies. Even with a rent subsidy, the total amount of the public assistance would not be sufficient because housing costs were so high. The social worker advocated for M with the child welfare caseworker's supervisor and was able to, after three weeks, get M on the waiting list for Section 8 housing. Lack of affordable housing forces many low-income households into over-crowded or unsafe conditions, and in this case, the mother had her child removed. The social worker provided support for M, but meanwhile her child was in foster care.

For direct practice or clinical social work, social justice needs to be a key organizing value. Swenson (1998) highlights this as follows: "Clinical social work should not be equated with practice based on the medical model, a focus on pathology, 'blaming the victim', or social conservatism." Clinical social workers must consider what a social justice perspective means and how it can be enacted in clinical contexts. They must think about work with individuals, families, and groups from a social justice perspective. Social workers provide leadership in assessing theories, practices, and service delivery arrangements from the point of view of increasing social justice. What does social justice mean when we sit with a client? It means profound appreciation for a client's strengths, contexts and resources. Experiences of race, ethnicity, gender, class, religion, sexual orientation, and ability must be perceived as central because these details contain meaning and shape client's worlds. It means we acknowledge and articulate the client's social realities.

We must also engage in the work of exploring our experiences of oppression, and of privilege and power. Only then can we engage in thorough analyses of professional and organizational power and actively work to increase client power relative to professionals and agencies, using a social justice perspective.

Social work's concern with social justice is a key factor in our interest in social policy. It means that our focus must include visualizing the person/family in the broader social context. By its very nature, therefore, social work is engaged in a struggle with the system since the client social workers represent are usually oppressed groups and persons. In addition to presenting key definitions of social work, it is essential to provide the reader with a clear conceptualization of social work and one that includes both direct practice and advocacy.

Social Control

Another important and often controversial topic in social work and in social welfare is the concept of social control. It is a topic that cannot be ignored, although often social workers would prefer to discount it. The words themselves have a negative connotation that social workers may be uncomfortable with. But, as students, we need to understand the broad functions of social control – and understand that the concept of social control has many differing interpretations.

Social control has to do with the concept of individual "liberty" vs. the "common social good." People living in a community (state, country, neighborhood) come together with some ideas about what is "good" for the community. These conceptions, based on ideology, can take many different forms. One way of ensuring that the "good of the community" is paramount may be to limit some individual freedoms. A clear example is when a community gets together to lobby for a traffic light on a corner where there have been several accidents involving the untimely death of children. The restriction on individual liberty is that a driver cannot speed through the intersection if the light is red. The classic example often cited is that, although we have freedom of speech, we cannot yell "fire" when there is no reason to in a crowded public place.

On a broader scale, the society we live in may require individuals to engage (or not engage) in certain behaviors in order to maintain stability and a sense of cohesiveness. Cowger and Atherton note that social control is a sociological term referring to societal processes that "support a level of social cohesiveness sufficient for the survival of the society as a recognizable functional unit" (Cowger and Atherton, 1974, p.456). They further note that from a functional sociological perspective social control is the "primary function of social welfare" (p.456). If the society is to remain cohesive, then it would seem that social control mechanisms would be quite beneficial. Indeed, philosophers like John Stuart Mill recognized that in a society such as ours citizens are required to obey the laws of the land. This holds true even in circumstances in which no one else is harmed. These restrictions on individual liberty are not meant so much to protect particular individuals from harm, but rather to protect the social order itself.

Cowger and Atherton delineate three forms of social control: "socialization" begins in the family, the educational and religious institutions where children learn what is required and expected of them; "direct behavior control" where the state can enforce laws formally through the direct power of the state; and "resocialization" which is the realm in which social welfare agencies, mental health and other human service agencies function to help individuals who are not functioning in ways in which they are expected to by society. (Cowger and Atherton, 1974)

However, questions arise with respect to **who** is making the decisions about **what** laws to enforce for **whose** benefit and at what cost. The most basic question is upon whose values are decisions made? Question can be raised, for example, about whether there will be a lack of social cohesiveness if there are laws that require women with little means of support to work for 30, or 37 or 40 hours a week in order to receive minimal benefits from the Temporary Assistance to Needy Families (TANF) Program. Will there be "less" social cohesiveness if we had a minimum family allowance program that automatically provided a family with support for a new child? Will there be a breakdown in social cohesiveness if persons with a mental illness who commit a misdemeanor are provided with community-based mental health treatment rather than a sentence in jail?

The question becomes: "who is making which rules that indicate who should give up his individual liberty for which overall societal good"? Or, who is determining what the significant issues are for the particular society?

As we can see, social control can also take on a punitive and coercive meaning. It is well-worth raising the question here about the function of our social welfare system and the role that social workers play with respect to social control issues. As social workers, we do not like to think of ourselves as "controlling" anyone. We are taught that each individual has worth and that on of our major roles is to "help" our clients become functional members of society "for his own good", while enabling each individual to help himself to grow. Yet, when we examine the structure of the social welfare institutions and agencies in which we work it becomes clear that the function of these institutions is often to maintain a *status quo* among populations that are considered by the majority to be "unworthy." In this society, work is rewarded and if one does not work (unless one is severely disabled) one is considered "unworthy" of receiving certain and reliable assistance. As noted in other sections, as more and more women became recipients of the entitlement program known as Aid to Families with Dependent Children (AFDC), and as the country moved towards a more conservative view, the more restrictive Welfare Reform program of 1996 was passed. At this time persons (in this case particularly women) who cannot work for a host of reasons including having lived in poverty, having limited educational opportunities as well as skill development opportunities, and beset by racial and/or ethnic stigma and oppression, are further "disentitled" from receiving some of the benefits of society. What is our role as social workers here? Many social workers work in public welfare settings or voluntary agencies in which they must deny eligibility for benefits for those individuals who are the targets of these policies. The social worker working in these agencies and systems must enforce the disempowering policies that exist. Hence there is often a conflict between the social worker's obligation to promote social justice on a broad scale, and assist the individual client, and the social policy mandate under which the social worker functions.

In other examples of the ways in which the structure of the state encourages social workers to be agents of social control we see the social worker who works with families in which there is an individual who has a substance abuse problem. It may become necessary for the social worker to make the determination to remove a child from the family if the substance abuse continues. Perhaps the social worker would rather spend some time with the client in order to help her cope with overwhelming issues in a different way. Or, social workers investigating a case of domestic violence may be forced to encourage a woman to have her partner arrested (under the policy of mandatory arrest) whether or not she wants to have him arrested. These brief examples demonstrate the powerful influence agencies have on the professionals who work for them, based on the overriding social welfare policies that the agencies must follow.

A more subtle form of social control can be encountered in the therapeutic process. Some maintain that social control may be encouraged in the therapeutic process. This means that words, alone, may be used to persuade an individual to give up his/her own view and accept the views of someone else. This can be seen in the mental health arena when a person who is labeled as "mentally ill" is not allowed to keep social security payments based on his "incompetence." Until this individual "accepts" the

diagnostic label and begins to act in a rational manner, the monthly payments will go to

a "guardian" of some sort. Questioning the judgment of the mental health professional is

not a wise decision, in this view of social control. The very labeling process which

identifies a pathological condition in the client, is a not very subtle form of social

control.

These examples of how the structure of social welfare services is enmeshed

with the notion of social control deserve serious consideration by social workers.

Questions about which liberties should be restricted in order to enhance the social good

are not simple questions. Should there be over 48 million Americans who do not have

health insurance because they are either unemployed, employed in jobs in which there

is no coverage, or immigrants not entitled to benefits? Should those with little skills be

forced to work for 37 or 40 hours a week, at a wage that is less than minimum wage

and with little or no opportunities for training and education? Who is being harmed?

Whose liberty is being compromised? What is the role of the social worker in these

situations? To whom is the social worker accountable? To the client? To the agency for

whom she/he works? To the views that encourage the implementation of these policies?

To the society-at-large who sanctions social worker? These are not simple questions to

answer. Our intention is to help the student understand the complexities of the systems

and policies that he will encounter as a professional social worker. As students we must

be mindful of these issues. The following examples will illustrate some of the points

just made.

Case Example

J is a six-year-old African American boy. He was referred to the Day Treatment Center due to an inability to control himself in the classroom. He has been diagnosed as oppositional-defiant with a conduct disorder. J has lived with his mother and her girlfriend for the past two years. Previously, he was in foster care for two years in a physically abusive home. He was there because his mother was in rehab, recovering from crack and alcohol addiction. Although J's mother abused alcohol and crack while pregnant, J was born negative for toxicology.

Recently J's mother and her girlfriend broke up; since then, J's appearance and behavior at the Day Treatment Center has deteriorated. When it is time to get on the bus to go home he cries and rants and raves, saying he does not want to. The program has called child welfare twice in the past three months due to bruises on J's face as well as him bringing a razor blade his "mother gave him" to school. J's mother says she loves all three of her children but feels overwhelmed by J. She says that her ex-girlfriend took care of a lot of the parenting and now she has to relearn those skills. As a temporary trial to see if she is capable of being a good parent to J, she's required to meet with J's clinician, once a week, as well as attend weekly parenting groups. If she does not fulfill these obligations, there is the threat of J being sent back to foster care. Even in fulfilling these obligations, if J's mom does not acquire appropriate parenting skills, J may be sent to foster care.

Case Example

A social work intern at an outpatient mental health clinic saw Robert, a twenty-seven year-old white man. Robert had a chaotic and unstable childhood. His father was a violent alcoholic who routinely brutalized his wife in front of the children. Robert had been incarcerated for three months after he had broken into the home of his landlady and had slashed both her and her nine-year-old daughter while highly intoxicated. He had returned to New York one year ago after spending three years in a rehab program and halfway house mandated by the criminal justice system. Robert had a long-standing history of alcohol abuse, which started at the age of fourteen. Since his return to New York and the end of his parole a year ago, Robert started drinking again. He claimed that his drinking was "social," and that he consumed no more than a "six-pack" every other weekend. He stated explicitly that his drinking was "under control" and that he had no interest in addressing his drinking in treatment. Robert was a voluntary client. Although there were no formal policies about abstinence at this agency, the intern's supervisor instructed the social work intern to refer Robert to a substance abuse program. The supervisor felt that Robert's judgement was impaired given the previous consequences of his alcohol use, and she was concerned about both Robert's well being and the responsibility of the agency. The supervisor felt it was unethical to do anything less than enforce strict limits about his participation in a rehab program. The supervisor compared not addressing Robert's alcoholism to a doctor in an emergency room who chooses to treat a patient's sore toe when the patient comes in with a massive heart attack. The intern was instructed to inform Robert that he could not be seen at the agency until he enrolled in a program for his alcoholism. Robert never returned to the agency after his second session.

Chapter 2 – The Agency Setting and Social Policy

The vast majority of social services are delivered through agencies. These agencies provide social services, child welfare services, mental health services, housing, vocational training, family counseling, and many other services. They are operated by voluntary agencies, governmental bodies or by for profit corporations such as nursing homes, correctional corporations, private hospital chains and so on. It is the social agency that forms the context in which services are provided.

Within each of these settings, the role of the social worker may vary extensively. Social workers may serve as care managers, group workers, or community organizers within the agency setting. As care managers the social worker may be responsible for providing therapeutic services, linking clients with other services, advocating on behalf of the client, and monitoring the client's emotional and/or physical health. As a group worker the social worker may be responsible for helping group members to engage in activities that will enhance their coping skills, activities that will focus on group member's abilities to relate to others, or helping group members to learn new skills. As a community organizer the social worker may help a tenant's group advocate with the legal authorities to gain heat in their buildings, or the worker may organize a coalition of several social service agencies to lobby the legislature to pass pro-social legislation. Social workers may also act as primary therapists in a mental health agency, or as discharge planners in a hospital. They may counsel children and parents in a school setting, or in a headstart program. These are only a few of the many direct service roles that social workers may engage in. In addition to these roles, social workers may supervise other social workers in an agency, they may develop new programs for their agency, they may write grants, engage in research or become executive directors of

social agencies. Looking at the roles of social workers in a broader context, they may

work as advisors to legislators, or become legislators themselves. In these capacities,

social workers have a major role in the policy-making process. However, even when the

social worker is engaged in direct clinical practice with individuals, developing agency

policies to better serve clients, implementing social policies, and advocating for more

socially just social policies they are playing a significant role. The level of responsibility

will vary according to the size of the agency as well as the resources devoted to social

work. In a host setting, for example a school district, only one or two social workers may

be available to serve two or three high schools. However, a social worker in a psychiatric

hospital may only have a half a dozen cases or so assigned to them due to the intensity of

each case. A social worker in foster care in the department of social services may

oversee a number of other social workers and therefore not have a substantial amount of

direct contact with clients. A social worker working in a homeless shelter may deal

primarily on a direct level of client service. These are only a few examples of the range

of responsibilities that social workers fill, as well as the variety of settings in which they

may operate.

The formal organizational structure of agencies differs widely, and the social

worker must learn to function in his/her own agency. There is also an "informal" structure

of each agency, reflective of the agency "culture". This means that each agency does

business in a unique way. Agencies may require certain dress codes, for example. In a

shelter for the homeless the dress code may be quite informal whereas in a public service

agency the dress code may be much more formal. The patterns of communication may vary according to the agency culture as well. In one setting, social workers may be encouraged to communicate with program directors, in another agency, this will be frowned on. The informal structure is equally as important, if not in some cases more important, than the formal structure of the agency. The formal structure may be hierarchical, as in a large, bureaucratic organization such as a hospital or a large family services agency with many satellite offices. In these cases it will be clear to the new social worker that s/he will report to a supervisor, who reports to his or her supervisor, who in turn, reports to a team manager, and so on up the line. Moreover, in an organization in which social work is not the primary discipline, as in a hospital, the chief social worker will be reporting to a hospital administrator and will have to work closely with the medical staff and the nursing staff. In a smaller, grassroots agency, the structure may be less of a hierarchy and encourage more communication between the social worker and all other levels of employees, including the executive director. However in each of these types of organizations, the less formal organizational culture will play a significant role as well. It may be possible that the social worker has a friend at a higher level in a bureaucratic organization, or makes friends with "the boss's boss." In these cases there are additional lines of communication that are open, although one has to be cautious about utilizing them. On the other hand, some large organizations encourage employees to get together with all levels of staff at functions, parties, events held outside the organization, etc. This may be part of the "culture" of the organization and the social worker should pay particular attention to both the formal and informal ways in which the agency operates. The benefits of recognizing these traditional (and perhaps non-traditional) means of intra-agency communication will ultimately benefit the worker who is concerned that certain policies in the organization may need to be altered, in order to better serve the clients. The bottom line is that we are there to serve the client as best we can. In order to accomplish this, we must understand how our own agency functions, as well as how the systems and policies that govern our agencies function. It is also important to understand where the funding in an agency comes from because ultimately, the funding source will be the driving factor in whom the agency can serve, how often the client(s) can receive services, how long a time clients can be seen for, and so on. It has been said that social workers operate within a variety of roles, work in a number of settings, and serve within a variety of organizational structures. In so much as these differences affect social workers in their jobs, so do the rules and regulations that govern them and set the parameters within which they are to work. By this it is meant that for each social worker in a particular agency, setting and role, there are rules, guidelines and laws that affect the social worker's role and govern the work or services provided by that social worker.

Factors Influencing Agency Settings

Key Factors

*Auspices: voluntary, governmental, private for profit

*Size: small, medium, large, very large (perhaps with multiple branches in different locations

*Source(s) of Funding: Governmental- federal, state, local; Philanthropic; Agency fund raising; fee for service; private insurance; Medicare, Medicaid

*Regulatory: Licensing Agreement, or Purchase of Services

*Affiliations: independent organization or part of broader network

*Social Work: primary discipline e.g. social service agency
Secondary discipline e.g. hospital or school

*Type of organization: formal, hierarchical with specialized roles and communication top-down, informal, loosely structured, generalized roles, communication can flow top-down and bottom-up, a mix of the above, i.e. a formal organization satellites office with informal style.

How the Agency Structure Affects the Social Worker and Service Delivery

In this section we will examine how the structure within an agency affects the social worker and to what degree this impacts the relationship with clients. Specifically, we will examine how the organizational structure of the agency impacts the worker's ability to deliver services (direct practice) and, additionally, how this affects the client.

It is also important to look at what are the structural factors in the organization. In social work agencies, as with other agencies in which individuals are working toward common goals, effective organization invites effective delivery of social services. Organizational factors include to the hierarchical arrangement, and the levels of management or responsibility of that agency. This arrangement may include levels in regard to responsibility, authority, power, and mechanisms through which the structure functions or operates. Organizational factors also include the mission of the agency, its vision and goals. Moreover, the auspice under which the agency operates as well as its relation to the community are important to consider. These factors will impact on how the social worker functions within the structure of the agency. There are a number of tactics which social workers can utilize in achieving a course of intended action while maintaining a level of independence within their agency. These include acknowledging a certain amount of variation for discretion and creativity in regulation, by not expecting too much in the way of praise and reward by the organization, by requiring a certain level of practical skills through which independence on agency resources are reduced, and by not easily succumbing to the requirements of administrative convenience. The challenge is to adequately fill the role of social worker and advocate, while remaining an efficient and effective practitioner exerting a level of independence in that role.

In examining the extent to which the structure of an agency impacts the practitioner and the services that are delivered, it is relevant to discuss the control that social worker has, or does not have, in his or her responsibilities and role. We can say that the social worker is empowered in a professional sense, and his or her level of or feeling of empowerment will affect his practice, and the effectiveness of that practice. Agency policies toward the practitioner, as well as toward the client, will affect the degree of empowerment felt by the practitioner. This means that the worker is comfortable in his ability to offer assistance to the client. Yet it must be remembered that the worker is tightly bound by the agency's goals, mission and funding source. This can sometimes create conflict for the new worker. For example, in a homeless shelter where the goal is to transition the client to permanent housing, some residents of the shelter may need more than the allowable time limit provided by the shelter. The social worker would like to let the client stay in the shelter more than the 30 day limit, however the funding source and the administrator of the shelter tell the worker that this is not acceptable. The client must leave when "time is up." This can lead to frustration, especially if there are few resources for the client in the community. In this example it is revealed that there was a major incongruence between the needs of clients and the rules that regulate the services that can be offered to them.

Case - Managed Care

A social worker in a child development center talked with her 16-year-old client about a recent hospitalization. The client explained that she had been delusional and was hearing voices, so her mother took her to the hospital where she was admitted. She was given psychotropic medications and released three days later. The patient was so depressed that she tried to commit suicide by taking pills a day after she was discharged. She was then readmitted for five days. The managed care company responsible for the patient's insurance urged the hospital to discharge the patient and the hospital complied, although the social worker argued that discharge was premature. The social worker than spoke to the clinic director and together they reached the Director of the managed care branch. They pointed out the possibilities of a client suicide and lawsuits. The managed care company agreed to six more days in the hospital.

It has been implied that current organizational models of management have empowered the manager to control performance but have little to offer to the worker regarding how to improve performance. In addition, these models are often outcome focused and rarely take into account the fact that worker or client skills are not standardized. Yet it is important to note that now, more than ever, we are beginning to focus on "evidence- based practice." Studies which can provide guidelines for the practitioner are becoming more common, although there is still a huge gap in many practice areas. Yet, there are concerns even in implementation of evidence-based practice. For example, mental health treatment is increasingly being "medicalized".

Consequently many insurers are willing to reimburse agencies only for medical treatment and very limited "talk treatment". Yet, many studies show that a combination of medication and talk therapy is more effective than simply medication alone. However the pursuit of evidence based practice is extremely relevant to the practitioner. As a profession, we must do the research to understand what works best, for which clients, and at what cost. The knowledge gained from these kinds of studies will have important policy considerations for the organization and funding of services.

Recently, many larger agencies have begun to function in ways that are similar to for-profit corporations. This may be due to the complexities of the funding process, wherein large agencies serve populations across the age range and with many complex and multiple needs. The agencies therefore must often contract with several different government entities, each of which has a different set of requirements and regulations which impact the agency. Agencies may then develop "management teams", "performance evaluations" and other mechanisms that apply to for-profit organizations as well. All human service organizations are now closely examining worker performance. Again, this is a result of demands for accountability, particularly in times of diminishing resources for human services, yet growing need. The call is "to do more with less" and to do it effectively and efficiently. This has an impact on the social worker in the agency, and can sometimes create a conflict for the worker. S/he is faced with the difficult task of operating within bureaucracies that may face an uncertain future, while having to provide the client with necessary services. A serious challenge for the social worker is how to continue to provide services within the changing nature of agencies and the diminishing resources.

Residents in a working-class neighborhood band together to shut down a shelter that provides services to less fortunate persons in the area. Opponents of a federal program, which provides assistance to single mothers with children, seek to abolish the program, claiming that the program only deters recipients from seeking gainful employment in the workforce. Despite evidence that giving cash to those receiving Food Stamps would save money and result in a more effective program, legislators and program administrators decide that Food Stamp recipients cannot be trusted to spend the funds given to them on food and the necessities of life. A statewide program designed to help poor individuals and families does not provide beneficiaries with enough assistance to lift them above the poverty line. Debate engulfs an urban community when an HIV prevention group distributes new syringe needles to the community's heroin addicts in an effort to deter the sharing of "dirty" infected needles.

Although the above examples are all drawn from various areas of social policy, all of them share one essential element. In all of the examples, the concept of values plays an integral role. Values play a primary role in all aspects of social welfare and public policy, whether they are held by the individual, the group, the community, the organization, or the society or culture in general. Karger and Stoesz (1990) described policy-making as a process consisting of formulation, legislation, implementation, and evaluation. At each level of this policy-making process, the values debate helps to shape and define the issues at hand, defining the scope of the issues, limiting the scope of debate, and determining acceptable and non-acceptable answers to social problem. In fact, values play a large part in the determination of what currently is and is not considered to be a problem. The proposed "solutions" to these problems must be consonant with values that exist within the culture, as well. The legislation of the 1950s and 1960s putting an end to segregation in the United Sates may have run counter to the prevailing racism existing in many parts of the United States, but was consonant with the values of equality that were present in the underpinning of our nation's founding. *In addition, while values are always conflicting in a pluralistic society, certain values are in ascendancy at some points while others are in descendency at different points in time.* The importance of values is not limited to the macro-level issues of policy development and implementation. As social workers, recognizing the importance of our own values and how they affect our relationships with the clients we serve is essential to effective practice. Recognizing and understanding the values of our clients is essential in accepting the client where they are, understanding their motivations and beliefs, and developing appropriate contracts or service plans fashioned around their own value systems. In all of our transactions, all perceptions and reactions are "value-laden and value-based" so that we can never be entirely objective in our work. Despite the obviousness of these statements concerning values within the clinical relationship, there are levels and value issues *that may not be* as apparent to those that work with individuals and groups in a clinical capacity. In fact, the very decision to focus on micro-practice issues may stem from a value-based position on the part of the individual practitioner or the agency in which he or she works. Consider the following example:

> *Mrs. S, an African-American woman, comes into an urban social service agency serving an impoverished community. She requests assistance in finding a job as she is in danger of losing her public assistance benefits if she cannot find a job in the next seven months. Mrs. S, who did not finish high school, is worried that she will not be able to provide for her two children, ages three years old and thirteen months old respectively, if she is unable to locate a job. She fears that she may even lose her housing in the future. She also is concerned that if she does obtain a job, she will not be able to obtain appropriate childcare, as there are no quality daycare centers in her neighborhood.*

Confronted with the above client's situation, it would be natural to begin to formulate ideas as to how one might assist the client in addressing her problems. Through further discussion with Mrs. S, we might begin to develop a plan of action that would address her immediate needs. The meeting of the client's immediate needs is essential, but in focusing specifically on the level of the individual client, the larger macro or community issues might be forgotten altogether. Behind this micro-level example are macro-level issues, which should be examined. There is the issue of the questionable policy of the public assistance program, as well as the issues of the neighborhood's lack of qualified childcare alternatives, the poor school system which failed to engage Mrs. S and allowed her to drop out, the historical legacy of racism—existing today—which has kept the large African-American neighborhood in poverty, and the economic practices and processes which provide few opportunities for Mrs. S to obtain gainful employment in a satisfying job. In focusing specifically on the individual problems of the client, the social worker is operating from, in part, a need to provide the client with immediate assistance. The social worker, however, is also operating from a particular American value that provides a context for the intervention: individualism. The cultural value of individualism in American culture has produced a resultant tradition of addressing problems on an individualized and selective fashion as opposed to a modality based on macro issues and viewing problems on a more universal level (Tropman, 1989). Social workers currently tend to focus more on clinical issues—on the private troubles of individuals—while often failing to address issues on the community or societal level. It is a common feature within American society that individuals are often asked to make changes in an effort to address problem that may actually be structural in nature. This is not without good cause, as addressing social problems on a community or structural level may be seen as a more complicated process. It is easier to address one person's poverty than to address the problem of the nation's poor. Therefore, even the unconscious decision to focus on immediate clinical issues related to the individual is, to some degree, a product of underlying values existing within society.

Before attempting to describe some of the common values that provide the context for social policy issues in the United States, it is important to keep several concepts in mind. One is that values may often be in conflict with one another. Existing within society, for instance, are the conflicting values of individualism and self-reliance and the values of helping those in need and social responsibility. The history of social welfare and public policy in the United States has shifted numerous times between these two concepts. Values may change over time and may result in shifts in policy and history is cyclical in nature, shifting back and forth between individualism and social responsibility.

Judeo-Christian Values

In understanding how values derived from Judaic teachings and the teachings of Jesus Christ influence the American value system today, it is essential to remember that we are not referring to a specific set of religious teachings, beliefs, or dogma. What we are referring to, however, are a set of teachings that are non-sectarian and relate to social standards and social discourse. Stemming from the tradition of the Jewish teachings comes the notion of social justice. Jewish prophets exhorted those around them to live according to the mandates given to the people of Israel and said that the mandate was also related to how Israel treated those less fortunate living within their midst, especially the sick, old, handicapped, and the poor. Charity began to be seen as a religious duty, Jewish doctrines taught that not only was it a duty to give to those in need, but that those in need had a right to receive charity.

The teachings of Jesus, building on this tradition of social justice, stressed the spirit of the Judaic laws as they related to the treatment of others. These teachings were encapsulated in the Golden Rule. Jesus, in his message of salvation for the poor, the sick, and the outcast, presented the message that all people—regardless of their position or status in society—were created by God and deserved to be treated with respect and dignity. The early Christian community portrayed in the Book of Acts shows a group of people, united in a common purpose, sharing all that they had in common. Those that possessed needed items gave them to the community to be distributed to those that needed them.

The values derived from the Judeo-Christian tradition, especially those of social justice, charity, and equality are still seen in American society. Through the ages, however, these values have found themselves in conflict with other prevalent values—values such as individualism and self-reliance.

Individualism

One of the most prominent values embedded within American society and debate about social policy is the value of individualism. This is the belief that success is achieved through one's individual strivings and efforts. If an individual is motivated, there is little to prevent the individual from achieving financial, personal, or social goals that a person sets for oneself. This basic value was fostered by the frontier ethic that existed in the U. S. The huge expanses of unclaimed lands seemed to beckon to anyone who had the motivation and individual strength to fashion a new life out of the untamed land. Success and achievement was attributed to the individual. The flip side to this, however, might be found in the corresponding philosophy that failure to achieve one's goals, to provide for oneself or one's family, or to suffer from want was due to individual failure.

Such a focus on the individual has greatly affected the way that society views the poor and the needy. Americans have traditionally sought to attribute fault on the "unsuccessful" members of society. If the cause of one's misfortune was outside of one's control—for example, the result of a flood or a natural disaster, or the result of naturally occurring processes like that of aging—then individuals are generally met with compassion or sympathy. These individuals would be considered "worthy" of assistance. In other cases, Americans tend to be quick in assigning blame or fault to those in need. This has led to a phenomenon known as "blaming the victim." Though those assigning blame to the affected individuals attribute the person's plight to a defect within the person. Ryan (1976) portrayed this social phenomenon in his book entitled *Blaming the Victim*. Ryan sought to demonstrate how this phenomenon had been applied to blacks over the years, but argued that every social problem has been analyzed within the framework of a victim-blaming perspective. Within this ideology, the deviance of a person or group from societal standards or norms is attributed to failed or incomplete socialization or as the cause of the problem, not as the result of detrimental factors affecting the person or group. Social problems are treated as individual problems resulting from individual deviance or the specialized deviance or problems of a small group of people (Ryan, 1976). Out of such modes of thinking comes concepts such as a "culture of poverty" or of an "underclass." These ideologies suggest that there are learned characteristics within marginalized groups that prevent their assimilation into productive society or inhibits the amelioration of the problem. The effect is still the same, though—the locus of the defect is within the individual or group of interrelated individuals, not in the structural patterns of racism, classism, or economics, for instance.

The value that Americans place on individualism has had dramatic effects on social welfare in the U.S. and in issues of service delivery. In addressing social problems and developing programs to address them, individualism has led the U.S. to pursue a policy of selectivity or exceptionalism. Within the framework of selectivity or exceptionalism, problems are seen as specific to certain persons and problems are treated on a person-by-person basis. This is the opposite of universalism. The Universalist framework sees problems, not as unpredictable and specific to isolated individuals, but as predictable and a function of social or structural arrangements (Ryan, 1976). To illustrate these two perspectives, Ryan used a medical analogy. In treating smallpox, one might examine and treat those individuals that became infected with smallpox on a case by case basis. The other alternative would be to vaccinate everyone within the population in order to prevent future outbreak of the disease. The former method would be indicative of an exceptionalist approach, while the latter would be more Universalist in nature. Tropman (1989) wrote that the U.S. has favored selective policies as they have the appearance of being less expensive and are targeted toward affected individuals. Individualism places a greater emphasis on individual or personal change as opposed to changing the external or social systems or structures (Tropman, 1989). This is true even when the cause of an individual problem is directly related to a public issue.

An ardent belief in individualism seems to reign during periods of economic success and prosperity. The poor during these boom times are viewed as being unmotivated, slothful or idle. Society begins to sing a different tune, however, when hard times fall on the country and the markets crash. During these times, the public clamors for government intervention to address the peoples' plight. When so many are affected, as during the Great Depression, what once was attributed to individual faults or failings are quickly attributed to the structures of the economy, to the cyclical patterns of capitalism, or other factors outside of the individual's control. The tendency to attribute poverty to individual characteristics is lost when millions suddenly find themselves poor for circumstances that were beyond their control.

The Ethic of Work

One of the most important values in understanding the American psyche is that of work often referred to as the Protestant work ethic. Inherently tied to the capitalist market system, the origin of this value has traditionally been attributed to the Protestant religious movement, especially through the writings and teachings of Protestant theologians such as John Calvin and John Knox. Within the Protestant framework, which originated with Martin Luther, individuals were either predestined to salvation by God's grace or they were predestined to remain outside of salvation. There was little one could do to achieve salvation, but had to rely on the grace of God. The question that arose, however, was how did one know that one was destined for heaven or hell? One's salvation status was thought to be evident in the individual's status in life and in the harmony of one's family and economic conditions. Financial prosperity was a sign that one had been saved. Furthermore, work was essential to the pattern of the person's life. Stemming from Luther's notion of a vocation or, literally a "calling", one's occupation or work was given by God. Fulfilling God's plan was achieved through the patterns of work. It was the believer's obligation to follow one's calling. To not work was seen as a sign of an unmoral life. The belief became widespread that those that did not work were lazy, slothful, and immoral.

Many have suggested that the issue of whether one works or not is the primary issue in making the distinction between the "worthy" and the "unworthy" poor. Tropman (1989) suggests that work often denotes worthiness because work indicates that a person is trying to achieve something and is trying to control one's environment, not just passively waiting whatever might occur. In a book entitled *Why Americans Hate Welfare*, Gilens (1999) proposed that Americans view welfare unfavorably because of public perception that welfare recipients are "undeserving" and would "rather sit at home and collect benefits than work hard to support themselves". Gilens suggested that Americans' distaste for welfare is not over a violation of individualistic values, but is due to the perception that the welfare rolls are filled with undeserving recipients. Americans are in favor of government support for those in need, but only if those receiving support are deserving.

Like the value of individualism, works bearing on an individual's worthiness and moral standing is often dispensed with when masses of formerly employed people suddenly find themselves unemployed, as they did during the Great Depression. During periods of economic hardship, people are more likely to attribute unemployment to the structures and pitfalls of the capitalist system, which is, by nature, subject to alternating periods of booms and busts. Nevertheless, even during periods of expanded relief such as occurred during the New Deal, work relief programs in which recipients worked for government-provided wages were preferred over direct relief programs in which cash or in-kind benefits were given.

One's past or present work status is a factor in public opinion regarding social welfare programs. For example, she wrote that Social Security retirement and disability benefits, for example, are not commonly thought of as "welfare." This is due to the fact that people generally pay into these programs through their past work efforts. Public assistance is seen as "welfare" because the public pays for the benefits.

Social Darwinism and Laissez-Faire: Against Interference in the "Natural" Order

Social Darwinism came about when Darwin's theories of natural selection within the natural world were extrapolated onto the realm of human society. Darwin's theory of natural selection stated, in essence, that organisms that are better suited for a given environment will have greater success in reproducing and have a better chance of their offspring reaching maturity. Those organisms that are less suited to exist in a particular environment will have less success in reproduction and raising their offspring to reproductive age. Lesser-suited organisms will, barring any biological or environmental changes, cease to exist while better-suited organisms will thrive. When applied to the societal realm of humans, Darwinist theory was used to support the notion of withholding assistance from the poor and the needy. Those that could not survive within the economic and social world were seen as unfit.

While these ideas are collectively referred to as Social Darwinism, these types of beliefs were espoused by Darwin's predecessor, Thomas Robert Malthus. Malthus' theories were presented in his *Essay on the Principle of Population*, first published in 1798. Malthus asserted that the population of an area will outstrip the area's ability to provide food and subsistence for the population unless there were various checks on the population. These checks included moral restraint, vice and misery. Moral restraint, the preferable means of checking the population, included the postponement of marriage until one had the means to successfully provide for one's family. Misery and vice, which were viewed as the result of not practicing moral restraint, included accidents of nature, miscarriages, pestilence, epidemics, famine, war, and other hardships. Malthus proposed that the poor laws of England should be repealed. By assisting those who could not support themselves, society was attempting to circumvent the laws of nature. The poor laws allowed for increases in the population without increasing the levels of food production, thereby spreading a limited amount of food over a greater number of people and diminishing the amounts available to more productive and worthy members of the population. The poor laws, according to Malthus, promoted poverty and dependence, and took away the natural checks that spurred individuals toward activity and economic independence.

The philosophy of Malthus, combined with the thoughts of classical economists

such as Adam Smith, helped to usher in an era dominated by a laissez-faire philosophy.

This philosophy dominated during the nineteenth century. Trattner (1994) described the

laissez-faire philosophy in the following way:

> Human happiness, or rather the greatest happiness for the greatest number, was
> the purpose of life and the goal of society. Society, it was believed, was
> composed of isolated individuals, each of whom was the best judge of his or her
> own interest. The sum of each individual's good led to the good of the whole. As
> a result, any interference with the individual was a blow or an impediment to the
> social good or welfare. Since wealth was a primary source of happiness,
> unfettered self-interest and the accumulation of wealth (and property) was the
> ideal, the economic welfare of the nation was not a matter of predetermined
> policy, but one of free and natural growth (p. 52).

Though Social Darwinism and Malthusianism have lost favor as theoretical

systems, remnants of these ideologies still exist. There are, for example, those who believe

that educational ability is biologically predetermined, suggesting that little can be done to

improve one's situation. By emphasizing the biological predisposition of individuals, the

effects of altering or improving one's environment or increasing opportunities for the

needy are viewed as relatively ineffective. The modern debate as to whether public

assistance fosters dependence and hinders a recipient's sense of urgency and self-reliance

hearkens back to Malthus' theoretical system. A laissez-faire philosophy remains

prevalent in society and its adherents believe that governmental interference in the

economy is counterproductive and violates the natural workings of the "free market."

Equality and Status

The United States was founded on the theoretical principles of liberty and

equality. That these principles did not apply to many of the country's inhabitants—

African-Americans and Native Americans, for instance—is clear, yet the value of equality—in theory or in reality—is important in understanding the system of American values. The importance of equality was, in part, a reaction to the highly stratified class systems of England and other European countries from which the colonists emigrated. The colonists came to this country with dreams of founding a new utopia where the unlimited possibilities of the frontier beckoned to any that were willing to realize their destiny. Opportunities in the colonies and in the frontier lands were open to all, according to the myth. Free of the class entanglements and limitations of Europe, American culture came to incorporate an almost mythical belief in the equality of individuals.

Within such a context of equality, it was believed that social status, as well as economic status, was a result of the individual's achievements. Unburdened by class structures, the individual was free to advance as high in social standing as he (women were not necessarily included in this scheme) wished. This is the basis for the myth of the "American Dream". A popular tale reincarnating itself throughout American history is of the poor young man who, through hard work and the right motivation, climbs the socioeconomic ladder until he has become a wealthy man of high social standing. Within this scheme, high status and social standing is earned as a reward for one's hard work and efforts. This system is based on the belief—quite false—that life is fair for all and that all people are placed on a level footing (Tropman, 1989). As social workers, we are all too aware that this is not the reality. Nevertheless, the belief in the "American Dream" and the equality of opportunity afforded to all still exists.

Incidentally, the idea that the poor threaten those of higher class standing because they threaten the mythical values to which they attribute their success in life is *in your face rich mofo's*

commonplace. The presence of the poor calls the dominant values of social mobility and

the fairness of life into question for those of higher classes.

Discrimination and Prejudice

Paradoxically, a society that has traditionally espoused the value of equality has

also vigorously discriminated against individuals and groups that are "different" from the

norms and standards of the dominant white males that have traditionally served as

America's elite. Though the most glaring examples of such beliefs in practice might

come from the centuries of enslavement, segregation, impoverishment, and

discrimination against African-Americans or from the wholesale extermination of the

original Native Americans that inhabited the "New World", other examples abound. Over

the centuries, African-Americans, Native Americans, Jews, Catholics, Irish, Italians,

Chinese, Japanese, Latinos, immigrants, gays and lesbians, and many others have born

the brunt of societal prejudice and discriminatory practices in the United States.

Discrimination and prejudice against blacks was a prominent feature of American

social policy throughout most of the nation's history, and it continues today, though in

less blatant forms. For instance, much of America's antagonism toward welfare is due to

the continued perception that welfare recipients are black and that blacks are, according

to a centuries-old stereotype, lazy and less committed to the work ethic than whites

(Gilens, 1999). According to Gilens, this stereotype that grew out of the need to justify

the existence of slavery still exists in society and is perpetuated by the media.

Women have traditionally been excluded from the societal benefits granted to

men. The history of women in the United States may be characterized by systematic impoverishment, forced dependence, subordination to patriarchal authority. Since colonial times, men have controlled the economic, social, political, sexual, and reproductive rights of women. The roles of women have traditionally been dictated by patriarchal and capitalist powers that have generally placed the woman in the "proper" role of the wife, managing the affairs of the home and dependent on the male breadwinner. In Abramowitz's *Regulating the Lives of Women* (1996), the author proposed that much of social welfare policy favors this conventional "family ethic"; social welfare programs are designed to reward those fulfilling their proscribed roles while punishing those who actively choose or are forced into alternative arrangements. While acknowledging the role of the work ethic in society's concept of the "deserving" or "undeserving" poor, Abramowitz wrote that a woman's compliance with the conventional "family ethic" determines whether society views her as worthy of assistance.

While all women have been affected by gender bias and discrimination, the subjugation of women of color has been especially severe throughout American history. This trend has continued to the present day and the role of the social pariah once assigned to the aged or the infirm is now played by the poor minority mother.

Independence

A value that has affected Americans view of charity is the concept of independence. Closely related to the concepts of individualism, the work ethic, and equality, independence encompasses the belief that being independent is optimal for the individual or the family. Self-reliance and autonomy are the conditions to which all people should attempt to achieve. To be dependent on others, especially with respect to public assistance is a sign that one has given up trying (Tropman, 1989). Throughout

U.S. history, charity has been looked on unfavorably. This is due to the belie

creates a state of dependence in others. This belief persists today.

Conservatives often call for the end to all federal funding of welfare and to end

the social safety net. In the last decade we have seen the conditions of the poor worsen.

Moralist Opinions

Within virtually all of the values mentioned above is an element of moralist

tendencies. Those that are impoverished, ill, mentally ill, physically impaired, drug

addicted, or those in the criminal justice system are often collectively judged by society.

Society tends to ascribe bad or incorrect morals to the individuals in these groups. The

belief is that immoral behavior results in the problems of the afflicted individuals.

Stemming from the Puritan ethic of the New England colonies, a New Puritanism has

gained prominence in the United States, which emphasizes "proper behavior." This new

form of Puritanism proscribes abstinence from activities that are thought to be

immoral— promiscuity, gambling, and drug use, etc.—but also holds up the standard of

the "traditional" American family based on a patriarchal arrangement between a man and

a woman. The moralists within society tends to ascribe the actions or behaviors of

individuals or groups with qualities of good and bad or right and wrong. Moralism and

the tendency to judge others plays itself out in the development and implementation of

public policy. Some communities call for the eviction of families from public housing if

one member of the family is involved in illegal drug activities.

This value can be seen clearly in the current debates over needle exchanges. In

an attempt to prevent the spread of HIV and other diseases, various groups have

attempted to distribute clean syringe needles to individuals using heroin in order to deter the sharing tainted needles. The motive for this initiative is not to facilitate drug abuse or to condone heroin use, as critics suggest, but to prevent HIV infection in a highly susceptible population. Needle exchanges attempt to meet those addicted to heroin at their current motivational level. Their efforts, however, have met with severe criticism. In a recent legislative action in April 1998, the U.S. House passed a bill banning the use of federal funds for needle exchange programs. The bill was passed despite research presented during the debate that demonstrated that such programs help stop the spread of HIV and provide a first step in getting addicts to seek treatment. Speaking about needle exchange programs, Speaker of the House Newt Gingrich stated that support for such programs was indicative of "why we have been losing the war on drugs" and in 1998, Congress suspended the use of funds from the District of Columbia's budget toward needle exchange programs despite the fact that the District has the highest rate of new HIV infections. The restrictions against funding these programs is currently being debated. There are numerous reasons why such opposition to needle exchange programs exists despite endorsements from organizations such as the Centers for Disease Control and the National Academy of Sciences. Among them is the belief that abusing drugs—a "bad act"—is voluntary. Viewing heroin abuse in this way, it is easy to see how opponents believe that addicts inflict problems on themselves and are not worthy to be helped.

American social policy has often attempted to prohibit certain behaviors or practices that are deemed to be immoral. The belief that alcohol consumption inevitably resulted in drunkenness, lawlessness, and immoral behavior resulted in the passage of the Volstead Act of 1919, which began Prohibition. This stands as prime example of this way the United States has attempted to manage social problems. Another more recent

example concerns sex education and contraceptive distribution in the public schools.

Segments of society are of the opinion that prohibiting sexual activities is the answer to

the problems of teenage pregnancy and the spread of HIV and sexually transmitted

diseases (STDs).

Among the many issues that might cause the social work student to write off the

study of policy is the apparent complexity of social welfare problems. The perceived

complexity of social welfare policy issues is due, in part, to the interconnectedness of

political, social, historical, and especially economic issues. One cannot effectively

comprehend the dimensions of social welfare policy without some understanding of the

economic contexts surrounding social problems. Not only do many social problems

stem from economic problems, but the debate over possible solutions to these problems

are often motivated by economic opinions and ideologies and possible means of

addressing social problems will be drafted and implemented within economic

frameworks.

While the average social work student reading this book does not necessarily

need to understand the details of Keynesian economic theory or the ins-and-outs of

"supplyside" economics, a basic knowledge of how the economic system in the United

States affects social welfare and public policy is necessary in understanding how social

policy has evolved. Understanding the basic economic trends in the U.S. should make the

social worker a better informed and, therefore, more effective agent of change. By

understanding these things, the social worker empowers him- or herself to be more than

just an agent of social control, implementing policies blindly; the worker will better understand his or her role and the role of the client or group within the larger economic framework.

The American Capitalist System: The Theoretical Base

The American economic system is based on the classical formulation of capitalism. The theoretical base that provided the underpinning of the evolving capitalist free market system was formulated by classical economists of the eighteenth and nineteenth centuries, a group which included Adam Smith, Thomas Robert Malthus, David Ricardo, and John Stuart Mill. The collective essence of classical economic thought is represented in the idea of a competitive market in which goods (as well as services) are produced specifically for sale in the market. Within the system, the means of production are owned privately; private capital is invested in the production of goods and services. The commodities produced are then exchanged in a free market in which the supply and the demand for items regulate themselves by means of the competitive model represented by individual choice. Within the theoretical free market model, the system regulates itself, with wages, prices, and profits being determined by the laws of supply and demand. The classical capitalist system theoretically regulates itself without government interference or external controls on the market, a condition known as *laissez-faire*. The freedom of the producer and the individual consumers to pursue their own economic self-interest leads to the greatest good for all concerned. Adam Smith wrote that social welfare was best served by individuals pursuing their own interests without restraints; in this way, social welfare is maximized.

This then provides the theoretical underpinning for many schools of economic and political thought throughout the development U.S. policy, even to the present day.

Milton Friedman, a modern economist, proposed that only in a laissez-faire free-market workings of the capitalist system would society prosper. Early economists, even up until the 1930s, failed to fully recognize the cyclical depressions that periodically wreaked havoc on the economy. Furthermore, early economists were virtually blind to the issue of unemployment, assuming that, just as demand for a product always came to equal supply, so the demand for labor would always equal the supply. Within a free-enterprise system, it was assumed that those willing to work could always be utilized in one type of industry or another. This view remained intact until the Great Depression, when its masses of willing yet unemployed workers revealed the fallibility of such a belief. By failing to adequately address periodic depressions and chronic unemployment, freemarket economists failed to take into account two major features of the economy as we know it today.

Though the American economy may be theoretically based on classical capitalism, governmental policy has not always reflected the laissez-faire model. Even prior to the massive expansion of governmental involvement in the economy in the 1930s, the federal government had periodically added itself to the market system. Perhaps the most notable move toward regulating the market was the anti-trust legislation passed during the Progressive Era. The classical economists had proscribed a system wherein no one business or firm had enough economic power to influence the market and its prices. The rise of trusts and monopolies—a result of capitalism at its worst—came to be seen as a threat to the competitive system itself. Legislation to control monopolies and trusts ensued. In addition to regulating the market by means of legislation thwarting trusts and monopolies, the government has involved itself in the market in other ways.

Laws regulating labor and employment, such as those setting a minimum wage, regulating the length of the work week, and the setting of minimum prices are all examples of this, as is unemployment insurance. Subsidies for agriculture and business also reflect governmental involvement in the market.

Interventionist strategies increased dramatically during the New Deal. This was, in part, due to a shift in the dominant economic ideology. The new economic practices were based on the work of John Maynard Keynes, a British economist. Keynes' economic formulations factored depressions and unemployment into the regular workings of the free-market system. The classical capitalist system was now seen as not being self-regulating. A laissez-faire system was not fault-proof; something was needed to counteract the periodic failings of the free-market system and to provide employment for those out of work (Galbraith, 1952). Keynes proposed that the government could counter the failings of the free-market system by various methods, including public expenditures, the construction of public works, manipulating tax structures, developing appropriate monetary policies, and shifting interest rates. By means of this system, Keynes proposed a system of "managed capitalism" which would allow private capital to remain virtually untouched while addressing the needs of socially-oriented reforms. Through such a system, adopted in part by the United States, government became more intensively involved in the market. This type of system, not unlike those proposed by advocates of greater freedom of the market, has its share of critics as well. Since the early days of capitalism, there have been a plethora of criticisms of the system and its societal effects. Before examining some of the critical arguments against the American capitalist system, let us briefly look at the widespread social effects that ensued following the rapid rise of the free-market system in the United States.

The Rise of Capitalism and its Effects on Society

The emergence of capitalism in the late 1700s and continuing throughout the 1800s altered economic and social relations in radical ways. With the rise of capitalism came the need for wage laborers who tended to move from rural agricultural areas to towns and cities, where industrial jobs were to be found. This soon created a class of landless manual laborers in towns and cities. This shift from rural to urban areas often left families without the security of being able to support themselves by living off of the land and tended to break up the traditional extended kinship networks that characterized those settled on land and farms; often, there was a lack of a caring community in the city. Once settled in urban areas, wage laborers needed to remain relatively mobile in order to follow the shifting demands for labor, thus leaving them more vulnerable in times of crisis the farther they became separated from their kinship networks. As households became smaller and more specialized, they were often less able to help needy family members, especially as space became a limiting issue in the smaller houses, apartments, and tenements of the city. The move toward industrial wage labor within a capitalist framework tended to force the elderly and those deemed physically "unfit" out of working roles. Whereas in agriculturally-based families elderly individuals could contribute to the family's well-being by performing less strenuous—yet necessary—jobs, few industries would hire elderly workers when younger and seemingly more capable workers were available. With the rise of wage labor, a division was created between home and work. "These forces, combined with an increasingly sex-segregated labor market, added to the problems which women faced as they sought a new role within the new urban landscape—a landscape in which economic power was in the hands of the male "breadwinners". Incidentally, while notion that white women were not "fit" to labor outside of the home according to the "family ethic" predominated, this standard did appear to apply to women of color, who were more or less expected to labor (Abramowitz, 1996).

As the free-market system expanded, so did attempts to expand the wealth of the capitalists who owned the means of production. This created a process by which industries and businesses became more concentrated into larger centralized operations. With this trend came an increase in the struggles of workers, as more and more workers were uprooted or displaced (Burghardt, 1996). In addition, under the capitalist system, the connection between the producer, the process of labor, and the commodity produced became less and less clear-cut (Burghardt, 1996). Whereas in the past, one made a product and then sold it or traded it for another good that was needed, industrial workers now came to sell their labor for wages, which then allowed them to purchase products that they needed. Burghardt (1996) related how capitalism increased the alienation and exploitation of the worker and diminished the quality of relationships in society:

> Under capitalism... so many more commodities are produced not for immediate use but for market exchange. The social relations necessary for such large-scale production are so much more disparate and nonfamily based that social relations (between people) are turned into material ones and material relations between things are turned into social relations. People no longer interact except when they exchange their commodities, including the commodity of their own labor. Individuals exist for one another only insofar as their commodities exist.

> In its abstraction, labor itself becomes a commodity that is exchanged for subsistence wages within the mode of capitalist production. In essence, labor

power (the actual expenditure of physical and mental energy to produce commodities) is transformed into a particular exchange values (wages) by capital, which is represented not as a "thing" but in the personification of the capitalist. The human relationship of work and production is now abstracted into a battle over wages, prices, and profit (p. 418).

Taxation and the Continuum of Economic Ideology

A primary tension in the relationship between economic ideology and social welfare policy stems from perceived challenges to personal liberty and freedom. This tension is one between too much market or too much state. If the market is given total freedom to work without interference, individuals and groups may be caught in the inevitable problems and effects of market mechanism such as recessions, unemployment, and poverty. Surely poverty is a threat to the liberty of the individual. On the other hand, as the state becomes more involved in the market, individual and business freedoms may be curtailed by the controlling power of the state. The tension is further heightened, according to Kuttner between the principles of democracy and the market:

> Political democracy and market capitalism exist in an uneasy marriage. The democratic state proclaims equality. The market generates inequality. The ideological champions of the market *celebrate* inequality. In the civic realm the first democratic freedom is citizenship—membership in a political community, which implies security and an equal voice in governance. In the market realm, the first freedom is freedom of exchange—the liberty to achieve personal economic success or failure. Absolute freedom of exchange thus creates extremes of social inequality (p. 10).

Decisions about social welfare and public policy are made within these contexts.

One of the major areas in which this debate may be seen is that of taxation. The state's policies of taxation directly affect the economy. One of the functions of taxation is, beyond supporting the state and its works, to redistribute income to the benefit of particular classes or groups within society. By redistributing income, patterns of income and wealth generated by the market are modified. Some view the redistributive tax policies as impinging on individual freedom; heavy and progressive taxes are viewed as unfair. They take money away from those with more resources, thereby preventing them from reinvesting in the market, which would, as the argument goes, create more jobs and a stronger and productive economy. This, then, would benefit those that remain outside of the current economic prosperity.

Those on the other end of the ideological spectrum argue that the market inherently creates economic inequalities by its very nature. The state's role is to mediate and minimize the negative effects of the economy in the lives of those left in the freemarket's wake. Progressive tax structures would offset some of the effects of the market. Proponents of this type of redistributive plan might, like Kuttner, argue that efforts to promote economic equality do not necessarily have to cancel out efforts at economic efficiency and production, and that social justice and economic prosperity are not mutually exclusive. Those promoting this view might suggest the elimination of poverty creates more purchasing power for those that were formerly poor, thus fueling businesses and economic growth (Kuttner, 1987).

PART II – Historical Context for Social Welfare Policy and the Policy-Making Process

Chapter 4 – The History of Social Welfare and Social Work

The absence of a historical perspective can lead to confusion about contemporary social welfare policies, history gives us a sense about how and why particular social welfare programs developed.

Events do not occur in a vacuum- neither do social policies. There is a broader political, social economic and historical framework that underlies all of our current social welfare institutions and policies. It is important for a social work student in an agency setting today to understand these factors because they have a major impact on who, what, where, how and why you are able, or unable, to provide certain services for your clients. This section will focus on providing the reader with a historical perspective on our social welfare institutions.

First, it is apparent that values and views of the human condition that are prevalent at a given time in history ultimately influence society's response to human need. Two major conflicting values: that of the goodness of man and the opposing view, that humans are, at their core, shiftless and lazy, have historically guided social welfare policies. These two conflicting values are often held simultaneously, perhaps by different members of the same society. We can see this conflict in the United States today in our debate about how to deal with issues of poverty.

The Judeo - Christian Background

The ancient Hebrews developed a concept of social justice, which can be seen in the Old Testament. While rooted in a religion, the concept of social justice reflects an understanding that a person has a moral obligation to provide for others: the duty to give. The doctrine goes further—it speaks of the right of those in need to receive (Trattner, 1999). This concept is an early formulation of the concept of "entitlement". In fact, ancient Jewish laws stress that one must not provide for those less fortunate out of a sense of charity but, rather, out of a duty to justice. Thus, an early concept that those who are in need are entitled to benefits from others is established. During the time of the codification of Jewish law in the Talmud, the concept of "tzedaka" was elaborated on by the Jewish philosopher Maimonides.

Tzedaka

According to the Torah, giving tzedaka, which is charity given to the poor or less fortunate. This is a revered commandment that is considered to be one of the ways to be redeemed. Tzedaka is an essential and vital component of the Jewish religion. It shows how material possessions are not really owned by the person but bestowed upon them by HaShem, which should in turn be distributed as dictated by Him.

Every person is required to give some Tzedaka no matter what position they hold in society. Even if the amount of charity is small, it could mean that the contribution is more significant because of the limited means they have themselves to give. The only exception is when the person is unable to provide for themselves does the expectation to give leave. The basic guideline is 10 percent of the earnings, however if this percentage causes the person to then have to accept tzedaka is the guideline waived.

Giving a percentage of the earnings alone is not enough to fulfill the duty of tzedaka. The spirit of giving should be a compassionate and humbling experience. Even if the amount given is extravagant and excessive, it becomes meaningless if the giver is upset by giving the charity. It is unacceptable to turn away a poor person. Even if the amount is small or words of comfort, the person asking for charity should never be turned away feeling shamed. It is also preferable that tzedaka be given anonymously as this is not something to give the person giving tzedaka a sense of pride. If the person is unwilling to accept tzedaka outright then every effort should be made to sell the person something at a lower cost in order to assist them. It is allowed to donate something and have a name attached to the memorial.

If at all possible, people should try not to accept tzedaka. People should lower their standards of living or take a lower level job in order to avoid taking tzedaka unnecessarily. The only exception to this is if the person is unable to change their lifestyle without affecting their health. This is often true for the sick and the elderly.

Christianity, too, emphasized the values of doing good and providing for all in need, not from a sense of charity but as a social responsibility. Stemming from the idea that all people were created in the image of God, it followed that everyone should be treated with dignity and respect. These are values that are clearly part of our social work tradition today. The Church provided for the needy through the institution of the monastery, a place of refuge where basic needs would be met.

The Middle Ages

During medieval times European society was tightly structured and hierarchical. Serfs were obligated to work for landowners who were in turn responsible for the serfs well-being in terms of basic necessities. Fiefdoms were subject to the rule of the local nobleman. Monarchs controlled more substantial holdings; however the system remained fluid and subject to change as wars were fought and monarchs acquired or lost possession of their lands. Social welfare functions were carried out by landowners with respect to "their" serfs and by the Church. The primary economic system during the Middle Ages was a system of barter and trading of goods. Money as currency had not been developed and society was primarily organized around agricultural activities.

Transitional Times

Several key influences on our modern American concept of social welfare are derived from social, political and economic events in England and on the European continent, which occurred between the end of the Middle Ages and the 17th century. During this period, feudalism declined as the growth of new ways of manufacturing goods became more prevalent. This movement toward industrialization had several key ramifications, which ultimately impacted on individuals and their welfare. Key among them was a movement away from the land and toward the newly developing cities, the need for people who had subsisted on the land to learn the newer skills in order to find employment, and the transition from an economy based on barter and trade to an economy based on currency. The developing emphasis on a capitalistic economy, with a concomitant emphasis on individualism, has had and continues to have a profound influence on our own conceptions of social welfare functions.

Elizabethan Poor Laws

As industrialization progressed primarily in England during these times, the majority of people who had survived on the land became subject to displacement by landowners who could begin to use more efficient machinery and had less need of human labor. With displacement there arose a need to learn new skills. However this was not so easily accomplished. A new class system arose as those with skills progressed and as merchants, traders and bankers became more powerful. The political structure remained a monarchy with the King as the ultimate authority. Church and State were one. Taxes were paid by subjects to the monarch, who accumulated great power and wealth even as the "landless class" grew significantly. Other environmental conditions such as disease and famine led to increasing dissatisfaction with the ever-increasing taxation and governmental controls by those who were disenfranchised. However there were other forces of change at work as well.

During the period called the "Enlightenment" philosophers such as John Locke in England and later Voltaire in France and Adam Smith in Scotland, promoted theories considered radical at the time. These theories included limiting the government's regulatory role, promoting the advancement of knowledge through empiricism and scientific methods and the belief in the immutable progress of man. These philosophers argued that the role of government should be restricted with respect to interventions in citizen's lives; that scientific knowledge should be pursued; and that the marketplace would stabilize itself if forces of supply and demand were left unchecked. Further, Smith argued that a "free market" would be good for society because competition in the market place would encourage entrepreneurs to develop new products. Those theories were in sharp contrast to the prevailing role the government played from the 14th through the 17th century.

Throughout this period in England and in Europe, however, the government had played a significant role in regulating and controlling the population. This was particularly true for the new landless class. A series of restrictive measures, aimed at punishing "vagabonds" and restricting able-bodied men, and restricting their movement had been imposed during these years, together with severe punishments for those able-bodied men who had become beggars. At the same time, laws had been passed to assist the "worthy" poor, the aged, and the infirm.

The governmental role with respect to the needy was consolidated in the Elizabethan Poor Laws of 1601. These laws were an attempt to deal with the consequences of a transitional society: a society that was moving from feudalism to an industrialized society; a society that had major disruptions due to the poverty of the new "underclass" as well as due to famine, disease and natural disasters.

Key principles of the Elizabethan Poor Laws are in evidence in our social welfare programs of today. These key principles included a distinction between the "worthy" and "unworthy" poor, with the "unworthy" considered to be able-bodied men; that "relief" or assistance to those who truly could not provide for themselves, the "worthy" needy, should be a public responsibility, although it should be a locally financed and locally administered public responsibility. The actual function of dispensing aid to the needy should be operated by the Church, who would appoint local "overseers of the poor". The Elizabethan Poor Laws also established the principle that parents should be responsible for their children and children for their parents, to the degree possible.

These principles are reflected today as the debate within the United States as to whether States and localities or the Federal government should have final responsibility for the needy continues. Since 1996 it is clear that we have moved back toward a more local conception of where the responsibility should rest. The Personal Responsibility and Work Opportunities Act of 1996 reflects the "devolution" of governmental responsibility away from the Federal government and places it squarely on the shoulders of State and local government. We also see the Elizabethan Poor Law of "family responsibility" reflected in our current debate about the needy. This would seem to be a return to the more traditional notions that families are obligated to care for their own members. This represents an individualistic view of the reasons for need, and does not reflect the complex realities of a post-modern society in which "need" is not reflective of a lack of morality, but the product of a host of environmental and market conditions, acting with and upon individuals. We see today also aspects of the principle of separating the "worthy" from the "unworthy" poor. This is evident in our programs of "residual" social welfare: that is, assistance given in an emergency and for short periods of time due to unforeseen circumstances to those in dire crisis. However residual social welfare programs embody an underlying values framework which seeks to punish the receiver. This is in sharp contrast to assistance given as "institutional" benefits to those who have paid their dues into the system, primarily through the institution of "work."

The Elizabethan Poor Laws demonstrated the values conflict prevalent at that time in England: and still prevalent today. How should the needy be treated? Who are the needy? What is (should be) the role of government with respect to meeting needs? What is the role of the family? To what extent should "charity" be provided? And under what conditions? We can sees these principles in questions and debates raised today by citizens and legislators alike.

Case Example

> *Ms. B is a 26-year-old single mother. She has two children, ages 2 and 4. Both were born out of wedlock. She was denied assistance by the state agency. They referred her to the Employment Office of the agency and told her she should get a job. They said she should move in with her sister and her husband and their two children in their two-bedroom apartment. They felt the family could take care of the B's until Ms. B got a job.*

Protestant Reformation

The influence of Martin Luther's challenge to the Church in 1511 is pervasive. The main theme of Luther's challenge to the Roman Catholic Church was to see "God's hand in everyday work". Together with Calvinism, work became a "divine vocation", thus imbuing the concept of "work" as a divine activity. Thus, the opposite of work, or "idleness" becomes sinful and work reflects the main purpose for which we are put here. Calvinism was seen as promoting work as the only activity...and which serves to increase the glory of God. Today we define these views as part of the "Protestant Work ethic" and they are clearly present as we deal with questions of the nature and causes of poverty and how to treat the poor. We hear words like "those on welfare are just lazy" and "those on welfare simply need to get a job". These sentiments reflect, in part, the ideology expressed in the Protestant Work ethic: work is divine: not to work is to be influenced by evil. These views of the worth of work also reflect the Calvinist tradition of "personal responsibility" and individualism, as well as the religious idea of work as being an indicator of worth in the eye of God. The Personal Responsibility and Work Opportunities Act is based on the idea that public entitlements serve to reinforce "dependency" while work (of any kind) reinforces dignity and self-esteem, cherished values in our society.

The American Colonial Experience

American systems of social welfare are defined by those who colonized this country, primarily the English and Dutch in the early days, and later other Europeans. These early settlers brought with them the conflicting values of a system of care for the needy. However the early colonists encountered quite different conditions in the New World which also had an impact on how the needy would be conceived of and cared for. A country rich in natural resources with uncharted land opportunities for growth and expansion presented many opportunities. However conditions were extremely harsh, from the initial voyage across the ocean in crowded and unsanitary conditions to the forced deprivation, the harsh winters, the encounters with Native Americans, the diseases and near starvation conditions that existed-all these reinforced conditions of poverty and hardship that many encountered upon arrival.

There were many reasons to come to this new land, some were seeking freedom to practice their religion, others were sent here as convicts, poor, homeless, and as other undesirables. All brought with them their values and a sense of how society should work. Many of the values and ways of treating the poor, which had been codified in the Elizabethan Poor Laws, was clearly part of the cultural context of these new immigrants. The organized system of dealing with poverty was to acknowledge public responsibility for the poor at the most local level: the village or parish, as was done in England. Programs for dealing with children and other "worthy poor" were differentiated from the treatment of able-bodied men. Systematic opportunities for assistance in the community for children were provided through "apprenticeships" to local families, "relief" in the home was provided for the elderly and sick. Providing assistance in the home came to be known as "outdoor relief" and was the primary means of giving assistance to the needy.

While communities generally felt obligated to provide for those who were members of the community, a system of "mutual aid", strangers were viewed with suspicion. This was particularly true for male strangers and restrictive laws were passed prohibiting non-residents from receiving any help from communities to which they traveled: in effect, residency laws were established to keep strangers who might become a public burden out of a particular community. As the social and economic structures became more complex and the growth of cities continued, several factors became important. First, if one was skilled, there were many employment opportunities as the cities and industrialization proceeded. However for those lacking skills, it was quite a different story. While there was certainly a need for skilled laborers, persons with limited skills had no place.

The conflicting value of those early settlers is evident in the systems that were begun to provide assistance. "Relief" evolved from a system of mutual aid in the community, with families caring for indigent (resident) children and other worthy poor toward a more complex and differentiated system of "outdoor" or community relief. Able-bodied men, following the Calvinistic tradition and the Poor Law heritage were considered to be "sinners" and were viewed with hostility. They were often forced into indentured servitude or put in jail- thus beginning a long tradition in America of equating "poverty" with "criminality" and "moral lassitude."

Women

Women generally had no separate economic existence. They were considered property of their husbands. They were expected to contribute to the economic well being of the household. If widowed they could be considered "worthy of support" and might receive assistance from family, friends, or the local community. If they had children the local community might try to provide support.

Abramowitz (1996) reports that women were imported to stimulate the formation of families so that men would settle down and the crown would have a stable workforce. The states that offered women land for settling in America, eliminated the inducement when the independent female landowners chose not to marry. The slaveowners forbid the right to womanhood to black female slaves. Women were thought of as less rational and needing of guidance, and the raising of children was primarily the responsibility of the father. In the nineteenth century, liberal feminists attacked the denial of access to citizenship rights by women. Importantly, any equality was focused on equality outside the family not inside the family. This dichotomy between private and public life was not challenged.

Women's advocates in the 1800's argued for economic independence for women, and attacked the prevailing notions of beauty, contested the "occupation of women by men" and discussed ways that women were oppresses as a group rather than individuals. Maria Stewart and Elizabeth Cady Stanton in the 1800's were among the first black feminists who encouraged women to build a community support system, and they argued in favor of black women's activism and self-determination. They insisted that sexual and racial oppression were the fundamental causes of poverty among women and attacked religious justification of women's oppression.

Children with no method of support were to become apprentices to families that could support them. This arrangement however, was only true for white children and not for African or Native American children. Apprenticeship served an educational function as well as an economic function in which children would become trained in a specific skill leading to employment opportunities. Apprenticeship also served as a disciplinary or social control function that of teaching and maintaining disciplines among potentially "unruly" children.

Slavery

Slaves were considered to be the property of their masters. It was the master's responsibility to care for them and the community did not support them since they were *not* part of the broader society. Thus, slaves were not considered for community assistance.

Laws supporting slavery were seen as early as the 1680's in the colonies. The *Black Codes* were laws that institutionalized slavery by establishing slaves as property, not people; maintained dominance of whites; and protected the whites' ownership of slaves. It has been contended that these laws legitimized the racial subordination of African Americans and thus institutionalized racism.

Most slaves worked in the fields and supported the agricultural economy. The labored long hours were punished harshly for whatever wrongdoing their owners determined. Their food was rationed and only basic clothing was provided. While some slaves lived on the farms and plantation working both as house servants and on the land, others lived on large units with absentee owners. It has been attributed that the emergence of an indigenous African American culture to the slaves was a result of their physical separation from the "big house" and were able to establish their own religious practices, family life and kinship relationships and communities. The unique culture of the slaves combined the survival of elements of their African homelands with their unique interpretations of white institutions such as Christianity.

The word slavery does not appear in the United States Constitution, but the Constitution gave indirect permission for slavery. The Continental Congress delegates provided that three-fifths of "all other persons" would be counted in determining the number of Congressmen each state could elect to the House of Representatives. That euphemism for slavery established that slaves were not whole persons with equal right to representation. Further, the Constitution required the return of fugitive slaves to their owners thereby condoning slavery. It also set an ending date of 1808 for the importation of slaves.

Native Americans

The new immigrants' response to Native Americans was one of suspiciousness and cruelty. There were no attempts to understand the culture, religion and way of life of these "strange" people. Considered to be "savages", the Native populations were pushed off their own lands and moved to the West. Those who were not forced to move were subject to harsh regulations as well as to outright murder. However the singly most disruptive influence of the immigrants was the introduction of diseases heretofore unknown to the Native American population. Once introduced, these diseases spread rapidly and were extremely deadly since the native populations had no natural resistance to the diseases. The resulting displacement, disease and death of Native Americans have had serious consequences, still being faced today, by these populations. Native Americans were outside of the concern of the colonists for assistance.

The American Revolution

The American Revolution set forth principles still important for us today. A primary principle is the concept of equality, although equality was not applicable to all.

Equality clearly did not include Native Americans, slaves and women. A principle concept of the early days which has also had long term consequences is that of separation of Church and State- ultimately leading to "private" and sectarian vs. governmental forms of assistance and to a continuing debate about responsibility for certain areas of human life. In terms of assistance, while religious diversity flourished to some degree, each group developed means of assistance for their own group members. These voluntary institutions are very much with us today and serve a major social service function. Today we see agencies operated by Catholic Charities, Jewish Federation, and Protestant Welfare League, which play a major role in our social welfare system. Some of you, as students, will be placed in these agencies and/or work for them upon completion of your degree. Hospitals and nursing homes, mental health agencies and child welfare agencies, programs for women and substance abusers are operated by many of these private and voluntary agencies, although in our current system, many of these "sectarian" agencies receive a substantial portion of their funding from governmental sources and they serve all in need without regard to religious affiliation.

Another important consequence of the American Revolution and the signing of the Constitution is that the Constitution does not delegate responsibility to the Federal government for the welfare of the people. Rather, the States are charged with the public's welfare. This has had, and continues to have, a significant impact on the ways in which our current system for treating poverty works. Although, as we shall see later in this Chapter, there has been a period of the last 60 years in which the Federal government has assumed some major responsibilities for the general welfare of our country, throughout most of our history it is the States and the localities who have had major responsibility for poor and vulnerable populations. This has resulted in a highly fragmented "non-system" of care with as many different ideas and definitions of who should receive care and how it should be delivered, as there are states.

The Development of Institutions: 1800-1870

The significant factors in the new Republic's response to need was the continuous increase in new immigrants, many of them unskilled, the ability to expand westward which simply did not exist in Europe and the continued rise of industrialization. By the middle of the 18th century, as the population increased rapidly, so did poverty. The concept of an almshouse developed, borrowed from England. The almshouse would become the institution in the community to care for the sick and elderly who were unable to care for themselves. But for the able-bodied, punishment through enforced labor in a workhouse or incarceration in jail became the primary mode of dealing with poverty. Thus the moral issue of poverty as a sin continued. This resulted in a movement toward the rapid expansion of the workhouse, sometimes known as "indoor" relief. This also constitutes the beginning of the development of separate institutions in the community rather than having the poor live amongst families. These workhouses became one of the major forms of assistance during much of the 19th century.

Andrew Jackson's election to the presidency in 1828 spurred an era of reform ideas about universal education, expanded voting rights, and the temperance movement was born. While Jacksonian democracy prevailed there was a shift in ideology and values concerning the poor and how they should be treated. However the countervailing forces of Social Darwinist ideology and the Protestant Work ethic, tied to capitalism combined to form a powerful thrust towards a more punitive response to the "lazy and indolent" utilizing the institution of the workhouse. As local governments struggled to find the monetary resources necessary to help the growing population of the needy through raising local taxes, citizens and their representatives became more opposed to "public" assistance in the form of grants. Instead they looked more favorably on the concept of enforced work, primarily seeing it as a form of social control for those "deviants" who seemed unable to secure work. It appeared to the majority that poverty was on the rise and the solution seemed to be the enforced labor and residence in a workhouse. Conditions in the workhouse varied from poor to horrendous, often with disease and starvation as constant companions.

As conditions in the workhouse did not seem to be an effective means of controlling poverty and as stories about the conditions in these "asylums" became public through the works of Charles Dickens (England) and journalists in America, a reform movement began which has impacted on policies, services and programs even today.

Dorothea Dix was the key reformer of the era. She is best remembered for her efforts to differentiate juveniles, adult offenders and the "insane" and to advocate for specialized facilities for each of these groups. She also pushed for Federal responsibility for the care of the mentally ill.

By the time Ms. Dix began her crusade on behalf of the mentally ill, innovations in treatment had occurred and several private hospitals for the "insane" had been founded. It was Ms. Dix's contention that states could best serve (the indigent) mentally ill, rather than local workhouses. States had more financial resources than counties and could afford to hire "quality staff." It was also Ms. Dix's contentions that the Federal government should bear some responsibility for the mentally ill. After extensive research into the conditions of the insane; and after visiting jails, houses of correction and workhouses, she presented her findings. At first she presented to the State of Massachusetts, her home state. Following a successful change in that State she presented her findings and a proposal to the United States Congress in 1848. She proposed that the Federal government give land grants to the states in order for the states to build and maintain institutions for the mentally ill. Although Congress passed legislation in support of her proposals, President Franklin Pierce vetoed the legislation in 1854. His rationale was that the Federal government had no responsibility for the social welfare of the country: that social welfare was the responsibility of the States. The veto by President Pierce, and the placing of responsibility for the welfare of the people on the states is once again evident in the passage of the Work Opportunities and Welfare Reform Act of 1996. As is always the case in a pluralistic society, prevailing ideologies are complex. There was, therefore, during this time period a continued growth of private and sectarian charities that assisted specific groups. The general public was much more comfortable with the notion of private charity, which was felt to be a more appropriate means of providing for the poor, rather than a reliance on public assistance.

Examples of these charitable societies include the Scots Charitable Society, founded in 1657 (one of the earliest of these organizations); the New York Society for the Relief of Poor Widows with Small Children (1798), the New York Association for Improving the Condition of the Poor (1843). By the time the A.I.C.P. was founded there was some concern that charities were duplicating each other. There were also concerns about the "moral needs" of the recipients of charities. Male volunteers were to provide religious teachings to the poor as well as to prevent the duplication of charity. It is known that the A.I.C.P. probably served more as an agent of social control than that of a charitable organization, and it paved the way for the Charity Organization Societies later in the century that have had a significant influence on the development of social work as a profession.

Often overlooked in a discussion about private charity were the mutual aid groups, which were developed in the African-American community. These groups were rooted in the African value system and heritage. They revolved around the importance of family and survival of the tribe. Although slavery disrupted, and in many cases destroyed, natural families intentionally, African-American mutual aid societies managed to exist surreptitiously. Their purpose was to provide assistance to the sick and to serve as burial societies for the dead. Later on, these mutual aid groups took on functions of education and the provision of concrete benefits for those in need.

During the first part of the 19th century, childcare was changing as well. Children's institutions, primarily orphanages, were rapidly developing. Many were funded by both private and public monies. Although children were separated from adults, a key component of these institutional settings was to control the child: therefore an emphasis on order and obedience prevailed. During the latter part of the 19th century, newer forms of thinking about childcare emerged as a result of more sophisticated views of children and their needs, which were becoming more prevalent. In 1853 Charles Loring Brace founded the Children's Aid Society in New York. His mission was to provide education and shelter to needy children, and to remove them from their natural families when these families could not provide "proper" care. The concept that we know as "foster care" was developed by Brace who also felt that the urban environment was not good for these children. He further felt that the children should be given the opportunity to live in a totally different environment, in a rural setting. In this way, the children would be removed from the crime and delinquency that was increasing in New York City and given new opportunities with families in the rural parts of the country. Over a period of 25 years, 50,000 children were removed from their natural families by the Children's Aid Society. Many of these children became runaways and a backlash arose in those communities to which they had been sent. However the Children's Aid Society was also responsible for developing numerous programs in New York City which served poor children, and they continue to provide services to children today.

The Civil War Period

During the Civil War there was a growing need for health and social services for both the wounded and dying soldiers on the battlefield and for families and children left behind. Both private and public endeavors were begun to assist in the efforts needed. As the Civil War neared its end, the Federal government recognized that the "freed blacks" had multiple needs. Somewhat surprisingly, the government established a social service bureau within the War Department to assist these freed slaves. The Freedman's Bureau, established in 1865 provided an array of services and opportunities including health care, help in finding and building housing and the provision of social services. Perhaps one of the most significant contributions of the Freedmen's Bureau was assistance in the establishment of educational institutions including colleges, meant to help African-Americans gain access to high quality educational experiences. The Freedmen's Bureau was short-lived and ended in 1872. Once again, the Federal government asserted that they should not bear the responsibility for welfare activities.

Throughout the 1800's, Americans' views of the poor and how to provide for their needs showed the conflicts that we still see evident today. The role of government (mostly local at first, then State) expanded and contracted, depending on circumstances related to the numbers of the needy; wars; economic conditions and the political scene. As the social sciences began to develop, ideas about whether poverty was a "natural" state of affairs or was a moral condition shifted. A major influence on the thinking about the poor and poverty was a result of Darwinian philosophy being "translated" to the social sciences and becoming a social philosophy. Early in the century, the publication of Thomas Malthus Essay on the Principle of Population, had a major effect on thinking about the role of government in assisting the poor. The Social Darwinists believed that human society, analogous to biological communities, advanced through "survival of the fittest". Since the poor could not survive without intervention, these Social Darwinists reasoned that the poor were not meant to survive. They proposed that it was wrong for government to interfere in the natural order by providing any kind of assistance. Assistance was seen as causing overpopulation, surely a condition to be avoided.

However, as we have seen, there were countervailing forces based in part on the principles derived from the Judeo- Christian tradition and from the Elizabethan Poor Laws that suggested that certain types of needs should be met.

Scientific Charity and the Charity Organization Society

Many of the factors discussed above contributed to the rise of "scientific" charity. The continued growth of urbanization, and industrialization; the fact that poverty was not being reduced but rather was increasing; the belief that municipal assistance should not be provided; the growing numbers of private charities; and the faith that spurred the growth of capitalism and Social Darwinism, led to several important developments. First, the country was unprepared to deal with the rapid changes that were occurring, particularly with respect to the growth of the poor. While there was a great reduction in any type of governmental assistance, there was a huge increase in the numbers of private charitable organizations. With this rise, however, concerns about providing assistance to the needy were voiced by people who adhered to the social Darwinist philosophy. William Graham Sumner, a leading Social Darwinist from Yale University, for example, felt that the charities would only lead to inefficiency and waste. He believed (as did others of the time) that no assistance was preferable to any assistance; that those who could not provide for themselves were inherently "weak" and therefore would not contribute to the ascendancy of the human race.

However conditions worsened as unemployment rose due to economic forces. Private charities increased but so did calls to organize the charities. In the late 1870's the Reverend Stephen Gurteen, having studied such an organization in London, proposed that an organization be established to coordinate the efforts of all the private charitable organizations in a community. The organization, modeled on the Charity Organization Society that he studied in London, was first established in Buffalo, New York in 1877. Among the Charity Organization Society's organizing principles was that it was to serve as a coordinating body for all private charities to promote efficiency and avoid duplication of services. The C.O.S. developed registration lists of the poor served in the community and established the concept of cooperation among charities: It also borrowed the concept of "friendly visiting" from the A.I.C.P. However instead of male "visitors" the C.O.S. friendly visitors were women. The role of the visitor was to investigate the conditions of each person visited to "diagnose the cause of destitution", and to register the poor. The C.O.S. movement rapidly caught on and these organizations were developed in many of the major cities. Their emphasis on planning, coordinating and organizing resources in the community was part of the scientific movement of the times. These ideas were also prominent in the development of business and industry. The importance of the investigative methods of the friendly visitors in the development of the profession of social work needs to be stressed as well. The methods developed, and later promoted in professional papers, led directly to a method of social work practice, social casework, which still plays a prominent role in our current clinical practice.

The Development of Casework

The emphasis of the friendly visitor was on the individual's need for help, and the determination of the individual's "worthiness" to receive assistance. The C.O.S stressed the moral imperative for material aid only to the worthy, summarily rejecting the sturdy beggar, the alcoholic, the womanizer and the prostitute. Work was stressed as the means to eliminate poverty and therefore the C.O.S., in many cases, developed employment services. Religious values were a significant part of the work of the friendly visitors, who were middle class women and volunteered for the roles. It is of significance that the mission of the C.O.S. was not to provide more charity to the needy. The purpose of the investigation was to assess and document need in order to provide a more efficient and rational means of allocating resources. One of the unintended consequences of the friendly visitors, however, was the beginning of understanding that social and environmental forces were significant in the lives of the poor. This shift occurred as a result of the record-keeping activities of the friendly visitors, so the notion of "personal responsibility" for poverty needed to be somewhat reconsidered.

Before long, it was recognized that volunteer visitors needed some direction and training. Mary Richmond, from the Baltimore C.O.S. made a strong statement about the need for training of the volunteers in 1897 at a meeting of the National Conference on Charities and Correction. The first formal training program, lasting just six weeks, was begun at the New York School of Philanthropy in 1898. Several years after, the program was extended to a one-year program and by 1912 a two-year curriculum in social work was developed. The school became known as the New York School of Social Work and later the Columbia University School of Social Work. By 1919 there were 17 schools of Social Work in the United States.

The Settlement House Movement

By the end of the 19th century, American cities had grown at a staggering pace. By 1900 the proportion of Americans who lived in cities had reached one-third, and by 1920 it had reached one half. Many of the city dwellers were immigrants who were either poor to begin with, and/or were not trained and many did not even speak English. Conditions in these urban areas were overcrowded, with poor sanitation, and lack of suitable housing.

A response to these conditions, known as the Settlement house, emerged in England and was copied in the United States by the end of the 19th century. One of the most important Settlement Houses, as well as one of the first established, was Hull House, established in Chicago by Jane Addams in 1889. The Settlement Houses had several major aims: a primary aim was to live amongst the poor, in their own communities, and to provide cultural education and vocational training opportunities for new immigrants. The primary focus was not on charity, but on social and economic reform. Women were the predominant residents in the Settlement Houses and they focused their attention not only on vocational activities but also on cultural activities and on the children of the immigrants. These were highly educated women, and to a lesser degree men, and, as their concerns tended to be broad and they expressed concerns about the influence of the environment on the lives of the needy, they began to develop programs for children and youth (the concept of Kindergarten arose from the settlement house movement as did the first juvenile court), their concerns about overcrowded housing led them to advocate for housing and public health legislation, they were concerned about the need to teach English to the immigrants, they began arts and cultural programs for their constituents and they advocated for improved working conditions for men, women and children, and for recognition of the newly developing trade unions. Because many of the women had been trained in the social sciences, there was an emphasis on researching the conditions they encountered. It was the careful research produced, together with a skillful use of advocacy, which led to many of the reforms of the day.

Questions can be raised about the role of the Settlement Houses with respect to African-Americans. Although there were some efforts on the part of some of the Settlements to work with the African-American population (for example, some Settlement House residents worked with the African-American community to establish the National Association for the Advancement of Colored People (NAACP) in 1909), many feel that, on the whole, there was not a lot of attention paid to the needs of the African-American community by the Settlement House participants.

Members of the Settlement House movement were concerned with social justice. They promoted the idea of "community" and believed in a democratic vision for the neighborhoods in which they lived. The members of this movement have been contrasted to the volunteers and founders of the Charity Organization Society who were concerned with efficiency and on promoting morality among the poor. However, there were certainly similarities among the two movements in that both represented middle class values, both understood to some extent the importance of the environment on the lives of the poor both movements were concerned with gathering data and doing research, both movements relied on volunteers to accomplish their goals. A major difference in the methods each movement chose to implement its goals was that the C.O.S. volunteers relied on individual interventions while the Settlement House residents worked primarily with groups of individuals and with neighborhoods.

The Development of the Profession of Social Work

The C.O.S., and in particular, Mary Richmond, was extremely influential with respect to the casework curriculum in the schools. In 1917 Ms. Richmond published a book, *Social Diagnosis*, which discussed techniques for the assessment of the poor. In 1922, her book, *What is Social Casework?* Defined a casework method as processes which develop personality through adjustments consciously effected, individual by individual, between men and their social environment. The underlying and enduring principles established by Mary Richmond are an integral part of the profession today.

Although there were some contentious differences between the Settlement House philosophy and methods and the C.O.S., in the beginning of the 20th century there was an attempt to merge some of their ideas. Both movements are important to the development of professional social work and to social work education. Whereas the C.O.S. emphasized the individual and played a significant role in the development of social casework, the Foundations of group work, and, to a lesser degree community social work, are, to some degree, legacies of the Settlement House movement.

Early in the development of the professional schools, a debate emerged between two divergent approaches to a curriculum. Questions arose, as to whether there should be a strong emphasis on an academic curriculum, based on social scientific theory and having an orientation on reform and social policy, or whether the curriculum should be rooted in "practice wisdom" with a more practical emphasis on field work experiences and with strong relationships to social agencies. While the University of Chicago, with its connection to Hull House adopted an orientation toward social policy, many other schools emphasized the preparation of caseworkers more heavily. Ultimately a two-year curriculum was adopted, which is based on both academic learning and work in the field. As social work began to be practiced in a wide variety of settings, specializations began to be developed. For example, medical social work services were first introduced at the Massachusetts General Hospital by Dr. Richard Cabot in 1909. The first medical social worker was Ida Cannon. Psychiatric social work began as psychiatry itself was developing. "Casework" was felt by some community-minded psychiatrists to be an important adjunct to psychiatry. Social workers also worked actively with children and families, in schools and in the criminal justice system. At first, each field of practice developed its own curriculum and association, however by the end of the 1920's a more generic model for social work education was formulated. Today, the social work curriculum for all Master's students in the United States is an outgrowth of these early decisions modified over time, to be relevant to the concerns of social workers practicing in a variety of settings and with diverse populations. The accrediting body for Schools of Social Work is the Council on Social Work Education (CSWE) which sets standards for both undergraduate and masters degree programs in social work. While schools may differ somewhat in their orientation and in their major emphasis all masters programs are required to meet certain standards. This ensures that social workers trained at an accredited school of social work will have similar competencies and understandings of the issues relevant to practice today.

The Progressive Era

The period from the last two decades of the 1800's to approximately the start of World War I is known as "The Progressive Era." As we have seen, there were many changes in the definition of how assistance to the needy might be given, from the registration, coordination and friendly visiting practices of the C.O.S. to the development of the Settlement Houses and the beginnings of professional social work. We have also indicated that many of these developments arose together with the rapid rates of urbanization and industrialization and the rapid increase in rates of immigration. As the country moved away from agricultural activities, there was a movement towards providing more support for laborers, particularly in the form of better protection from harsh working conditions, lack of security in old age, unemployment due to recessions and so on. The initiatives to provide protection arose as a result of strikes and harsh conditions. It should also be remembered that in Europe the socialist movement was growing and gaining respect among intellectuals and academics. Some Americans were also influenced by the ideology promoted by the socialists. Americans who were part of the leadership of the Progressive movement included Jane Addams, John Dewey, the American philosopher and educator who had a significant influence on educational practices in the United States, George Herbert Mead, Eugene Victor Debs and others. The Progressive reform movement addressed political, economic and social conditions. The major social welfare outcomes of the Progressive movement revolved around the beginning provision of social insurance programs such as workers' compensation and the beginning of assistance to the elderly and dependent children; legal protections for workers, particularly with respect to child labor; the beginning of state and particularly federal governmental regulation for example the Intestate Commerce Commission was begun during this period. It was also during this period that women were beginning to make strides both in the labor market and by finally gaining the right to vote. It was also during this time that Prohibition was established. Many of the concepts and programs established during the Progressive Era became prototypes for the programs that would move the country toward the establishment of a (reluctant) social welfare state in the 1930's.

Social Work continued to develop as a profession during this period. While Schools of Social Work were developing, there were still issues of practice and method to be defined. Social workers were beginning to practice in a variety of settings, including medical, psychiatric, child welfare and criminal justice settings. Some stressed the importance of casework and the casework method while others stressed research, an interest in social policies and reform and administration. In 1920 the Association of Training Schools of Professional Social Work was established. Ultimately this body became the Council on Social Work Education and today sets the standards for all schools of Social Work that have accredited Master's and undergraduate BSW programs.

The primary emphasis of social workers during the first two decades of the twentieth century remained on the development of the methods of social work with the emphasis on social casework. In search of a method to call their own, the precepts laid out by Mary Richmond's book, Social Diagnosis, played an important role in defining what social work was and what social workers did. As the influence of Freud grew, social workers embraced many of his methods and concepts, as they seemed to "fit" with their own work. These were years in which the emphasis on social reform among social workers was not nearly as strong as the emphasis on developing a technical method and developing a profession that could be recognized as such by the public.

The Great Depression and The New Deal: The 1930's

Subsequent to World War I, the 1920's were generally a time of prosperity. Economic and social forces, as well as advances in scientific thinking, contributed to commitments to expanded services for children, mothers' pension laws, an emphasis on prevention of mental health problems through the child guidance movement and improved public health measures.

The crash of the stock market in 1929 dramatically changed the situation, however. Unemployment rates skyrocketed leaving people, often for the first time, hungry and without any source of income. This was not simply "the poor" who faced joblessness, for the first time the middle class was severely affected. The more traditional response of the charity organizations was simply not sufficient to meet the needs of these "new poor" and it became clear that drastic changes in the way in which "welfare" was thought about were necessary. It was common for the unemployed to suggest that, "We're about down and out and the only good thing about it that I see is that it is not much farther down we can go."

In the beginning of the Depression the federal government was slow to react. President Hoover rejected the calls for federal intervention. At the same time, the Governor of New York, Franklin Delano Roosevelt, had instituted an emergency unemployment assistance program, to be provided to those newly unemployed, and based on the fact that taxes had been collected from those who had worked prior to the Depression. This program served as the prototype for several of the New Deal programs after Roosevelt's election to the presidency in 1932.

Initially, the Roosevelt administration focused on the passage of emergency measure to address pressing needs.

Roosevelt then turned to the development of more permanent solutions. Programs instituted during Roosevelt's administration served for 60 years, until 1996, as the key social welfare provisions in the United States. Two major categories of programs have

Emergency Banking Relief Act   March 1933
        Banks were closed while the government inspected the health of all banks.
The President was given power over many banking transactions. The Federal Deposit
Insurance Corporation (FDIC) was formed.

Federal Emergency Relief Administration (FERA)   May, 1933
        Harry Hopkins, a social worker, in charge of $500 million for quick relief.

Civil Works Administration (CWA)   November 1933
        Gave the unemployed jobs building or repairing roads, parks, airports, etc.

Civilian Conservation Corps (CCC)   November, 1933
        2.5 million unmarried men worked on forests and parks for $1/day plus board
and job training.

National Industrial Recovery Act (NIRA)   June 1933
        Helped business and workers and set a minimum wage.

Public Works Administration (PWA)   May 1935
        Projects such as the Grand Coulee Dam.

Federal Securities Act   May 1933
        Established the Securities and Exchange Commission (SEC).

Agriculture Adjustment Administration (AAA)   May, 1933
        Tried to restore prices for farmers by cutting production and eliminating
        surplus. Established the farm subsidy principle.

Tennessee Vally Authority (TVA)   May 1933
        Helped farmers and created jobs where they were needed.

Works Progress Administration (WPA)   May 1935-1943
        Spent $11 billion on projects: construction of airfields, schools and hospitals
        and projects for writers, artists, musicians, actors, etc.

Farm Security Administration (FSA)   May, 1935
        $1 billion for migrant labor camps.

Resettlement Administration (RA)   May 1935
        Aided farmers not benefiting from the AAA.

Fair Labor Standard Act of 1938 (Wagner Act)
        Banned child labor: set minimum wage.

served as the foundation of our social welfare system. The categories represent social insurance programs, meant to provide assistance to those who have contributed to the workforce, but, due to market conditions and/or individual circumstances beyond their control, they are no longer able to work, and public assistance programs, meant to assist those who simply cannot help themselves. The cornerstone of Roosevelt's policies was the Social Security Act of 1935 which established, in principle and in law, a federal social insurance system for workers once they reached a certain age, as well as unemployment and disability provisions for workers. It also established in principle and in law, a state and federal program of assistance for needy children, the elderly poor and the disabled.

Social Security Act

1935 – Passed in response to the "Great Depression" and the severe economic hardships in the country. In reaction, the *Federal Government* assumes a *Central Role* in Social Welfare.

The *Social Security Act* establishes *basic programs-*

A) *The Social Insurance System*:

- Social Security benefits for seniors

- Unemployment Insurance

- Disability Insurance

B) *Public Assistance*:

- Aid to Families of Dependent Children

- Old Age Assistance

- Aid to the Blind and Disabled

Additionally, FDR focused on work as a means of addressing unemployment and the following programs were created:

Works Progress Administration (WPA) which was a job that employed at its peak 2.5 million men and engaged in 250,000 projects (e.g. road and bridge construction, library and public housing construction, painting of murals and cultural projects).

National Youth Authority – gave jobs to adolescents to enable them to stay in school.

Civilian Conservation Corps – employed young men to work in preservation of natural resources in conservation camps.

One of the key principles of this era in America, was the understanding that the federal government shared responsibility for the welfare of its citizens. This concept, known as "the welfare state" represents the idea that, in a complex society, the individual cannot meet all his or her needs at all times without some assistance from "The State". The concept of "entitlement" emerged from the policies of the New Deal, a concept of federal responsibility for (at least) some of the people's welfare.

It should be noted that Roosevelt believed in the primacy of work: many of the policies established during the New Deal were based on the ideas that assistance should be given on a temporary basis, in an emergency, to those workers who suddenly found themselves unable to work (i.e. unemployment insurance, disability insurance). In addition, there was a distinction between the social insurance programs and the public assistance programs which maintained the distinction between the "worthy poor" and the "unworthy poor". Those considered "unworthy" would receive public assistance, supported by the government, but at a price: the "means test", a humiliating experience for those who apply. In addition, the public assistance programs were shared programs with the States, allowing states some discretion in the administration of these funds. The social insurance programs, on the other hand, are not subject to a "means test". So long as one had worked and contributed to the nations' economy, one would be eligible upon reaching a certain age, for example, to receive social security benefits. These distinctions have maintained the concept that the "poor" are somehow not similar to the "worthy", creating destructive separations of groups of people. It has become clear over the past 60 years, that the primary targets of these policies have been women, children and people of color.

The legacy of the New Deal was the creation of the "welfare state", far less developed than the European welfare states created during the 20th century, nevertheless generating programs that benefit citizens in a variety of ways. The major programs of the welfare state generally fall into three major areas: education (which is often not even considered to be a "Social welfare" program but which, in fact, is a right of all children), the social insurance programs including social security, unemployment insurance, disability insurance, Medicare and so on, and the means-tested public assistance programs such as A.F.D.C. (now T.A.N.F.), general public assistance, food stamps, Medicaid, and so forth.

What role did social workers play during these times? Although it can be said that the major preoccupation of social workers had been, as noted, on the refinement of "method" and working with individuals, as the Depression affected a significant number of Americans, some social workers began to renew a commitment to social reform. It was realized by some, that major reforms would be necessary to deal with the huge economic losses suffered. In fact, a social worker named Harry Hopkins was appointed by Governor Franklin D. Roosevelt to direct the first unemployment relief program enacted (in New York State). Known as The Wicks Act (1931), this program provided temporary emergency funds for work relief and home relief and served as a model for the Federal Emergency

Relief Act that was later instituted when Roosevelt became President. As governmental

relief efforts became more widespread, both for social insurance and public assistance

programs, there were more opportunities for social workers to enter into public service

positions. As a result, more and more people entered into professional schools of social

work and the number of qualified social workers increased significantly. Another outgrowth

of these times was a resurgence of interest among many social workers in social reform. Of

significance also, was that many social workers assumed leadership positions during the

New Deal, and thus influenced the social policies that developed. For example, Harry

Hopkins, a social worker and confidant of President Roosevelt, helped to design and was

put in charge of the Federal Emergency Relief Administration (FERA). In this capacity he

was responsible for the distribution of $500 million for emergency relief funds.

From the 1940's Through the 1960's: The Great Society and the War on Poverty

World War II was significant for America not only because of the vital role the

United States played in ending the War, but also because of the increase in employment,

especially for women, during the War itself. Prosperity increased for many after the war

was over as well. There was a movement away from cities, as suburbia began to grow,

there were more opportunities for higher education, and there was a generalized feeling

of comfort. What was not discussed was the fact that many remained (or became) poor;

and, as mentioned previously, the majority of these were women, children and minority

groups. John Kenneth Galbraith first called attention to the poor (albeit the minority

poor) with his book, *The Affluent Society* in 1958. Michael Harrington pointed out in his book, *The Other America: Poverty in the United States* (1962), that there was significant poverty in the United States although the poor were mostly invisible to the majority. He estimated that there were over 40 million poor Americans in the beginning of the 1960's.

The "Cold War" with the Soviet Union, the paranoia about a "communist takeover" and the witch-hunts of Senator Joseph McCarthy contributed to the lack of major federal social policies being enacted in the 1950's. An exception was the amendment to the original Aid to Dependent Children provision of the Social Security Act which became Aid to Families With Dependent Children in 1950, thus somewhat expanding the definition of eligibility. When John F. Kennedy was elected President in 1960, he was the youngest to have achieved the office of President. On the foreign affairs front, he was primarily concerned with the growing gap between the Soviet Union and the United States with respect to defense issues. He was also concerned with stimulating the economy. However an extremely significant issue was coming into national prominence which was to have a major impact on the nation. That was the growing attempt by American Blacks to gain access to the "rights" of Americans: the Civil Rights movement. The beginnings of the Civil Rights Movement occurred in the 1950's but, by 1960 there was more attention paid to the increasingly serious protests over the severe discrimination faced by the African-American community and the sometimes violent responses to these protests. Not only were American Blacks not allowed to vote, they were not allowed to use the same restaurants, restrooms, schools and other public facilities that Whites had access to. While overt discrimination took precedence in the southern part of the United States, African-Americans in the North were discriminated against too, but perhaps somewhat more subtly. Under pressure, Kennedy eventually introduced the Civil Rights Bill in 1963, which was passed after his assassination in 1963.

Initiatives in the Kennedy Administration

- **1960**   A law signed by President Eisenhower gave disability payments to disabled workers of any age and their dependents.

- **1961**   The age at which men were able to collect old-age benefits was lowered to 62.

- **1962**   Manpower Development and Training Act – (MDTA) This act enabled disabled workers to get technical job training.

- **1963**   Community Mental Health Centers Act – This act gave federal funding for the construction of mental health centers which were designed to offer preventive and outpatient services.

The Civil Rights movement, under the leadership of Dr. Martin Luther King, Jr., promoted non-violence while asserting equal rights for African-Americans, however major changes were slow to occur. By any count, the American Black represented the poorest, sickest, least well educated, and most highly unemployed population: it was thus becoming increasingly clear to some that more drastic measures needed to be taken. The Civil Rights movement addressed not only the political disenfranchisement of the blacks, particularly in the south where they were not allowed to vote (let alone hold office), but also the economic and social consequences of discrimination. It was also becoming increasingly clear that poverty and race were linked and that, proportionally, the poor were representative of the African-American community.

President Lyndon Johnson assumed the presidency upon John F. Kennedy's assassination. Not only did he inherit the problems posed by the extreme levels of poverty and racism encountered by the African-American community, he inherited other domestic initiatives such as the result of Kennedy's emphasis on providing job opportunities (through the 1962 Manpower Development and Training Act). However he also inherited a foreign policy nightmare: the War in Vietnam. The conflicts caused by the War in Vietnam, the extreme feelings of either opposition or moral justification of the war, often by members of the same family; the rapid increase in the number of American troops sent to Vietnam; and the instant media coverage of the War efforts resulting in Americans seeing for the first time what War really looked like, created an extremely difficult political condition for President Johnson and ultimately he made a decision not to run for President in 1968.

Despite the increasing militancy of young Americans in opposition to the War effort, and the movement away from nonviolence of the American Civil Rights movement, the Johnson administration was responsible for significant programs promoting social welfare legislation. In the language of militancy, he instituted a "War on Poverty" in 1964 with the passage of the Economic Opportunity Act. The primary goals of the Economic Opportunity Act were to allow poor communities to develop their own programs to deal with poverty. The emphasis was on "community development" and neighborhood social action. The goal was to create local Community Action Programs under local control, which would be able to challenge and change the structure of more traditional community programs; integrating them and making them responsive to the specific needs of a local neighborhood. Under the Economic Opportunity Act, individual communities established Community Action Boards, which were nonprofit agencies that could design proposals for neighborhood improvement. The proposals, if accepted, would be funded directly by the Federal Office of Economic Opportunity, bypassing local bureaucracy. A significant aspect of the legislation was the encouragement of local participation by those who would be most affected by the programs. This was a new development in American public welfare policies, and seemed an outgrowth of a focus

on participation in the growth of the country, originally called for by President Kennedy.

These ideas were considered controversial by many: who would actually gain

control of these organizations? Whose goals would be adopted? What role would local

community people play?

Social Welfare Initiatives

The Great Society (Kennedy/Johnson Era)

Entitlement/Benefits:

- expansion of social security benefits; in terms of dollars and populations covered;

  SSDI benefits

- enactment of Medicare and Medicaid programs

- passage of Food Stamp Legislation

Programs

- The War on Poverty

- Economic Redevelopment

- Headstart

- Community Mental Health Centers

- Civil Rights Legislation

- Job Corps

- Vista

- Model Cities

- Legal Assistance for the Poor

- The Older Americans Act

The decade of the 1960' is considered to be a time of social reform, a time in which the social conditions of the U.S. were undergoing rapid change, a time of general optimism and hope. However it was also a time of increasing violence during which a President, a Civil Rights leader and a candidate for President were boldly assassinated; a time when students and the "establishment" frequently clashed, sometimes resulting in violence, and a time when there was significant migration to urban areas as well as serious unrest in many cities. The unconventional political tactics of the civil rights movement brought national attention to the problem of racial discrimination. As a result, Congress passed the Civil Rights act of 1964; the most comprehensive legislation to date designed to eliminate racial discrimination. Despite the policy and programmatic innovations of the 1960's, poverty and racism were certainly not eliminated.

What was the role of social workers during these times? During the 1940's and the 1950's many social workers once again were somewhat less interested in public social services and more interested in working in the voluntary agency sector. Social work methods of group work were developing, but social casework remained the primary focus for many. Psychiatric social work had assumed major importance during World War II, and social workers began to be interested in family dynamics became a focus for social workers where both group work methods and casework were important. The programs of the 1930's had stimulated more interest in public social policy and, by the early 1950's some social workers were becoming interested in community social work. However as a result of the emphasis on neighborhood action during the Johnson era, community organization activities in social work moved forward at a more rapid pace and grew to include community development activities, social planning activities and to incorporate social action and advocacy activities as well.

Retrenchment and Conservatism: 1970-Present

From the late 1960's through the 1990's, the beneficiaries of our social welfare programs have been changing. At the outset of the "New Deal" social welfare legislation to the 1950's, the fastest growing programs were the social insurance programs providing assistance to the elderly. However, during the latter part of the 1950's and into the 1970's, the Aid to Families with Dependent Children program rapidly grew. There was growth in numbers of this program and the numbers of non whites grew as the number of roles was growing. For example, there were a growing number of poor women and children who were African-American receiving assistance through the A.F.D.C. program. The percent of poor African-Americans far exceeds their proportions in American society. As the "welfare" rolls grew, to be African-American became equated with poverty in the public's mind. Thus, "poverty" and "race" came to be associated by the general public. Martin Gilens points out in his book, *Why Americans Hate Welfare* that contemporary images of the poor, often played up by the media, foster the association between poverty and race (Gilens, 1999). Other minority groups, including those from Central and South America, Native Americans, Asians, experience high proportions of poverty. In fact, poverty has essentially become a forum for the frequent promotion of racial prejudices and stereotypes.

Nixon Years (1969-1973)

The Nixon years were characterized by a retrenchment of many social programs and a movement towards a more conservative social philosophy. Nixon was generally opposed to federal interventions in the lives of the people, yet, surprisingly, he promoted several new social welfare directions and an innovative social program called the Family Assistance Plan. The proposal was to provide poor, unemployed families with a minimum allowance provided by the Federal government, of $1600 a year. The program

was to provide the difference between marginal wages, and the designated poverty line,

and in order to meet the eligibility criteria, work would be required. The work

requirement would apply to both men and women. If this proposal had passed, it would

have essentially nationalized the way benefits to the poor and the working poor were

administered, setting a national minimum "floor" for benefits and a federal administrative

structure. Although the Family Assistance Plan did not pass, some of the core ideas, i.e. a

federal minimum as opposed to state discretion for certain benefits, became part of the

reorganization of the categorical programs of Old Age Assistance, Aid to the Blind and

Aid to the Disabled into the Supplemental Security Income program of 1973. This

reorganization represented a considerable change in the administration of these

programs, and made the federal government responsible for all public assistance for the

adults poor who were considered to be unemployable. A minimum "floor" for benefits,

which had to be provided by all states, eliminated the great disparity in aid to this

population that had existed when the states themselves were responsible for determining

benefits. The Supplemental Security Income program provided the first guaranteed

annual income to the needy, blind and disabled, under federal statutes. Other significant

social welfare initiatives passed during the Nixon administration such as the

Comprehensive Employment and Training Act (CETA) which promoted the concept of

training for entry into the workforce and subsidized jobs in both the private and public

sectors. Despite this, Nixon espoused a generally conservative ideology. Nixon was

forced to leave the Presidency as a result of the illegal break-in of Democratic

headquarters at the Watergate.

Nixon Initiatives

- **1969** President Nixon identified that there needed to be reform in welfare programs to provide order and purpose to overlapping programs. From 1969-1972. President Nixon amended and revised the Food Stamp Program, Medicare and OASDI. He added a family planning program to the Public Health Act.

- **1970** Occupational Safety and Health Administration (OSHA) - This office was established to have federal oversight on industrial safety and health standards.

- **1971** Work Incentive Program – This became WIN II and initiated that all AFDC recipients had to register for work or training programs, except if they had children under age six.

- **1972** COLA – Automatic cost of living adjustments were added to the Social Security Benefit.

- **1973** Rehabilitation Act of 1973 – Protected the physically disabled from discrimination.

- **1973** Comprehensive Employment and Training Act (CETA) - This was established to help the unemployed work in subsidized public service jobs, without requiring a means test.

- **1974** Supplemental Security Income – This program converted the "adult categories" of needy aged, disabled, and blind individuals from state welfare programs. Under SSI, Old Age Assistance (OAA), Aid to the Blind (AB), and Aid to the Permanently Disabled (APTD) had a uniform federal guarantee.

Nixon was not successful in developing the **Family Assistance Program (FAP)**, which was designed to provide a national program for AFDC recipients, guarantee an income higher than standards the welfare recipients were getting in some states, and had a work requirement. His effort at establishing a national health insurance was also defeated. However, Nixon also played a role in strengthening the Social Welfare System:

- Expanded Headstart

- Expanded small business loans for African-American businesses

- Increased Food Stamp Funding

- Established "bloc grants" to enable states to spend money on their own priorities

- Established revenue sharing from the U. S. Treasury to state government

- The "Philadelphia Plan" sponsored by the Department of Labor encouraged "affirmative action" in hiring minority workers in large corporations

Ford and Carter (1973-1980)

During President Gerald Ford's term, the rates of unemployment rapidly rose, as did the rates of inflation. It is not surprising that the poverty rates, which had declined during the 1960's and early 1970's, primarily due to redistribution of income through the social insurance programs, began to rise. During the Ford administration, there was scant attention paid to social programs. Jimmy Carter became President in 1978. Although a Democrat, the Carter administration was fiscally conservative also. Carter was considered a "populist" and an outsider in terms of the federal government. Inflation was a major issue during this time and Carter, in fact, cut the budgets of many social service programs. However in the area of mental health, there were several significant achievements made. Other proposals for advances were the Carter plan for the "Better Jobs and Income Program". This proposal would have created a jobs program for those who could work and a guaranteed income program for those who could not. However it did not pass Congress.

In summary, during the 1970's "real" economic growth in the United States was severely limited and inflation grew at an extremely rapid rate. The middle class continued to gain mobility and to flee the central core of the cities, leaving a growing sense of urban decay and poverty. The country was beginning to age, as the life span increased. The divorce rate began to rapidly rise, drugs become more available, the deinstitutionalization movement for the mentally ill assumed great importance. While poverty for the elderly was reduced, the poverty rates rose for single parent families, most of who are black and Latino. Between 1970 and 1978 there was an increase in growth for social welfare expenditures from 145.8 billion to 394.5 billion, a significant increase. Much of this increase was due to the expanded use and costs of entitlement programs; e.g. Medicare/Medicaid related to hospital and nursing home costs.

1980-1992: The Reagan-Bush Attack on Welfare

When Ronald Reagan became President, inflation was extreme, taxes were high, and many expressed that government had become "too large" and a sense of conservatism was growing. Those expressing this philosophy reflected a fear of "big" government, and a belief in the free market system. Reagan fully believed in this ideology and one of his first Acts was the Omnibus Budget Reconciliation Act (OBRA) of 1981 which instituted the Block Grant program, consolidating and cutting many categorical social service programs and giving responsibility to the States to determine how these monies should be allocated. Reagan's political philosophy was to reduce the role of the Federal government, increase tax cuts (especially for the wealthy), and increase spending for defense and, in general, to reduce spending for social programs. The general feeling was that since poverty had not been eliminated, the country needed to review its priorities. It was suggested that the government itself was the cause of the country's economic problems and the "solution" was to reduce the role of the federal government with respect to social programs. Reagan's "new Federalism" proposals called for States to assume major responsibility for welfare activities, with particular emphasis on the A.F.D.C. program.

It should be noted that by 1981 there were approximately eleven million recipients of welfare, seven million of whom were children and by 1990, 51 percent of all black children under age 18, 27 percent of Hispanic children and 16 percent of white children were living in single parent families. Under these circumstances, the association between poverty and racism became important in determining social policies resulting in a severe backlash directed at the A.F.D.C. programs. The Reagan administration promoted the idea that welfare recipients are "lazy", "malingerers" and engaged in "fraud", although there is very little evidence of that. Studies have shown that most A.F.D.C. recipients do not stay on welfare for extended periods of time. Further, the benefits received through welfare provide no incentive to remain on the rolls. On the contrary, since these programs were not designed to reduce poverty, but to provide "temporary relief" for women and children, there is little incentive to remain on the rolls. Rather, public perceptions have been fueled by stories in the media about "welfare cheats" and, has been noted, a disproportionate percent of recipients are members of racial and ethnic minority groups; hence subject to stigmatization.

Despite the growth of those women and children in need, the percent of the federal budget that was allocated to social welfare programs grew much more slowly under Reagan, although states welfare expenditures continued to increase. While the poverty rate had remained relatively stable in the 1970's it increased during the years of the Reagan administration, primarily for single-parent families often headed by minority women and for their children. The major attack of the Reagan years on the social welfare system was directed at the means-tested programs as opposed to the social insurance programs. It might be useful to consider, once again, who is served by each of these programs: for the most part, the means-tested programs are directed at poor women and children, and towards the unemployed, while the social insurance programs are primarily directed at senior citizens and those who have contributed to the labor market.

Among other proposals, the Reagan administration proposed those adult recipients of A.F.D.C. be required to work for their benefits. Congress and the President agreed that a major reform of the welfare system was necessary and in 1988 the Family Support Act was passed and signed into law. The emphasis of this "reform" was on work: the Job Opportunities and Basic Skills program (JOBS) was the major provision of this Act and required that single parents receiving welfare get a job. If this was not possible, the recipient was required to enroll in a training or education program. This measure applied primarily to women, another measure of the feminization of poverty. States were required to reduce the grants of those who refused to join the program. Another provision of this Act was the addition of vigorous methods of collecting child support payments: this was intended to help states recoup money spent on the program. As we shall see shortly, many of the concepts underlying this Act have been incorporated in the welfare reform program of President Clinton. These include the idea that remaining on welfare is a choice made by individuals and that if these individuals really tried they could get jobs (that would pay sufficiently) and thus become productive members of the society. It does not take into account women's needs, including the lack of adequate day care for their children, the lack of opportunity available for sufficient education and training, and the structural racism (for many of these recipients are members of minority groups) that is built into the marketplace.

Despite the measures taken by Reagan to address the economic condition, the situation did not dramatically improve. Nevertheless, Reagan was one of the most popular Presidents in America and many of his policies are, in fact, reflected in our contemporary social welfare policies.

Nevertheless, we should note that some of today's most pressing social problems are an outgrowth of the social, economic and political conditions and policies of the Reagan, and subsequently the Bush administration. Further, the states were encouraged to develop their own approaches to welfare. The diminishing attention to public subsidy programs for housing the poor; the decrease in livable housing stock, particularly in the cities; the policy of deinstitutionalization of the mentally ill, the increasing mobility of the American public and the growth of the single-parent family, and other factors. While definitions of the homeless population are quite varied, thus the count of the homeless constantly shifts, homelessness remains a significant contemporary social problem. The Reagan administration did support the McKinney Homeless Assistance Act in 1987, but this Act was really "too little, too late" to effectively address the problem.

Reagan Initiatives

* Immigration Reform and Control Act – Required employers to vouch for the legal status of their workers, offered amnesty to illegal workers who had arrived prior to 1982.

* Job Training Partnership Act of 1982 – Funds given to states for job training

* McKinney Homeless Assistance Act in 1987.

* Family Support Act of 1988 – Provided funds to states for training projects and childcare to help AFDC recipients into the workforce.

George Bush became President in 1988 and continued the conservative tradition. Although in general agreement with an anti-large government philosophy, the Bush administration supported the Americans with Disabilities Act of 1990, which dramatically increased protection from discrimination for those with disabilities. Overall, however, the emphasis in the Bush administration, similar to the Reagan administration, was on the free market system, the private sector and the idea that the states should have more control over social welfare policies and expenditures. Thus, for example, states were able to get "waivers." Further, the states were encouraged to develop their own approaches to welfare. States received permission from the federal government in order to permit them to design more stringent regulations for recipients of assistance programs. This was an attack on the A.F.D.C. program whose rolls had continued to swell. Wisconsin became one of the earliest states to apply for a waiver and instituted a program that cut benefits to A.F.D.C. recipients by 15 percent in those families where teenage children did not attend school for an identified number of days.

In New Jersey unmarried mothers on A.F.D.C. who had an additional child were denied benefits for that child. Another development during Mr. Bush's presidency was the Family Support Act of 1988. This act required single parents on welfare to participate in the JOBS program (Job Opportunities and Basic Skills). Recipients had to work in order to receive public assistance unless they had a child under age 3. This foreshadowed the Welfare Reform Act of 1996. The Americans with Disabilities Act promised persons with a disability, or who were discriminated against, a chance to enter the labor market.

The Clinton Presidency: "The End of Welfare As We Know It"

When Bill Clinton was elected President in 1992, the economy was stagnant, there was a continuing major shift to a "post -industrialist" society, meaning a move away from manufacturing to a service-oriented society, and there was a huge gap which was continuing to increase between the rich and the poor. There was also a growing gap between the so-called "middle class" and the very wealthy, as well as a new group of the very wealthy who came from the banking and investment sectors as well as from the growing computer sectors.

Clinton was elected on a platform which promised attention to revitalizing the economy; a favorite campaign slogan was "It's the economy, stupid." He focused his attention on domestic issues and supported a family leave proposal, attempted a policy to reduce discrimination among gay military personnel (the "Don't ask, don't tell" policy) which has backfired to a large degree, and expressed concern about the plight of children in America. His first major policy initiative was to appoint his wife, Hillary Rodham Clinton, to chair a task force to rewrite health care policy. His concern was to find a way to provide universal health care coverage and control the rising cost of health care. One

of the key aspects of the proposal was that, while basically financed by employers, the

federal government would provide subsidies to those who were not working and to help

poor business support the cost of health insurance. Coverage was to be "portable", thus if

an employee changed jobs, s/he would not lose coverage. A second highly significant

aspect of the proposal was the concept of "managed competition" which meant that

Regional Health Alliances would be formed in each state in order to have purchasing

power over the cost of health insurance. There was to be an oversight mechanism created

at the federal level in order to ensure that costs remained "reasonable."

There was serious opposition to the health care proposal from a conservative

Congress as well as from the powerful insurance lobbyists and physicians. Congress did

not act on the health care proposals, and, in the next congressional election, the

Republicans gained a significant majority in both Houses of Congress. This group

represented an extremely conservative ideology, and, led by the House Speaker, Newt

Gingrich, promised a new "Contract With America" which would essentially dismantle

social programs which started with the New Deal. Clinton took a "centrist" position with

respect to many of the issues raised by the Congress. He felt that the welfare system

needed to be radically changed, although he expressed concern about the need for

education and job training. However his central position was similar to the more

conservative trends that we have seen as part of the American tradition; the centrality of

work and a sense of "personal responsibility." This placed the major reason for being

poor not on the external aspects of the environment but rather squarely on the shoulders

of the poor themselves. Again, as in previous times, the burden of welfare change fell on women and children: the A.F.D.C. program was the primary target of welfare reform proposals. The reality of welfare was that there were 5 million families receiving assistance in 1993, 39 percent of the family heads receiving assistance were non-Hispanic white, 37 percent were black, 18 percent were Hispanic but most remained on the welfare rolls for less than two years, with more than one fifth of the recipients averaging six months or less. Yet, the public perception of welfare recipients remained highly stigmatized. It suggested that recipients "enjoy" being on welfare, that they are "lazy" and that, if they could only work, they would develop a sense of dignity and worthiness.

In August 1996, President Clinton signed into law the **Personal Responsibility and Work Opportunity Reconciliation Act.** The provisions of the legislation did what Clinton had promised to do: *they ended the system of public assistance that had been in place since the New Deal, a 60 year old federal policy of guaranteeing some level of financial assistance primarily to women and children, but also to other poor.* Instead of federal guarantees, the new law provided block grants to the states that were allowed to establish specific eligibility criteria for the receipt of benefits. There were some federal guidelines however. First, the amount of money guaranteed to the states would decline over a period of six years. Second, all recipients would be forced to find some type of work, and would be subject to a lifetime limit of five years of benefits. Legal immigrants who were not citizens at the time the law became effective would not be eligible for food Stamps and SSI, and it was left up to the states as to whether this group would remain eligible for Medicaid. The new program created by the Personal Responsibility Act is called Temporary Assistance to Needy Families (T.A.N.F.) The name of the program indicates the ideology behind it: the federal government should not assume responsibility for creating a serious program to support the needy, assistance should be temporary and work must be encouraged. *The end result of this Act is that the safety net for poor women, and especially for children, does not exist.*

Highlights of 1996 Welfare Reform Bill

The new welfare law has abolished the Federal guarantee of welfare benefits, principally Aid to Families with Dependent Children, and instead gives states block grants they may use as they wish, *within Federal guidelines,* to aid the poor. Eligibility criteria and benefit levels, which already vary from state to state significantly. The new law also establishes work requirements for most people seeking welfare or other benefits; states that do not meet these requirements may lose some of their Federal grant.

Examples of Specific Provision

Single mother; youngest child is over the age of 5

The mother will be required to work within two years of receiving benefits, perhaps sooner. Since the youngest child is over the age of five, the mother will not be able to sidestep work requirements. States will generally be required to have 25 percent of adult welfare recipients working at least 20 hours a week (and 50 percent working 30 hours a week by 2002). Mother and children will be guaranteed health coverage under Medicaid as long as they would qualify for welfare under current law.

Single mother; youngest child is 1 or younger

States may exempt parents with children under one from work requirements, and may disregard them in calculating participation rates.

Single mother; youngest child is 5 or younger

States may not penalize mothers with the youngest child under 6 years old for not working if she proves that she cannot find suitable, affordable child care.

Unmarried mother under 18

She will generally have to live with an adult and attend school in order to receive welfare benefits. She will not have to live with her parents or guardian if she or her child is likely to suffer serious physical or emotional harm, sexual abuse or exploitation as a result of such living arrangements.

Missing father

A woman will be required to provide information about the father of her child as a condition of receiving welfare. If she does not cooperate with state authorities, she will lose at least 25 percent of her family's welfare benefit. Using a national data base, the Federal Government will help states locate the father and force him to pay child support. States may require genetic testing of the child and parents in some cases.

Legal immigrant family

Noncitizens who have been in the country less than 10 years will generally be ineligible for food stamps and Supplemental Security Income, a cash assistance program with an average monthly payment of about $420, for the needy aged, blind and disabled. Immigrants arriving in the future will be ineligible for most other Government benefits as well. States will be allowed, but not required, to cut off cash assistance, Medicaid and social services for noncitizens now receiving such aid. In assessing an immigrant's need for assistance, the Government will assume that the income and assets of an immigrant's sponsor are available to the alien.

Convicted drug abuser or drug dealer

If convicted of a drug felony under Federal or state law, a person may not receive cash welfare benefits or food stamps. A state may override this ban.

Childless nonworker

A person 18 to 50 years old who is not raising children and not working may receive food stamps for only three months in a three-year period, with three additional months allowed if the person gets and then loses a job. The Congressional Budget Office estimates that in an average month, one million jobless individuals who are willing to work and would take a work slot if one were available will be denied food stamps under the new law.

Low-income disabled child

The Supplemental Security Income program for children will be cut and, over the next six years, 315,000 low-income children with disabilities will lose or be denied access to benefits. The program currently provides eligible children up to $470 a month and, in most states, access to health care through Medicaid

The 1996 welfare reform did end the federal responsibility for welfare and did dramatically change the system for public support.

Administration of George W. Bush

Since 1980, under the Administration of Ronald Reagan, we have witnessed the overall retrenchment of the "welfare state." The key themes of the George W. Bush administration were a continued emphasis on state and local control, the reduction of federal government oversight, the promotion of volunteerism and the push toward privatization. Overall, the market had a freer hand with less regulation and there was an overall restraint in social welfare policies. There was, in addition, an emphasis on tax relief, mainly for the wealthy.

The Bush presidency was marked by the terrorist acts of September 11, 2001 (9/11). The country experienced the most terrifying and devastating attack on U.S. soil when hijacked planes were flown into the World Trade Center in New York resulting in the death of almost 3,000 innocent people. A third hijacked plane was flown into the Pentagon and hundreds died while a fourth plane was brought down in a field in Pennsylvania by the brave passengers who prevented the hijackers from flying into the Capitol. These acts, by jihadists who oppose our way of life, spurred President Bush to declare war on Iraq on the presumption that Iraq had "weapons of mass destruction" aimed at the U.S. This was never proven to be factual but the United States has been engaged in war in Iraq since 2003 and currently is engaged in a war in Afghanistan. While the Bush administration retrenched spending on social welfare, the wars cost billions of dollars, paid for by taxpayers. The wars have been controversial, as has the handling of prisoners of war, with many fearing the violation of human rights of war prisoners. As well, citizens in the U. S. have been subject to incursions of privacy which have been justified by the need to protect the country from further attacks.

More specifically, in the realm of social welfare policies, the Bush administration placed emphasis on turning over the provision of family and children services as well as drug and alcohol services to faith based organizations. The administration also opened a controversial debate about the future of Social Security and retirement benefits. Claiming a "crisis at hand", the administration proposed privatizing social security which would allow contributors to take a percent of their financial input and invest it in their own private accounts, namely in the stock market. While the stock market soared this may have seemed like a good idea. However, as we now know, the stock market, the housing market, and, indeed, the global economy was rife with fraudulent practices resulting in a major recession, a huge loss of jobs, and a bursting of the "housing bubble" by the end of the Bush Administration.

A major social policy that did pass in the Bush administration was the Medicare Prescription Drug Improvement and Modernization Act of 2003 (known as Medicare, Part D.) This legislation allows Medicare recipients to have some of their prescription medication covered, with caveats to be explained. First, a Medicare recipient must purchase a private, supplemental prescription plan or a Medicare "Advantage Plan" (also private). These plans are in addition to the government sponsored "regular" Medicare plan to which all persons over 65 as well as certain others are entitled to. Next, it should be noted that there are hundreds of these private plans and not all plans cover the same medications. Thus, if a senior citizen is taking multiple medications for several conditions (which is often the case), it may not be possible to find one plan which covers all of the individual's needs. All of these plans have deductibles (in addition to the regular Medicare deductable). One of the most onerous provisions of the policy, however, is the "doughnut hole". This occurs when the recipient has paid a certain amount for their medications (this amount has changed over time). Once this expenditure is reached, the recipient must pay "out of pocket" until $4,350 of their own money has been spent. At that point coverage of medication costs will resume. This can present major difficulties for seniors who must find the plan that covers the medications they need but still must pay huge amounts out of pocket if they take multiple medications. Another provision of the policy is that the Federal government was barred from negotiating with the pharmaceutical companies to lower the cost of medications. This was seen as a boon to the pharma companies who could charge what they wanted to without having to justify the high costs. This is also unlike the Veteran's Administration which is allowed to negotiate with the drug companies. This policy exemplifies the ideology of the Bush administration: reduction in government intervention in people's lives, with more reliance on the free market (in this case private Medicare Advantage Plans and the pharmaceutical industry) to regulate supply and demand.

Barack Obama

Barack Hussein Obama was elected President of the United States in 2008. He is the first African-American to reach the office of President. President Obama is of mixed racial background: his mother is a Caucasian woman from the U.S. while his father was a black man from Africa.

Mr. Obama began an unlikely campaign for President in late 2007, while he was the Junior Senator from Illinois. Following Mr. Obama's undergraduate years at Columbia University, he moved to Chicago and became a community organizer working in the ghetto neighborhoods to promote better living conditions. He then studied at

Harvard University where he obtained a law degree and spent some years teaching constitutional law.

Mr. Obama's presidential campaign was predicated on a platform of change from the "old ways" of Washington. His formidable democratic candidate in the primary was Hilary Rodham Clinton. Although it seemed unlikely at first, Mr. Obama won the democratic primary and went on to beat Senator John McCain in the presidential election. Obama's promise was to address the overwhelming dissatisfaction in the country. This dissatisfaction included the growing war in Iraq and its toll among soldiers and their families; the ever-increasing debt that the country had allowed to grow; the bursting of the housing bubble; the job losses that were starting to mushroom and the rise in health insurance costs leaving millions of Americans without health insurance or, at best, with minimal coverage. He also vowed to re-engage with other nations and extend American diplomatic ties which had suffered greatly during the Bush Administration. In his presidential campaign, Mr. Obama was able to enlist the assistance of thousands of volunteers; most often young people who were energized by his ability to engage the issues and his mantra of "yes we can" which became a major campaign slogan. He also appealed to African-Americans and to other minority groups as well as to many "liberals."

Upon assuming the Presidency in 2009 the key issues facing the nation were primarily economic: the recession was deeper than at first believed; the automobile industry was facing huge losses; the housing bubble had burst and many people were facing foreclosure of their homes; the banks seemed to be failing; health care costs were rising precipitously; the nation's debt had reached trillions of dollars, and the war in Iraq was costing more and more. Moreover, the war was extended to Afghanistan where it was felt by some the focus should have been from the beginning. With all of these concerns reaching a crisis point, the new President had to choose a focus immediately. His first major legislation was the American Recovery and Reinvestment Act of 2009 which was an act meant to stimulate the economy. It should be noted that there was much controversy surrounding Obama's policy initiatives. The controversy stems primarily from the opposition party and concerns that party's view that the government should not "interfere" with the free market. This opposition has assumed greater and greater force, with each of Obama's policy initiatives. In fact, the country at this time seems polarized, and, with the growth of the anti-government movement known as the Tea Party, the level of anti-Obama rhetoric has markedly increased. Opponents have decried the President's "abuse of power" and, among multiple other critiques, many have claimed he is "leading the country toward socialism", primarily based on the health reform measures that have been signed into law. (See below for details).

Nevertheless, President Obama has signed several policy directives into legislation including the reauthorization of the State Children's Health Insurance program of 2009 (SCHIP) which extended health coverage to children and families who are above the Medicaid eligibility criteria but still cannot afford health insurance. He also signed the Matthew Sheppard and James Byrd Jr. Hate Crimes Prevention Act of 2009 which extends the categories of crimes which can be prosecuted as hate crimes. The Patient Protection and Affordable Health Care Act of 2010 and its companion the Health Care and Education Reconciliation Act of 2010 is perhaps the most significant policy initiative to date. These two acts attempt to restructure the way health care is provided in the United States and are the only major health care initiatives since the passage of Medicaid and Medicare in 1965. While the health reform measure seems complicated, its essence is the following: first, health insurance companies will be regulated so that they will not be able to deny coverage to anyone who has a "pre-existing condition". This has been a practice of many of the private health insurance companies who fear that someone with a pre-existing condition will cost them too much money, whereas a healthy person will not. Next, the bill will require everyone to have health insurance and will provide subsidies to those who cannot afford to buy health insurance on their own. There will be requirements for employers to provide health insurance to employees (with subsidies if necessary). A major change from the current status will be to fill the "doughnut hole" by 2020. This ultimately will affect seniors who now must spend their own money as described above, once they reach a certain dollar amount in their expenditures for prescription medication. The legislation will also reduce Medicare premiums for seniors who are not enrolled in Medicare Advantage plans. There will also be a prohibition on lifetime limits in expenses. As well, young people will be allowed to participate in their parents' health insurance policies until the age of 26, a significant increase over the current age limit.

While this is significant reform, many of the provisions will not take effect for several years although aspects of the law do go into effect immediately. This health insurance reform also has an effect on mental health policy. The Paul Wellstone and Pete Dominici Mental Health Parity and Addiction Equity Act of 2008, which took effect in

2009, must be in compliance with the new health reform policy. This means that employers who provide mental health coverage cannot require separate deductibles for mental health care. Further, mental health and substance abuse treatment must be equivalent to medical care in that there must be coverage for in-network, out-of-network, emergency and prescription coverage, just as there is for medical benefits. Insurance companies providing mental health coverage may not impose annual or lifetime dollar limits that are less favorable than medical limits. It should be noted that the Mental Health Equity Act only applies to those large employers who have been providing mental health benefits and does not apply to non-employer health insurance benefits (although certain states may require mental health coverage). It should also be noted that any large employer that does provide mental health benefits may "opt out" of the requirements if, in the first year of compliance with the law, claims of the beneficiaries exceed two percent of previous claims.

While we are in only the beginning of the second year of the Obama presidency we can note that there has been a significant attempt to reform health insurance. Yet many questions remain about the implementation of legislation. Further, the economy appears to be improving yet there are still many people who have lost their homes and/or their jobs. As far as the deficit, it is still huge and Obama has, in fact, increased the number of troops in Afghanistan while promising to "wind down" the war in Iraq. We cannot yet know the effect of the opposition to Obama's domestic policies. We do know that President Obama was awarded the Nobel Peace Prize in 2009, very early in his Presidency. The prize was awarded for his efforts to strengthen international diplomacy.

The Social Welfare Benefit System in the United States

This section is included to provide the student with a brief overview of the present social welfare system in the United States. For many clients and those served by social welfare agencies the availability of benefits is important to their survivals. Students as part of their internships and in their ongoing professional practice should familiarize themselves with specific details of the programs and their application procedures. As stated in the history section there are two major categories of benefits in the United States, Social Security and public assistance. Social Security which dates to 1935, is a universal program that provides benefits without requiring a *means* test. It is incredibly important in that it provides a financial support to retirees, the disabled and funeral services of workers who die. The American Association of Retired Persons in their overview of Social Security and its importance writes:

> Social Security is much more than a retirement program. It is a family income protection program that reflects the commitment of the country to the economic security of workers, retirees and their families. Social Security protects workers and their families during their working lives and thorough their retirement. It's the primary source of retirement income for most Americans. Six out of ten (60 percent) of today's beneficiaries derive more than half of their income from Social Security. In most low-income households of retirement age, Social Security represents 80% or more of their retirement income. In addition to paying benefits to retirees and their spouses, Social Security provides a guaranteed foundation of income for workers who become disabled, and for the spouses and dependent children of wage earners who die or become disabled. In fact, one in three beneficiaries today is not a retired worker.
>
> - An estimated 97% of children under 18 can count on monthly benefits if a working parent dies.
> - About 90% of workers and their families have protection in the event of a long-term disability.
> - Anyone who qualifies for Social Security benefits receives a monthly check and can count on that check keeping pace with the rising cost of living.

Social Security provides a strong, unshakable financial base that does not depend of a person's investment savvy. It was not designed to compete with the stock market as an investment vehicle. Nor was it designed to provide all the money one needs for retirement. Because of its lifetime guarantee and its annual cost of living adjustment, Social Security has dramatically improved the economic status of older Americans. Women and minorities are most likely to depend almost exclusively on Social Security for several reasons. Minorities because their employment opportunities are often more limited and they are more likely to have lower wages and work in jobs without benefits such as a pension. Women, too, are more likely to work in lower wage jobs lacking pension and often experience time out of the paid workforce (frequently due to family care-giving responsibilities). Thus, as noted Social Security covers retirement benefits and benefits to survivors. (AARP Social Security, 101 AARP Website, 2008)

In addition to the categories identified above there are three other categories under Social Security that are important: Medicare, Disability Benefits, and Supplemented Security Income. Medicare is a health insurance benefit and is available to anyone over 65 who is eligible for Social Security. Health care benefits are provided under the four parts of Medicare. Medicare taxes paid while the individual works finances hospital insurance (Part A) that helps pay for inpatient hospital and skilled nursing care and other services. The other three parts of Medicare that are generally paid for by monthly premiums are: medical insurance (Part B) that helps pay for doctors' fees, out-patient hospital visits and other medical services and supplies; Medicare Advantage (Part C) plans that allow people with Parts A and B to receive all of their health care services through one provider organization; and prescription drug coverage (Part D) that helps pay for medications doctors prescribe for treatment.

Disability benefits can be paid at any age if the individual has worked long enough and has a severe physical or mental impairment that prevents him/her from working for a year or more or if they have a medical condition that is expected to result in their death. Millions of Americans receive Social Security Disability benefits each year, and each year more than 2.5 million new applications are filed. The Social Security Administration defines disability in terms of ability to work. Persons who cannot work for a year or more, or whose condition is likely to result in death, may qualify for benefits. Disability examiners at states agencies, consulting with SSA doctors, determine disability based on clinical evidence and examinations. Unfortunately, these examiners do not meet the applicants.

Supplemental Security Income (SSI) makes monthly payments to people who have low incomes and few resources. To get SSI, the person also must be 65 or older, blind or disabled. Children as well as adults may qualify for SSI disability payments.

The amount of SSI payments that a person can receive depends on their income, resources and where they live. The federal government pays a basic benefit and some states add money to that amount. Check with the local Social Security office for the SSI payment amount in one's state. Generally, people who get SSI also can get Medicaid, food stamps and other assistance. The person does not have to have worked to get SSI payments. SSI payments are financed through general tax revenues, not through Social Security taxes.

Public Assistance Benefits

The most important public assistance or *means* tested program designed for poor families is TANF (Temporary Assistance for Needy Families). As was reviewed in the history section TANF is recent – 1996 and replaced the 60+ year federal

program. Under the welfare reform legislation of 1996, (the Personal Responsibility

and Work Opportunity Reconciliation Act- PWRORA- Public Law 104-193), TANF

replaced the welfare programs known as Aid to Families with Dependent Children

(AFDC), the Job Opportunities and Basic Skills Training (JOBS) program and the

Emergency Assistance (EA) program. The law ended federal entitlement to assistance

and instead created TANF as a block grant that provides States, territories and tribes

federal funds each year. These funds cover benefits, administrative expenses, and

services targeted to needy families. TANF became effective July 1, 1997, and was

reauthorized in February 2006 under the Deficit Reduction Act of 2005. In addition

to TANF, the other five state-administered public assistance programs are Food

Stamps, General Relief, Medicaid, Refugee Assistance and State-Local

Hospitalization (SLH).

Fairfax County, Virginia describes on its website the process which may be

typical for most states as follows:

Applying for Public Assistance

- The individuals call or walk in to a Department of Family Services (Human Services, Welfare Services) office for information and receive the application and directions for filling out. No appointment is needed. They will be seen the same day they come into the office. Or, they may call to set up an appointment.

A language interpreter for non-English speaking customers can be provided, if

needed. For some programs the person may not need a personal interview or the

interview may be held over the telephone.

- The applicant may bring others with them, or in some cases, send someone in their place.
- During the interview, the entire application process will be explained to them.
- They are told of any missing information or documents you'll need to bring in.
- The application is processed beginning on the date the agency receives the information.
- A Human Services worker determines if they are eligible and notifies them.
- If eligible, they begin receiving benefits.
- Periodic reviews of their eligibility are made while they are receiving benefits.

What personal or family resources are counted as assets?

- Cash on hand
- Stocks and bonds, including U.S. Savings Bonds
- Money in checking and savings accounts, certificates of deposit and/or shared accounts
- Property, including pleasure craft, such as boats and recreational vehicles. A car or truck counts differently depending on how it is used. The home you own is not included as a resource if you are living in it.

What is counted as income?

- Wages
- Support payments
- Pensions
- Veterans benefits
- Alimony
- Dividends
- Public assistance
- Fellowships and veterans'

- Interest and similar payments
- Retirement or disability benefits
- Workers or unemployment compensation
- Old age, survivor's or strike benefits
- Scholarships and education grants

What identification does the applicant need to supply?

- Personal identification: driver's license, Social Security card, etc.
- Proof of status, if alien
- Proof of residence: copy of lease, utility bills, driver's license, etc.

(Fairfax County, Virginia Website May 2008)

Concluding Observations

Although, Social Security and Public Assistance benefit programs are important and assist millions of individuals and families, our programs compare to other industrialized countries (Eastern Europe).

Chapter 5 – The Policy-Making Process at the Federal, State and Agency Levels

To understand how social welfare policies are initiated, debated, and administered, it is necessary to know something about the government structures that provide the context for these processes. An analysis of these governmental structures should incorporate discussion of the separate domains of the executive, legislative, and judicial branches of government at both the federal and state levels, as well as an examination of the interplay of these three main divisions of government in the United States. Furthermore, a discussion of governmental structures should include a discussion of how federal, state and local levels of government interact (or fail to interact) in the development and administration of social services. An understanding of the functions and workings of the various structures at the federal, state, and local levels is not only essential in understanding how social welfare policies are developed, enacted, and administered' but provides a knowledge base for the practitioner who seeks to implement changes in policy or in empowering clients to address needed changes in the system, as well.

The Federal Government

The basic structure of the federal government is set forth in the United States Constitution. The Constitution provides that the national government is to be divided into three branches—the executive branch, the legislative branch, and the judicial branch. Each branch functions separately according to its given powers, but a system of checks and balances exists between them.

The executive branch includes the President, the Vice-President, executive departments (such as the U.S. Department of Health and Human Services, the U.S.

Department of Housing and Urban Development, and the U. S. Department of Education), and independent agencies (such as the Veterans Administration). The executive branch is primarily responsible for enforcing laws and carrying out policies.

The legislative branch is represented by the United States Congress, which is bicameral in structure in that it has two houses: the Senate, with equal representation by each state, and the House of Representatives, with proportional representation by the states. The function of the Congress is to draft and enact legislation. This process begins when a Senator or a Representative introduces a bill in his or her respective house. The bill is then assigned to the appropriate committee within the original house. The committee, comprised of both Democrats and Republicans, studies the bill and then either tables the bill, at which point the process stops, or it may amend or rewrite the bill. The committee then reports on whether the bill should be passed into law, given its favorable or unfavorable recommendation. The bill is examined, debated, and possibly amended by the original house and is passed or defeated. If the bill passes, it is sent to the other house where it is debated and amended if necessary. If it is amended, it is sent back to the house in which it originated. The same version of the bill must be passed by both houses in order for a bill to become law. If both houses cannot agree on a single version of the proposed legislation, a conference committee is convened whereby selected members of both houses meet to construct a compromise bill; a compromise bill is returned to both houses and must pass in each. Once both houses of Congress pass a bill, the piece of proposed legislation is sent to the President for his approval. If approved the proposed legislation becomes a law. If the President vetoes the bill, Congress may override the executive veto if two-thirds of each house votes to do so.

1) Chart of Federal Government Structure

Legislative Branch	**Executive Branch**	**Judicial Branch**
Bicameral congress	President	U.S. Supreme
(a) Senate	Vice President	Lower Court
(b) House of Representatives	Cabinet and	
	Executive/Department	

The third branch of the federal government - the judicial branch - is responsible for interpreting existing laws, determining laws' constitutionality, and settling lawsuits. *The judicial branch at the federal level is comprised of the U.S. Supreme Court which has nine justices appointed for life by the President with confirmation by the Senate. There are also 11 courts of appeal, 91 district courts, and three courts of special jurisdiction.* Though the judicial branch may appear to have less impact on social welfare than the other two branches, it may have a dramatic influence as it renders judgements on laws or presidential actions. The Supreme Court has dramatically altered the social landscape by means of its decisions. Marbury v. Madison, in 1803, was the first instance where a law passed by congress was declared unconstitutional which greatly expanded the power of the court by establishing its right to overturn acts of congress, a power not explicitly granted in the Constitution. In 1857, Dred Scott v. Sanford involved a slave who was taken from a slave state to a free territory. Scott's contention was that he was entitled to his freedom. The court ruling that blacks were not citizens and could not sue in Federal Court intensified the national debate over slavery. In cases like Brown v. Board of Education of Topeka, Shawnee County, Kansas invalidated the racial segregation of schools in 1954. Roe v. Wade, 1973, legalized abortion by deciding that a woman has the right to an abortion without interference from the government in the first trimester of pregnancy, because it is part of her right to privacy. The political nature of the Supreme Court is, to a certain extent, determined by the President, who nominates the Justices of the Supreme Court when there is a vacancy. However, the cases that are selected also reflect the justice's opinions that the issues are important and "ripe" at that particular time in history.

State Governmental Structures

The structures of the state governments are determined by their respective state constitutions. Though there is some variation in structures between states' variation is controlled by the fact that state constitutions cannot contradict the Constitution of the United States. Like the structure of the federal government, state governments are also characterized by executive, legislative and judicial structures. State government often tends to be more responsive to citizens through the mechanisms of state initiatives and referenda. These mechanisms entail that a certain number of citizens' sign a petition in order to initiate legislation, amend the state constitution, or have an issue submitted for popular vote. Often, initiatives and referenda are initiated by concerned groups of citizens united over a particular issue. The voters within a state may also recall, or remove, officials from office.

CHART OF TYPICAL STATE STRUCTURE

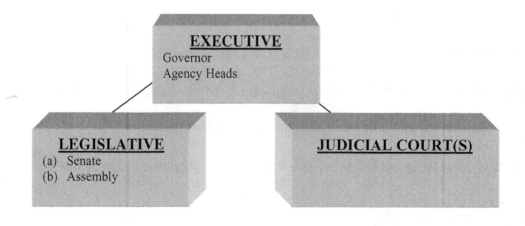

The division of power within the structure of the state is parallel to that of the federal government with a few variations. State governments have three branches: legislative, executive and judicial. In the executive branch, the chief executive of a state is a state's governor, elected by popular vote, typically for a four year term (some states have two year terms.). In addition, the state legislature is generally bicameral in composition, except for Nebraska. The upper house is usually called the Senate and the lower the House of Representatives, House of Delegates or the General Assembly. The judicial branch is comprised of minor or lower courts, trial courts (district, circuit, superior, common pleas), appellate courts (though not in all fifty states), and the state supreme court. This system of state courts also includes justices of the peace, family courts, juvenile courts, municipal courts, county courts, etc. In the last two decades the role of states in social welfare has increased markedly.

The Welfare Reform Act is an example of this new "federation" and provides states greater authority and autonomy including the authority over eligibility rules and benefit levels previously removed only by statutory enactment and judicial interpretation. The new welfare legislation permits states to deny aid to any poor family or category of poor families. It includes reductions in food stamps and prohibits using block grant funds to provide vouchers or other non cash assistance to families. The President and Congress have returned to the states functions that have become political and financial liabilities.

This new federalism also presumes and facilitates different priorities among the states. Will states sharply reduce their spending on poverty-related programs? Will states maintain services if they are not mandated to do so? Will there be a 'race to the bottom' among the states regarding benefits and eligibility?

Questions are many: As states are granted more freedom, will policy differences among them widen? Will such disparities be accepted? How will the disparities be viewed in light of social justice for individuals? What will determine priorities among resource allocations? How will states analyze their new programs, and how sophisticated in their statistical capacity? If a recession hits, can the states absorb the reductions in federal aid without reducing or eliminating services? Can states be trusted to protect the rights of vulnerable citizens? There is evidence that states will design and implement policies that will affect the profession of social work itself and its clientele regardless of income status and we need to be politically aware of the changes.

Local Government

Local forms of government are prescribed through state constitutions, which set forth the procedures by which local governments are established. Local government bodies include the city, county, township, and village.

In many states counties or large cities are a major political entity. In most counties, one town or city is designated the county seat where the board of commissioners or supervisors meets. Cities have their own policy structure, however, almost all have some kind of central council, elected by voters, and an executive officer, assisted by department heads. There are three general types of city government: the mayor-council, the commission and the city manager. These local officials levy taxes, borrow and appropriate money, build highways, and administer national, state and county welfare programs. These government bodies are playing an increasingly important role with respect to social policy issues. Counties often have the primary responsibility derived from the state for providing services such as: Public

Assistance and Child Welfare, Mental Health, Aging. And they either directly provide

services or fund other agencies and organizations to provide these services. Larger

metropolitan areas, example New York City or Los Angeles, will also be the provider

and/or funder of services.

In the last two decades there has been increasing interest in "providing the

service closer to the consumer" and with a diminution of direct federal involvement,

states and cities and counties have assumed greater importance. (This is discussed below

in more detail and examples provided.).

The Relationship between Federal, State and Local Government in the Provision of Social Services

The modern relationship existing between federal, state and local governments is

the result of historical trends, political processes, and administrative and economic

realities. Through its history, the United States has tended to favor a model based on

decentralization, with the power of decision-making left to the states. The framing of the

U.S. Constitution and the subsequent Bill of Rights outlined the powers given

specifically to the federal government, with the understanding that all other powers

would be reserved by the states. Incidentally, this fact may have prevented the

development of comprehensive federal social service programs earlier in the nation's

history.

Regarding current structural relationships and social services, most public social

services operating on all levels are financed by federal and state funds. A common setup

is that the federal government will provide funding for social services to the individual

states who distribute the funds to a plethora of state and local programs and agencies.

Perhaps administratively, the state is the most important level, for social services funding, as all federal funds not given directly to recipients must be channeled through the states. Federal grants-in-aid and block grants exemplify this funding model. The interplay of governmental structures has become more complicated with the advent of for-profit agencies working within the system of providing services.

The division of responsibilities and powers between federal and state bodies presents many interesting issues with respect to modern social realities. It is important to note that the poor and those in need of social services are not equally distributed between states and localities. For example, urban areas tend to have larger concentrations of poor individuals and families than non-urban areas. States with multiple urban areas, therefore, might have a disparate number of those needing the various services aimed at assisting the poor and welfare reform impacted cities differently than rural areas. While welfare roles dropped from the mid 1990s it doesn't mean the poor are better off.

Local government e.g., cities or countries often have a significant role in social welfare. Municipal or local governments can decide to provide services directly e.g., a county mental health or drug program, a County Child Protection Service or contract out to voluntary nonprofit agencies or they can do both and provide some services directly while contracting out others.

Understanding the nature of the structure of government and ultimately the delivery of social services is important. It can also be very confusing. The charts and texts that follow give different types of structured examples of arrangements for social welfare funding and service delivery.

EXAMPLES:
EXAMPLE 1
Models of Structural Relationships-Examples

Model of Structural Relationships

Between Levels of Government
RE: Social Services

(Note: This model is not applicable for all types of social services in the United States)

Example- selected child welfare services

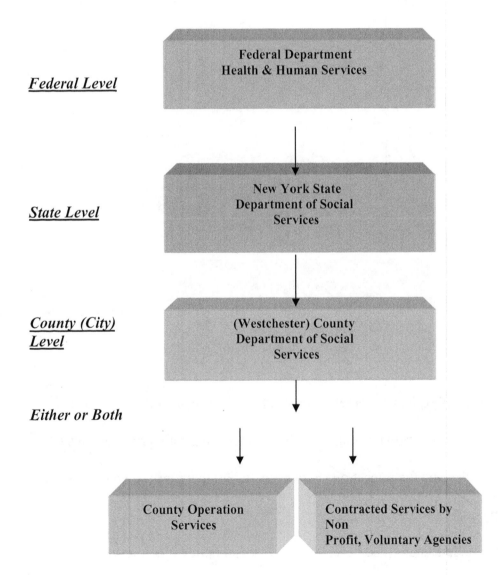

EXAMPLE 2

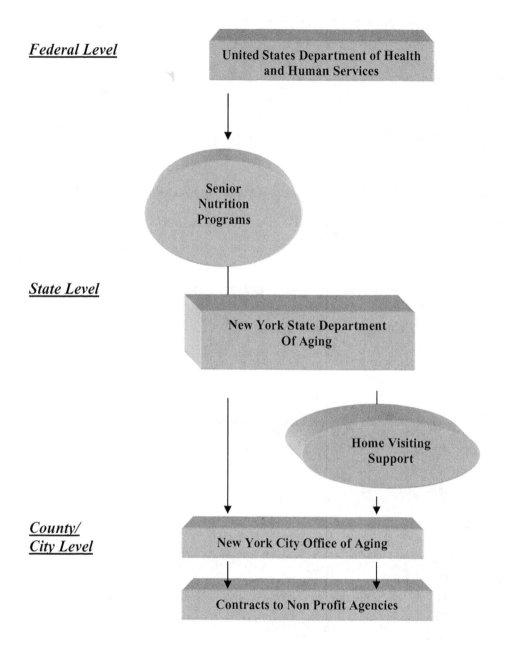

Federal Level

United States Department of Health and Human Services

Senior Nutrition Programs

State Level

New York State Department Of Aging

Home Visiting Support

County/ City Level

New York City Office of Aging

Contracts to Non Profit Agencies

Although complex, it is extremely important for the social worker and the social work student to have a rudimentary understanding of these structural arrangements so that he/she can understand the impact on services including the impact on agencies' workers and on clients.

In further understanding the development of social policy it is important to describe two key factors that shape this policy. These factors are (a) the context in which social policy is shaped and (b) an overview of the process by which policy is shaped and ultimately implemented.

The Context of Social Welfare Policy

In discussing social policy, it is necessary to understand the key role of government. Although not discounting the roles played by philanthrophy or the private sector (e.g. managed care firms) the role of government at the federal, state and county or local level is paramount in social welfare. It is governmental agencies that control the key resources and set crucial directions with respect to social welfare. The 1996 adoption of the Federal government of "welfare reform", as we discussed earlier, fundamentally changed the direction of public assistance in the United States. This federal action not only changed the millions of lives of public assistance recipients but in fact set the direction that was operationalized by state and local governments. The power of the federal government is not limited to public assistance but also it's actions with respect to numerous programs, e.g. Medicare and Medicaid, Headstart, Aging Assistance. It is also true that actions by state governments also have significant consequences on it's resident's in their area of social policy.

In thinking about government, at the federal and state levels the key "actors" fall into three distinct categories – the Executive, the Legislative and the Judicial branch. The chart below illustrates these groups at the federal and state levels.

Briefly, the Executive (the President or Governor) and their agency heads have great power in that (a) they set directions and establish an agenda, (b) propose legislation, (c) develop budgets, and (d) use power to influence the media. The Legislature has power to develop, approve and/or reject legislation, exercise "oversight" of program activities, develop, and pass budgets. Judicial can oversee

FEDERAL

Executive	**Legislature**	**Judicial**
• President (elected)	• US Senate (elected)	• US Supreme Court
• Cabinet members (appointed)	• US House of	(appointed)
(e.g., HHS, Department of	Representatives	• Other federal courts
Justice)	(elected)	(appointed)
• Civil Service		

STATE

Executive	**Legislature**	**Judicial**
• Governor (elected)	• Chamber 1 –	• Supreme Court (state)-
	Assembly	(appointed)
• Heads of Agencies	• Chamber 2 - State	• Lower state court
(appointed)	(elected)	(appointed or elected)

activities as to whether they violate previous laws or mandate by decree governmental actions.

At the county or local/city level the patterns of the structure may vary but usually also include an *Executive* (an elected county executive or appointed county administrator/an elected mayor or appointed local manager), and a *Legislature* (elected county legislators or city council members). County or local executives or legislators have significant power within the localities they represent. The power of local officials is considerably less than federal or state counterparts on broad social policy issues. Local officials do have significant power to the degree that they contribute local funding or set direction for the development of programs.

Influencing governmental officials as a member of an organized group is a key role that needs to be recognized. Interest groups and lobbyists often conduct advocacy. Lobbyists are professional paid advocates who work on behalf of interest groups and causes. Powerful interest groups, e.g., the US Chamber of Commerce, the National Rifle

Association, and the American Medical Association, have the financial resources to pay

for teams of lobbyists. Further, on key issues, e.g., health care legislation, well funded

interest groups expand their lobbying activities and begin to engage in heavy use of the

media to influence public opinion. In contrast to the resources available to business or

corporate organizations, social welfare interest groups have considerably fewer

resources. The number of full time lobbyists they employ is often quite limited. Often,

they may use part time lobbyists. To augment this lack of resources, social welfare

organizations, e.g., NASW, may ask members to voluntarily become involved in

lobbying.

The role of all interest groups is to shape policy. This is done directly via public

officials and legislators or by influencing the media. The role of the media is often to

shape public opinion which, then, has a key role in shaping policy.

Other groups that try to influence social policy are provider and consumer

groups. Both types of these groups have a large stake in policy and the accompanying

programs and services that emerge. With respect to provider organizations, as social

workers we should be aware of the role of NASW. On the national level, NASW either

independently or in collaboration with interested social welfare or health organizations is

most frequently actively involved in issues of interest to social work. NASW may

actively advocate for issues such as increased child welfare funding, developing

regulations to insure social workers are reimbursed by managed care organizations, or

that social work is a designated profession in nursing homes. Every year NASW joins

forces with other social organizations to lobby the federal Executive and the Congress to

sponsor an enhanced social welfare agenda. Core issues for social work most frequently

relate to promoting policies that improve the condition of the poor, families and minorities. At times, NASW, especially at the state level may focus on issues directly related to the professional survival and growth, e.g., licensing, and increased funding for MSW education.

Consumers are also actively seeking to influence legislation. Over the past several years the role of consumers as active participants in policy making has grown substantially. A key example can be found in the area of mental illness and the emergence of the Alliance for the Mentally Ill. The Alliance with a primary membership of family members of the mentally ill has emerged in the past decade as a powerful interest group on federal and state mental health issues. On the federal level, they all are very strong advocates for funding of studies of the causes of mental illness and of enhanced services. Another example of consumer of family advocacy groups can be found in the area of violence. In response to the emergence of violence as a major national, state and local issue, victims' organizations have been established and become strong advocates of legislation guaranteeing victim participation in the determination of sentences for offenders and for victims' assistance services. These examples are multiplied hundreds and thousands of times since a key defining feature of American democracy is the involvement of its citizens in government.

Understanding the Policy Process

Through the diagram below, the authors provide a shorthand overview of the policy process:

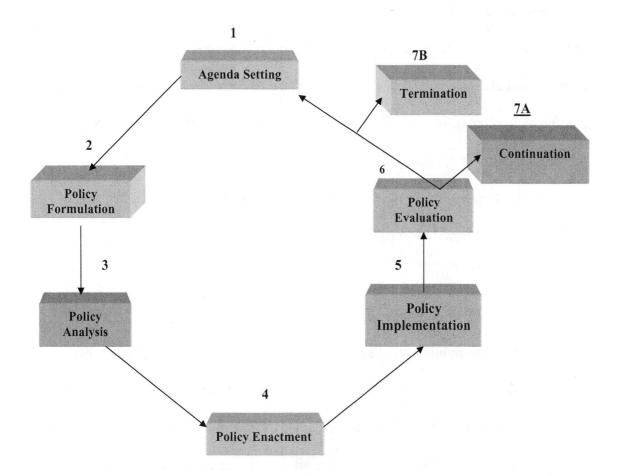

Definitions

Agenda Setting – Issues become part of public agenda being considered by the executives or legislature for action.

Policy Formulation – Problem is defined in more detail and possible solutions proposed.

Policy Analysis – The possible solutions are reviewed and the pros and cons of alternatives examined.

Policy Enactment – A policy is enacted in the form of legislation passed or executive action taken.

Policy Implementation – Refers to the actions needed to insure the policy creates programs and services.

Policy Evaluation – The impact of the policy and the processes by which it is being implemented are evaluated. This can lead to (a) the termination of the policy or (b) a modification of the policy (which means it needs to become part of the agenda, again) or (c) a continuation of the policy.

These elements of the policy process are discussed in more detail below and illustrations are provided for further clarification.

1) Agenda Setting

For a social welfare issue to even be considered for policy action, it must become part of the public policy agenda. Specifically, this means that key policy institutions (the Executive – President, governor, mayor, director of an agency, the legislature – Congress, State Legislatures or City Councils, or the Judicial – federal or state courts) must be willing to review and discuss the issue. Policy practice means that a policy issue needs to be placed on decision makers agendas in agency, community or legislative settings.

How specifically are we assisting in this process? It is now recognized that two of the key steps are (a) to develop community interest in the issue and (b) bring the issue to the media attention. This latter step is crucial because it is through the media that the broader public and key decision-makers become aware of the problem. Perhaps, these steps are best illustrated by several sets of examples.

Example 1:

An unfortunate tragedy occurred in 1998 in New York City. A young woman named Kendra Webdale was pushed in front of an onrushing subway train by a chronic schizophrenic young man named Andrew Goldstein and killed. Although several other incidents of this nature had occurred over the past 15 years none generated the reaction and had the political impact of the Kendra Webdale case. Why? The Webdale family was middle class, well educated and was actively involved in pushing the issue. By 1998, in New York City and New York State the most powerful interest group for mental health issues had become the Alliance for the Mentally Ill. The Alliance consisting of primarily family members of the chronically mentally ill who were concerned about two major facts with respect to New York State's mental health system, (a) it had become increasingly fragmented and insufficient resources existed in the form of community services and (b) it lacked an outpatient commitment statute. (Outpatient commitment statutes had been adapted in the majority of states in the United States. Outpatient commitment forces a mentally ill person to get psychiatric treatment through court actions and if they fail or refuse they can be involuntary hospitalized in an inpatient unit or even face the possibility of jail). At the time of the incident the state government was under the jurisdiction of an administration who was more readily attuned to social control measures than the expansion of social programs. Via major media attention (TV, radio, and newspapers) the issue was continually presented. In "amazingly quick speed" for legislative action, an outpatient commitment law (known as "Kendra's Law") was adopted. Further, compelled by all of the publicity, the governor and legislature offered significantly increased revenues to expand outpatient mental health services.

Child abuse has become recognized in the past 25 years as a major social issue in the United States. The emergence of child abuse is directly related to the role of the media. Johnson writes in an article entitled "Horror Stories" and the "Construction of Child Abuse" that:

> "Everyone recognizes that the mass media's power extends beyond the mere transmittal of information. Their power (and some of their history) also derives from their ability to elicit emotions. Eliciting emotions often paves the way for action... Sensationalized mass coverage is often an important aspect of social problems and claims making". *(Johnson, p.10)*

Johnson goes on to describe his research on child abuse and calls them "horror stories". He provides one such example: "The Baltimore Police found Patty Saunders, 9, in the 23 × 52 inch closet where she had been locked for half her life. She weighed only 20 pounds, and stood less than three feet tall. Smeared with filth, scarred from parental beatings, Patty had become irreparably mentally retarded" (Newsweek, October 10, 1977:31). *(Johnson, p. 10)* He points out it was the major role of the media that in fact caused child abuse to be seen as a significant social problem nationally and in individual states and localities. As a result national and state legislation was enacted and program actions occurred. (However, as we will discuss later, media attention and immediate policy actions may not lead to well-targeted program interventions or strategies.)

The creation of community interest and getting media attention is not sufficient to guarantee that a social issue becomes prominent on the agenda for public policy action. There are other factors that very much impact on whether an issue becomes a priority for action. Let's illustrate this fact by discussing youth violence. In the late 1980's through the mid 1990's there were significant increases in youth homicides. The already very high rates of youth deaths grew dramatically. Organizations such as the Children's

Defense Fund were strongly advocating major action including gun control measures, introduction of funding for violence prevention programs and increases in after school programs. Yet, overall the issue failed to generate significant wide spread support to create major changes. Why? Youth homicide most often involves guns and any action to develop gun control involves confronting the National Rifle Association (NRA). Further, youth violence most often involves kids killing other kids in poor minority communities. The homicide rates for poor and minority teenagers are significantly higher than for white or middle/upper class teenagers. Further, most often the deaths that occur are individual events. Most youth homicides do not become the focus of major media attention. On occasion where a mass murder occurs, i.e., Columbine High School in Colorado, major media attention results. Yet, our unwillingness to grapple with the more fundamental issues, e.g. poverty, racism, educational problems, leads us quickly away from in- depth discussions of violence and factors that contribute to it's occurrence. Further, as we noted in our earlier writings on Children and Families we often pay "lip service" to the issue without truly addressing the major concerns from a social justice perspective.

There are other observations that are important to consider in discussing agenda setting. They are:

(a) agenda setting is not accomplished instantly; rather having an issue prioritized for public action often occurs over years and requires constant reinforcement

(b) it is essential for social workers to understand that they can not address many of these social issues alone. Rather, working with others, e.g, advocates, neighborhood groups, is key to creating sufficient interest to begin to have the problem achieve recognition.

(c) doing "home work" in the form of solid, in depth research is essential. Knowledge of the "facts and figures" is important. Information gathering is a fundamental first step for promoting agenda setting and further action.

(2) Policy Formulation

After a social issue has become part of the "agenda", a process called "policy formulation" occurs. The process includes a further definition of the problem, information is then collected and discussed, alternative approaches or directions are screened and a preferred direction is finally chosen. The process does not occur in a specific sequence because policy making is not neat, logical or rational. Thus the key element of the process is research and analysis. The chart below provides a greater elaboration of key questions to be addressed in the process.

Problem Definition/Causation	*What Is Being Done/What Is Recommended To Be Done About The Problem?*	*What Are Possible Responses to Problem?*
❖ Who defines the issue as a social problem? ❖ Who is specifically affected and how? ❖ How does the media portray the issue and how does it effect public perception? ❖ How does political/ philosophical orientation impact on the definition and causation of the problem?	[suggested program response, legislative, action, advocacy] ❖ By the government (at what levels) ❖ By provider agencies ❖ By political parties ❖ By advocacy groups including social workers ❖ By communities and community groups	❖ Develop alternative strategies, i.e. programmatically, legislatively, entitlement ❖ What are the pros and cons of these strategies ❖ What political and advocacy actions can be developed to pursue these strategies?

Problem Definition and Possible Causation

As we note in the chart we need to first examine the definition and causation of

the problem. Defining a problem and possible causative factors is often dependent on

political or philosophical values. For instance, domestic violence can be defined as being

the instability of an individual. It also can be defined in broader terms, e.g.

"powerlessness of women in a male dominated society", it can be further defined by

economic stressors that impact on the individual or it can be seen as being caused by

multiple factors. We have seen this issue played out with respect to many problems.

HIV/AIDS was, especially in the first decade of its known existence, attributed to illegal

(e.g. drug use) or immoral behaviors (homosexuality). This philosophical stance greatly

hampered developing the federal response to the problem. Thus, the first step is to more

clearly define the problem or issue and who is specifically impacted and how? The

general rule, although not without exception, is that if significant numbers of individuals

and families are impacted and if the impact is severe then it will be treated more

seriously and expeditiously. In reviewing the issue of child abuse, we observe that when

it was thought to be a limited problem it was not a major concern. Through research

when it was identified as being more significant in scope and it impacted on different

class, economic, religious and racial groups it was given greater credence. (Note the

relationship between research on this phase and the actions needed to have an issue

placed on the policy agenda). It further needs to be noted that selected social issues, e.g.

homelessness, are not universally present in every community in the United States.

Homelessness is a much more significant issue in large urban environments that in

suburban or rural communities. Yet, as research and data collection began in these individual cities in the United States the dimension of a national problem emerged.

Homelessness is also an excellent example of the dilemmas of problem definition and

discussions of causation. In the 1980's there was significant variations in the estimates of

homeless populations. Part of the variation was caused by questions about definition

(was someone in the shelter homeless or did they have to live on the streets? Were

Marie and her 3 children living with a sister and her two children living in a one-

bedroom household because she couldn't find housing at the welfare rates and therefore,

part of the problem? How do you count the homeless? Homeless people move often so

how do you count the number of individuals who live in NYC subway tunnels?).

Definitions are often affected by political needs (advocates wanted to enlarge the number

while HUD officials wanted to minimize the numbers).

Also, as we noted, to discuss further attribution of causation significantly plays a

role in deciding policy options. In the United States with our emphasis on individualism

we have traditionally seen failures as being caused by deficits of the individuals. The

Horatio Alger myth or being able to "pull oneself up by their bootstraps" has been a

guiding philosophy. The systematic nature of problems was often ignored. A more recent

classic case of this observation can be seen in Ronald Reagan's campaign for the

Presidency when he picked up a Sunday business section of a newspaper and read aloud

a number of job opportunities and suggested those on welfare didn't have to be there

because jobs were plentiful. There was no discussion of the fact that many on welfare

lacked basic skills and education, and had to concern themselves with childcare or health

problems. Thus a key task for a policy advocate is to clearly define possible factors that

can cause the problem. Here good research is essential. This research could/should involve intensive literature reviews, discussions with key informants, community leaders, groups impacted by the problem and others.

Resulting from these initial activities a detailed presentation that defines the problem, indicates who is impacted and how they are affected and outlines possible causative factors should emerge.

Review of Current and Recommended Future Actions

The research discussed in the section above should include an examination about what is currently being done about the issue and what is being recommended. The task involves reviewing government policies and programs, philanthropic and provider agency actions and programs, recommendations of political organizations, key players, advocacy groups and organizations, communities and community groups led by consumers. Compiling this inventory provides the background to explore the development of policy or program recommendations. The scope of research may vary depending if the intended goal is to impact on national policy or on state or local policy.

Example- Violence by the Mentally Ill

An example of this type of endeavor was implemented by the authors. The authors received funding from the Office for Victims of Crime of the US Department of Justice to develop a training initiative to address issues facing the victims of mentally ill offenders. Because this had been a neglected and understudied issue, an essential initial task was to "more fully describe the issue and define it, identify its dimensions and causes, and highlight possible actions." The initial research required an extensive review of the literature, interviews with key informants, and conducting regional and

> *national focus groups with diverse participants- e.g. family members, criminal justice providers, mental health providers, and advocates. From this research it was possible to develop goals for actions and recommendation changes e.g.- changing legislation to let victims of mentally ill offenders be part of the judicial process, to develop coordinated and linked program response between mental health and criminal justice systems, to increase awareness of mental health providers to assess the potential of violence by their clients, and to train victims assistance staffs to provide needed support for victims of mentally ill offenders.*

Developing Possible Responses To The Problem

After compiling the inventory we discussed previously it is crucial to examine alternative policy/program approaches. As they are developed, key variables to be considered are:

- cost

- political acceptability

- availability of competent provider agencies

- acceptability to community (ies)

- acceptability to clients

- legal issues

- technical problems

- attitudes by funding or regulatory agencies

- ethical issues

To the degree possible alternative policy directions should be articulated. The pros and cons of each policy or program directions must be reviewed. Further, even in this stage it is necessary to consider the political and advocacy actions that are needed to pursue these directions. As part of these development activities a more formal policy analysis process discussed in the next section should be pursued.

Example- Homelessness

Homelessness is a major problem for a number of American cities. Yet for many of these cities developing a response involves major issues. Assuming that the community decides to formally address the problem [Note since the homeless are a powerless population, communities often are not inclined to devote resources to assist them] numerous issues need to be addressed. Homelessness is not a single problem. The homeless population is often made up of diverse groups, e.g., single mothers and their children, the mentally ill, drug and alcohol abusers and poor or low wage earning men. Do you develop approaches for each group? Do you choose the group(s) that are the most numerous? the most problematic? In designing a response do you limit your response to developing housing? Do you add an outreach and service component? (Many of these homeless individuals are very reluctant to use resources and outreach may be essential; further, for some groups, e.g., the mentally ill, services are a key to keeping them in shelters). Who is going to provide services: the government? voluntary organizations? church groups? Examining options requires research and review before a program or policy direction can be established.

Undertaking These Tasks

Undertaking these tasks seems overwhelming. Rather than identifying this work as being done by a single individual, the social worker interested in policy work needs to see himself as working in collaboration with others. Whether it is working through NASW (on a local, state or national basis) or other professional or community groups these tasks require linked action. Further, as part of the development work in all areas of policy work the goal is to establish collaborative relationships. Through this collaboration needed manpower and skills can be identified and joint activities implemented. Approaches, strategies and skills to promote collaboration will be discussed later in this section.

Chapter 6: Policy Analysis and Evaluation at the Federal, State and Agency Levels

Policy Analysis

Policy analysis can be an important tool for assessing the values of specific policies being developed or offered. They can be utilized to assess the adequacies of a policy either emerging from one's own group or by other organizations. In conducting a policy analysis the values of the individual or group form an important factor by which the proposed policy is reviewed.

There are numerous approaches to policy analysis and each may use different frameworks. For simplicity and because it has benefits for social workers to use we have chosen to present the model utilized by Donald Chambers.

Chambers suggests six basic factors that an analysis requires and highlights options within each factor and discusses factors to be utilized in conducting an evaluation. The chart below represents an abstraction of the Chambers model:

CHAMBERS MODEL

OPERATING CHARACTERISTIC	EVALUATIVE CRITERIA	ANALYTIC ACTIONS
1) **What are the Goals & Objectives** (goals is a general statement of desired outcomes; objective is a specific and operational statement about a desired outcome) Manifest/latent goals_____?	*Clarity* – is it understandable? *Measurability* – can I measure it? *Concern with ends* – are possible/intended outcomes stated?	❖ Examine *manifest & latent* goals; ❖ review legislative history & act itself; get viewpoints from official and unofficial sources

2) Forms/types of benefits and services ❖ Material goods or commodities ❖ Expert services ❖ Positive discrimination ❖ Cash ❖ Credits and vouchers ❖ Market or wholesale subsidies ❖ Loan guarantees ❖ Protective regulation ❖ Power over decisions (sometimes multiple benefit programs)	*Cost effectiveness; target efficiency (how well does it reach target group? stigmatization potential (will it label clients?); consumer freedom of choice*	❖ Research studies – process & outcome; ❖ Client input/reaction studies or observations ❖ Key observer feedback
3) Eligibility Entitlement Rules (who gets what, how much, and under what conditions?) ❖ *Prior contributions* (i.e., social insurance programs) ❖ *Administrative rules* (i.e., selectivity with choosing clients; intake rules no active drug abusers) ❖ *Private contract* ❖ *Professional discretion* (judgements by professional i.e., client does not fit appropriate diagnostic category; abuse did not occur) ❖ *Administrative Discretion* (i.e., patrol decides when to intervene in domestic quarrels ❖ Means (income) test	❖ *Potential for alienation and stigmatization of clients* ❖ *Potential for missing target group* ❖ *Potential for overwhelming cost or over/under utilization* ❖ *Potential for individual or family description*	❖ *Research* ❖ *Observation* ❖ *Opinions from key parties* – i.e. consumer providers

4) *Administrative/Service DeliverySystem* ❖ Centralization/ decentralization ❖ Provider auspices – gov't or contracted or both ❖ Client/citizen empowerment ❖ Standards or utilization review of system ❖ Service approaches (defined vs. open) ❖ Administration review/appeal	*Integration/continuity* Linked or fragmented system & impact on client? *Accessibility* – is it readily available for client/recipient? *Relatedness to Ethnic Racial Diversity* How well are key groups served? *Accountability* – is it accountable to public? To clients?	❖ Research – process and outcome ❖ Observations ❖ Feedback from key participants (i.e., officials, providers, clients)
5) *Financing Methods* ❖ Prepayments/insurance ❖ Publicly regulated private enterprise contract ❖ Voluntary contributions ❖ General revenue appropriations ❖ Changes (to clients) for services	*Ability to generate funding continuity* *Ability to insure secure benefits overtime* *Ability to protect against inflation recession and depression* Ability to protect against demographic changes (i.e., unusual large cohorts of aged) *"Hidden" rewards to key players & side effect profits*	❖ Research – process and outcome ❖ Financial analysis and projections Feedback from key participants officials, providers; clients ❖ Review of additional or emergency governmental funding requests
6) *Interactions Between Operating Characteristics Between This Policy/ Program and Others* ❖ Co-entitlement ❖ Dis-entitlement ❖ Continuing effects ❖ Unintentional duplication of benefits and services	*Undesirable interactions* that hinder clients or programs *or undermine desired outcomes*	❖ Research – process and outcome ❖ Feedback from key participants (i.e., officials, providers and clients)

A policy analysis is a tool that can be beneficial in examining policy alternatives. Further, a policy analysis using a model like Chambers' provides an opportunity for social workers to utilize their values about social justice to determine directions and their support or rejection of policy options.

Policy Enactment

Policy enactment means that a policy is either adopted by a legislative body at the Federal (Congress), state (State Legislature) or local (County Legislature) levels and becomes law or is adopted by the executive (President, Governor, Mayor or County Executive) through an "order." It then represents the official direction that government entity will follow to address a specific social issue.

Adoption of a policy by a legislative process is a crucial and complicated procedure. We will discuss this in more substantial detail later in this chapter as we review how social workers can influence the process. The key elements of the process involve, among other tasks: identifying political strategies, developing a support base, e.g., coalitions, assessing the political factors (favorable or unfavorable towards the policy), having the policy introduced as "proposed legislation", engaging in promoting the legislature (e.g. lobbying and education) and fostering final adoption.

Policy Implementation

Once a policy has been passed and legislation emerges we operate under the belief that those effective programs or actions will occur. We further believe that these programs or actions will have an impact on the social problem being addressed. Yet, more often than not our beliefs may in fact be illusions. The outcomes may not be as intended and the social problem or issue can be exacerbated.

—   Why may there be poor results after a policy has been enacted? Palumbo and Calista suggest that there are often numerous reasons. They note:

1. Much legislation passed at the national, state, and local levels is symbolic; it is usually a promise that something can be done about an intractable social problem that has lingered on the public agenda for years (i.e., welfare dependency).

2. Legislation is often not based on a sound program theory that correctly identifies what design conditions will get the target groups to behave in the desired fashion because we do not have such theories.

3. Socioeconomic and political conditions change so that the solution promised in the legislation may not be appropriate a few years later (i.e., the economy loses unskilled manufacturing jobs that welfare recipients could fill).

4. Administrators discover during implementation that a different type of program or organizational structure would work better than the one envisioned in the legislation.

5. Insufficient resources are committed to the program.

6. Implementers don't have the know-how to make the policy work.

(Palumbo and Calista. Implementation and the Policy Process-Opening Up The Black Box p.4)

Social workers must in fact be acutely aware of the forementioned factors that influence implementation. This is crucial if social workers developing policy actions are intent on producing meaningful change and not *symbolic* change. Further, to the degree possible thatsocial workers need to insure new or modified programs and policies are responsive to client needs. Additionally, to influence the actual implementation process social workers must be in the "game for the long haul."

As we noted, the passage of legislation does not automatically equate to change. The social work community needs to continue to review agencies and their implementation actions, to work with coalitions and partners to continue influencing agencies and the resources and directions they establish for programs emerging from enacted policy. Further, social workers need, with their partners, to continually assist and evaluate the impact of new policy actions.

Let us illustrate with a selection of examples below key tasks that social workers can and should be providing.

Example 1

In a specific state social workers through their NASW chapter joined with other mental health advocates to have the legislature pass a bill in which the state downsized and closed numbers of the state's psychiatric hospital beds. The law required that the financial resources saved were to be directed towards establishing community mental health programs. These social workers and other advocates instituted a process by which they reviewed, in detail, all actions that the State Mental Hygiene agency was utilizing in implementing this legislation. Quickly, they found that the funding formulas, rules and regulations that were adopted by the state were cumbersome and a burden to voluntary providers and favored state operated programs. They met with key state officials and convinced them to change these rules. They further began to compile a listing of all new community programs developed under this legislation and gave reports summarizing this data to the State's governor and legislators. This was intended to keep continued support for this policy.

Federal action to change welfare (1996), as discussed earlier, lead to major actions at the state and local levels (county, city). In numbers of states and localities, NASW chapters and child and family advocates have established committees that review and evaluate the rules and procedures that the states and localities established with respect to women and children receiving public assistance. In numbers of cases they have battled state and local Departments of Social Services to insure fairness for public assistance recipients. In some situations the advocates have taken direct action or even court action. Line workers based upon data they collected from their clients have provided much of the feedback to these advocates.

Evaluating and Assessing Policies and Programs

It is essential for the promotion of social justice that there is a continuing emphasis on evaluating and assessing policies and programs. Passage of legislation aimed at addressing or alleviating social problems is not a guarantee that the needed actions are occurring to address the issue. Often, the policy actions may be too limited, or not well focused or designed to impact on the issue. We know by experience that lack of impact is quite commonplace.

The fact that a program has been implemented and is available does not mean that program is effective, well developed or addresses the populations affected by a social problem. A prime example of less than successful program initiatives is the community mental health centers program. Started in the mid 1960s one of its "stated goals" (in response to the initial phase of deinstitutionalization) was to create systems of care for discharges from long term psychiatric centers. Repeated studies of CMHC's over nearly twenty years document their failure to serve the serious mentally ill, especially former state hospital patients. This was not to suggest that CMHC's did not have some utility in promoting the development of community based mental health service but they did not serve, at least initially, as a resource for the severely mentally ill being discharged from state hospitals.

Further, as we discuss in the next section, the policies enacted may have inherent flaws (e.g., they are symbolic in nature, they may not be meaningful for the population). Policies may not be built upon a sound theoretical or experiential base. Frequently, legislators in a rush to be seen as responding to social issues, may not carefully assess the directions needed. A recent example is seen in the passage of federal legislation to promote the development of Mental Health Courts (Oct 2000). This legislation was a response to a continuing concern about the necessary "criminalization of mental illness." Yet, the legislation was built only upon the experience of 3 or 4 model Mental Health Court programs that had not been evaluated. Further, the legislation because of its origins fails to define mental health services to courts as a possible funding option and thus the legislation is of very limited utility.

Program and policy evaluation and assessment are necessary and important vehicles for examining the impact of policy and programs. They are especially essential in social welfare and crucial for social workers intent on promoting social justice. Richard Hoefur writing in Social Work (1994) notes:

> Evaluation is a vital enterprise for social programs. Well-done evaluations are helpful for program administrators, program worker, clients, policy makers, and the public at larger in whose name the program is conducted. Each stakeholder group can learn some things that are primarily of interest to itself, but the most significant contributions of a competent evaluation are important to all stakeholders. Good evaluations provide useful information. They illuminate program strengths and weaknesses. They can lead to improvements in individual programs. In the long run, they also lead to a more effective and efficient mix of programs to clients.

(Hoefer 1994, p.233)

Policy assessment or policy evaluation refers to the "objective, systematic and empirical examination of the effect the ongoing policies and programs have on their target in terms of the goals they are meant to achieve." This assessment can be done on federal, state or local policies. Implicit in the assessment process is an attempt to assess broad policy impacts rather than a specific program evaluation or outcome study.

These definitions of policy evaluation assume that the goals and objectives of programs and policies are clear, that we know how to measure costs, and that we can impartially weigh benefits against cost in evaluating a public program. In short, these definitions view policy evaluation as a rational activity. Yet, this is not always the fact.

Ideally, the evaluation of a program would include all of its effects on real world conditions. Evaluators would want to (1) identify and rank all of the goals of a program; (2) devise measures to describe progress toward these goals; (3) identify the "target" situation or group for which the program was designed; (4) identify non-target groups who might be affected indirectly by the program ("spillover" effects) and non-target groups who are similar to the target groups but did not participate in the program or receive its direct benefits ("control group"); (5) measure programs' effects on target and non-target groups over as long a period of time as possible; (6) identify and measure the costs of the program in terms of all of the resources allocated to it; and (7) identify and measure the indirect costs of the program, inducing the loss of opportunities to pursue other activities.

The policy evaluation described above represents a daunting but crucial challenge. The complexities of the challenge are both technical, e.g. can we readily identify the intended target populations? Can we effectively measure the impact of the services or benefit?, and political, e.g. can we truly and rationally identify the purposes of the policy, which often is symbolic? And can we identify possible unintended side effects? Further, we need to in fact examine impacts of programs on non-target populations, e.g. providers. Does a child welfare policy increase the burdens and demands on the staff and increase burnout and turnover? Additionally, we can not confuse policy outputs (what a government agency does, e.g. spending dollars) with policy impacts, e.g. improved mental health care for the elderly poor.

Because this challenge is so complex it is often in the best interest of practicing social workers and others to seek help from research or policy analysis experts. A key role for the social worker is to know how and when they need to turn to others. These policy evaluations are key because without this information the social worker and other advocates are not able to determine if a social policy is successful or if other changes are needed.

Program evaluation, in contrast to policy evaluation, has a narrower definition. It refers to the process of making judgments about a specific program intervention with respect to its effectiveness, efficiency and adequacy. These judgments are based upon data collection and analysis. Program evaluations can have a useful role with respect to policy evaluation. Reviewing multiple evaluations of specific interventions or programs, e.g. family preservation care, assist us in making judgments about family preservation as a policy direction.

Program evaluation can most easily be described as follows:

***PROGRAM EVALUATION*-**is intended to answer the key question

(1)   **(2)**   **(3)**   **(4)**   **(5)**

Who does *What* to *Whom* with *What Outcome(s)* and at *What Cost?*

DEFINITIONS:

(1) Who-staff/workers-characteristics

(2) Does What-intervention methods and strategies (i.e. short term individual

casework)

(3) To Whom-clients served and their characteristics (i.e. age, sex, ethnicity,

education)

(4) What Outcome-what are the results? Changes? (i.e. functional or problem

improvement)

(5) What Cost-how much does it cost to provide this service? Is it less or more costly

them alternative approaches

Conducting evaluations involves addressing key technical and political

issues best summarized by the illustration below:

Social workers often, if they do not have extensive training in research or

who are not expert researchers, avoid discussing evaluation. This posture may

remove the social work practitioners from making needed contributions to policy

or program development. The roles for social workers include:

Participating in critical discussions of specific evaluation projects and social

workers should be eager to participate in discussions about the merits of specific

research projects by critically examining their choice of criteria, their interpretations of

findings, their methodological choices, and their instruments.

Even when they have not conducted their own studies, social workers can cite and

draw on the research of others as they evaluate specific programs. For example, when evaluating a social program that lacks a bilingual staff they can cite available research that examines whether and when persons who speak only a foreign language are deterred from seeking or using services when no translators exist. These suggestive findings can be used to evaluate specific programs even when they have been obtained in other settings and with different kinds of programs; we can infer, for example, that findings about the impact of a bilingual staff on services given to refugees could be applicable to many settings.

Nor should social workers be reluctant to use professional wisdom as well as theory drawn from the social and human services in their evaluation activities and in their reviews of policies and programs that exist within the human services. To rely solely on empirical research is often limiting since it may not exist in the area of interest to us. We would consign ourselves to silence on most issues if we wait for only empirical data. When social workers confront policies and programs that appear to conflict with professional wisdom or specific theories that are widely respected, social workers should draw on these to criticize or support specific policies or programs.

Policy Continuation or Termination

Based upon multiple factors which include (1) public reaction to the policy or program, (2) political reaction, (3) provider reaction, (4) formal policy assessment, (5) media reaction/attention a policy may be continued or terminated. If termination occurs then it is likely for the policy cycle to begin again.

Social workers may have an initial impulse to stay away from what they perceive to be the complicated process of social policy and change. However, as evidenced above, when broken down into understandable pieces, the processes of policy development, implementation, and evaluation can be straightforward and easy to understand.

Fields of Practice for Social Workers

Social workers provide services in many fields or areas. The breadth and scope of the areas for social work practice and the populations they service represent one of the fundamental benefits to having a social work degree. Among the populations they serve are youth, the physically disabled, the emotionally disturbed, the elderly, the homeless, criminals, and their victims, among others. Social workers can work many settings, including social agencies, mental health programs, criminal justice settings, hospitals, nursing homes, senior centers, schools and after schools and pre-schools, domestic violence programs, legislation and government policy making organizations, and other settings. They also play many different roles, e.g. care managers, therapists, advocates, community organizers, and researchers. It is therefore, impossible within the limits of this text to provide examples from each area. We therefore have chosen to focus on only several fields of practice to provide examples.

PART III –Contemporary Social Welfare Programs and Policies

Perspectives on Fields of Service:

In this section of the book we look at three populations that are of great importance

to social work and which are greatly affected by social welfare policies and programs. The

populations discussed are children and families, the mentally ill and the elderly. The status

and treatment of each of these populations is discussed from a social justice perspective

which provides the main focus for this text. These populations are highly dependent on

governmental policies or actions or inaction. For each of the three populations we provide,

(a) an overview of key present issues, (b) a discussion of the historical background with

respect to policies and programs, (c) a review of the current systems of care, and (d)

conceptual models that social workers can utilize in promoting policies and services that

enhance the well being of these populations. The discussions are designed to enable

students to understand key policy issues as they impact on the three populations.

Chapter 7 – Children and Family Services

America is supposedly a child-centered nation and much of our political rhetoric

and/or TV/media presentations are often devoted to "how can we improve life for

children and families?" Yet, as you will see in our presentations, much of this dialogue

ignores, from a social work/social justice perspective, a focus on the overall condition of

children and families, especially those that are most at risk. From numerous perspectives,

this is a country that most often neglects the needs of children and their families.

Further, as is highlighted below, conditions for poor children and their families have not

improved in the last number of years. Although the comments below were written many

years ago they remain appropriate today.

When we examine how a society cares for its children we are peering directly into the heart of a nation. Today, the United States, the wealthiest country in the world, has more children living in poverty than any other industrialized nation. Millions of children wake up to dangerous neighborhoods, dilapidated and violent schools, impoverished and stressful homes and futures devoid of opportunity. Further, the country that pioneered strategies to prevent child abuse that now spends more money fighting it than do all other industrialized countries has the highest rate of child abuse.

-Duncan Lindsey, 1994, *The Welfare of Children*, p. 3

Further, the Children's Defense Fund in a dramatic 2002 report entitled "The State of Children in America's Union" summarizes the major problems facing children and families today as follows:

The state of millions of children in the richest most powerful democratic nation in the world is morally shameful, economically costly, and politically hypocritical.

- An American child is reported abused or neglected every 11 seconds; 581,000 children are in our foster care system – 127,000 of them are waiting for adoptive families.

- An American child is born into poverty every 43 seconds; one in five children is poor during the first three years of life – the time of greatest brain development.

- An American child is born without health insurance every minute – 90 percent of our nine million uninsured children live in working families.

- An American child or teen is killed by gunfire every 2 hours and 40 minutes – nine every day; 87,000 children and teens have been killed by guns since 1979. It is safer to be an on-duty law enforcement officer than a child under 10 in America.

- Millions of American children start school not ready to learn, and millions more lack safe, affordable, quality child care and early child-hood education when their parents work.

- A majority of American fourth graders can't read or do math at a proficient level.

- Seven million children are home alone on a regular basis without adult supervision often after school when they are at greatest risk of getting into trouble.

- Nearly 12 million children are poor, and millions are hungry, at risk of hunger, living in worst case housing, or homeless. Almost 80 percent of poor children live in working households.

> \- Children's Defense Fund, 2002, p. IV–V

In a December 2003 Op-Ed article in *The New York Times*, Bob Herbert writes:

A broader look at the levels of serious distress being faced by increasing numbers of Americans comes from the latest Index of Social Health, which is published annually by the Institute for Innovation in Social Policy at the Fordham University Graduate Center in Tarrytown, N.Y.

The institute analyzes government statistics in a wide variety of areas, including infant mortality, children in poverty, teenage suicide, health insurance coverage and homicide rates, as a way of monitoring the "social wellbeing of the nation."

The latest index, which covered the year 2001 (the latest year for which complete statistics were available), showed the social health of the nation taking a steep dive. It was the biggest decline in the index in two decades. and preliminary data for the years since 2001 show the decline continuing, according to Dr. Marc Miringoff, the institute's director.

The categories that worsened in the latest index were children in poverty, child abuse, average weekly earnings, affordable housing, health insurance coverage, food stamp coverage, the gap between rich and poor, and out-of-pocket health costs for those over 65.

Two indicators reached their worst levels on record, food stamp coverage (which correlates with increases in hunger) and income inequality.

"These numbers are usually invisible to us," said Dr. Miringoff. "They tell us an untold story, not just about the poor but the working poor and the middle class as well. It's shocking to see such a sharp decline in just one year. It tells us that something's going on with the basic fabric of our society."

> \-Bob Herbert, New York Times, 12/14/03

The Children's Defense Fund dramatically concludes its judgment on the present

status of children by noting:

These facts are not acts of God. They are our moral and political choices as Americans. We can change them. We have the money. We have the power. We have the know-how. We have the experience. We have the vision. And we have the moral and social responsibility. What we lack is the civic and spiritual engagement of enough citizens, and political, faith, and media leaders to pierce the profound lack of awareness about and indifference to preventable and solvable child suffering; the poisonous politics of self-interest and greed; narrow ideological agendas which reflect the belief that government should help the rich and powerful most and the poor and powerless least; and the political hypocrisy of leaders at all levels of government and in all parties who leave millions of children behind while pretending to do otherwise.

- Children's Defense Fund, 2002 p. V

What we have are children and family policies at multiple levels-federal, state, and local and they often conflict with each other. Numbers of these programs, e.g. welfare reform, may not have been passed to promote the well being of children and families but for other purposes, e.g. save money. Additionally, many of our policies may overtly and covertly promote social injustice rather than social justice.

Key Facts About Children and Families

• There are an estimated 70+ million children under 18 years of age and this number is expected to reach 74 million by 2010. "America's children continue to grow in racial and ethnic diversity. In 1998, 65 percent were white, non-Hispanics; 15 percent were black, non-Hispanic; 15 percent were Hispanic; 4 percent were Asian/Pacific Islanders and 1 percent were American Indian/Alaska Native." (America's Children: Key National Indicators of Well Being, 1999, p. iii) There are expected to be especially large increases in non-white and minority children over the next decade.

• The nature of the family keeps changing. Children living with two parents are declining to approximately 65%. Further, there are large differences between racial and ethnic groups. More of white children, non-Hispanic, lived with two parents compared to 36 percent of black children and 64 percent of the Hispanic children. As noted above, with the expected increase in non-white children there is expected to be an increase in children in non-white family households. Further, the growth in the proportion of young families (with parents under 25) rose over the past decades and is likely to increase further. Additionally, even in two parents households increased numbers of these families involve "mixed families", e.g. divorced adults marrying and linking children with different birth parents.

- The percentage of births to unmarried women has risen, although it has tapered off.

- The location of where children live differs by racial and ethnic group. Most black and Hispanic children live in central cities while most white children live outside of central cities.

Beyond the general information provided above we will now review issues with respect to children and families that represent problematic areas for social work.

Children/Families and Income Insecurity

Children as an age group are the most likely of any in the United States to live in poverty. Approximately 1 in 4 children live in poverty and families with children are 3 times more likely than families without children to be poor. The ratio of poverty among families with children varies markedly by racial group (14% for whites, 39% for blacks and 32% for Hispanics). These poverty ratios are especially true for young families (31% for whites, 67% for blacks and 46% for Hispanics).

Further, our concern is not only with families in poverty but with the many other families who live on the "edge". The present economic downturns increase the number of families having difficulty.

A crucial factor in the lives of children, especially with respect to economic well being, is often the change in family structure, e.g. divorce. This is a crucial issue for social workers. The Family Research Council writes:

> The biggest threat to the material well-being of children is the insecurity of the modern family. Family breakdown deprives a child not only of security, stability and happy home life, but it also threatens the economic support and well being of the child. In some instances, the child may have to suffer only a decline in living standards, but far more often, single parenthood means a plunge into poverty. A huge gap exists between the poverty levels of children living with two parents and children in single-parent homes. Over half of the children in single-parent homes live in poverty—this is five times the rate for other children. *(Family Research Council, "The Breakdown of the Family Forces Women and Children Into Poverty," Opposing Viewpoint on Poverty, p. 126 & 127).*

The economic deprivation dramatically impacts on the quality of life of families and the Children's Defense Fund, notes:

> "Many poor families manage by cutting back on food, jeopardizing their health and the development of their children, or by living in substandard and sometimes dangerous housing. Some do without heat, electricity, telephone service or plumbing for months or years. Many do without health insurance, health care, safe childcare or reliable transportation to take them to or from work. Some borrow money if they can. Some beg. Some have small amounts of unreported income or feel compelled to engage in illegal activities" *(Holly Sklar, "America's Unfair Socioeconomic System Causes Poverty," Opposing Viewpoints on Poverty, p. 108).*

Although the economic boom of the late 1990's was helpful in aiding more poor people to obtain jobs the downturns in recent years has reversed the trend and family homelessness and use of food handouts is at an all time high.

The Shrinking Welfare Safety Net

Of additional concern to social workers is the issue of welfare reform. Welfare reform has traditionally provided the economic safety net for poor families; but what has been the impact of welfare reform? But the passage of the 1996 federal welfare law was marked by reports showing large declines in the welfare rolls, an increase in

recipients finding employment, and a slight decline in the overall child poverty rate.

Political leaders of all parties declared America's experiment with welfare reform

(and similar state experiments that preceded it) a resounding success, yet often, the

children suffer.

Yet as social workers we must examine the issue beyond "glib proclamations"

of politicians. We need to take a deeper look at early evidence of family well-being,

drawing on new national survey data, a review of studies by states and private

research institutions, and a compilation of findings from informal community-based

monitoring projects, among other sources. This research suggests a more troubling

picture with some families faring better off welfare, while others are having a more

difficult time.

Many being forced from the welfare rolls are working at low paying jobs without

benefits. Further, private charities, food banks, and shelters are reporting increased

demands. Bob Herbert, in his Op Ed column "Change the Channel" in The New York

Times on December 14, 2003 writes the following:

> The problem is, if you peel away the headlines and look more closely at reality,
> you'll see some things that aren't so amusing. In New York City, which is now
> just emerging from the recession, there are more homeless people than at any
> time since accurate records started being kept in the late 1970's.

> Each night more than 39,000 people – nearly 17,000 of them children – seek
> refuge in the city's shelters. "It's the greatest number of homeless since the Great
> Depression," said Patrick Markee, a policy analyst with the Coalition for the
> Homeless.

> The faces of the destitute are changing as more and more families with children –
> in New York and across the nation – find themselves without the money
> necessary for food or shelter.

The U.S. Conference of Mayors released a report yesterday showing that over the past year hunger and homelessness continued to rise in major American cities. A survey of 25 cities showed an increase of 17 percent in requests for emergency food assistance and an increase of 13 percent in requests for emergency shelter. (Herbert)

It seems increasingly clear that based upon the information from the recent US Conference of Mayor's report and the Index of Social Health the shrinkage of the safety net and economic downturns are producing starkly negative results for children and families.

Violence in Families/Violence in Youth

Violence within the family (spousal violence and child abuse) and violence by youth represent significant social issues. It is important as we discuss issues affecting children and families that these issues of violence are explored. This is a key area of concern for social workers.

1. Violence in Families

(A)   *Spousal Abuse*: Domestic violence causes more injuries today to American women than rapes, auto accidents and muggings combined. The FBI estimates that between two and six million women are battered each year or about one woman every 15 seconds. A current or former husband or boyfriend kills four women every day and one of those women is beaten to death by the offender's hands, feet, or fists.

The 2000 report from the Bureau of Justice Statistics on Intimate Partner Violence indicated that:

- Nearly one million violent crimes are committed against persons by their current or former spouse, boyfriends or girlfriends and 85% of these were against women.

- Approximately 1800 murders in 1998 were attributed to intimate partners and women were 75% of these victims.

- Only about half of the intimate partner violence was reported.

- 40% of the women who were victims of intimate partner violence lived in households with children under the age of 12.

> -Bureau of Justice Statistics, Intimate
> Partner Violence, May 2001, p. 1

What has also begun to emerge is that there is a significant overlap between domestic violence and child abuse. It has also been reported that domestic violence leads to an increase in homelessness for women and children and increased involvement with substance abuse and use of emergency rooms. Further, the impact of domestic violence on children includes stress, emotional problems, lack of school attendance and often isolation from family and friends.

(B)   *Child Abuse and Neglect*: The other major component of family violence is child abuse and neglect. It is a major problem of significant importance. Every day the media reports on dramatic cases of child abuse.

To begin our review of this topic is to review the definitions of child abuse and neglect and look at its scope. What is child abuse? The federal Child Abuse Prevention and Treatment Act (CAPTA), as amended, provides the following definitions. A *child* is a person who has not attained the lesser of the age of 18; or, except in cases of sexual abuse, the age specified by the child protection law of the State in which the child resides. *Child abuse and neglect* is, at a minimum, any recent act or failure to act on the part of a parent or caretaker which results in death, serious physical or emotional harm, sexual abuse or exploitation; or an act or failure to act which presents imminent risk of serious harm. *Sexual abuse* is the employment, use, persuasion, inducement, enticement, or coercion of any child to engage in, or assist any other person to engage in, any sexually explicit conduct or simulation of such conduct for the purpose of producing a visual depiction of such conduct; or the rape, and in cases of a caretaker or inter-familial relationships, statutory rape, molestation, prostitution, or other form of sexual exploitation of children, or incest with children. Each state is responsible for providing its own definition of child abuse and neglect. More information can be found at the National Clearinghouse on Child Abuse and Neglect website.

What is the scope of child abuse and neglect? It is a major national problem. Data on child abuse indicates that over 3.1 million cases of child abuse were reported each year and that over one million were substantiated. In examining this issue, it was found that cases of child neglect were most significant (46% of all cases), followed by physical abuse (24%), other (17%), sexual abuse (11%) and emotional abuse (5%). 2001 data shows that over 1300 children per year die from abuse and neglect but this may be an undercount. The greatest proportions of child abuse victims are the very young. Among recent victims, 39% are under the age of five, 69% were under the age of ten. With respect to neglect 80% involved children under the age of five and more than 40% of the victims are under the age of one. The National Clearinghouse on Child Abuse and Neglect (reports from 1998, 2001 & 2003) notes that in 83% of child fatalities one or both parents were involved and in 17% of cases non-parent caretakers were the perpetrators.

What is the impact of child abuse and neglect? Children exposed to abuse are more likely to be at 4–12 times higher risk of alcohol abuse, drug abuse, depression, and suicide, often become abusers themselves and are more likely to become socially withdrawn, engage in violent behaviors as juveniles and adults and to be arrested.

2. *Youth Violence*

In discussing violence we must in fact address the issue of youth violence. Youth violence, although it has declined, especially in respect to homicides, in the last several years, is still substantial. Overall, Merindoff indicates that "the United States still leads the industrial world in its youth homicide rate. Rates in two age groups – under 15 and 15–24 – are significantly higher than in any other industrialized nation, 10 times higher than Canada, 15 times higher than Australia and 28 times higher than France or Germany. By sheer volume the numbers are staggering. In 1994 over 8000 young people or 22 per day were homicide victims every day in the United States. Overall homicide is the second leading cause of death for males 15–24 and the leading cause of death for African American and Hispanic youth (Merindoff). In addition to being victims, youth are frequently perpetrators and have higher rates of homicide, rape, robbery and aggravated assault. The consequences of being involved in violence are dramatic; higher rates of PTSD, increased sleep and anxiety disorders, school problems and difficulty concentrating. Studies have continued to demonstrate the continuing importance of the youth violence issue. For example, studies following the events of 9/11 in New York City found that nearly two thirds of youth experienced high levels of anxiety related to violence in their homes, schools and communities prior to 9/11.

Child and Family Health

Children, especially those from poor and low income families are significantly more likely than children from middle income families to have poorer health. Further, with growing problems with insurance coverage, increasing numbers of children from low income families are not covered for medical care. Without insurance coverage these children often don't receive needed services. Further, these uninsured children were more likely to miss school, and have untreated medical problems, e.g. vision. Often, these medical problems affect school performance.

Historical Overview of Child Welfare

The problem about a singular focus on child welfare is that the manner in which it was historically constructed and is presently operationalized shortchanges women. Elizabeth Hutchinson noted in a key 1992 article:

> Almost from the outset, the child welfare system accepted the unequal power structure of a patriarchal society. Child welfare scholars, policymakers, and practitioners have studied, planned for, and served children and their families without giving special attention to the needs of female caregivers – as if children's needs could be met whether or not their caregivers had access to resources for providing sufficient care. The child welfare literature has failed to address the possibility that the well-being of children might, under current societal structures, come at great costs to their female caregivers, assuming instead that mothers' needs and children's needs are not met by the same programs. (Hutchinson, 1992, p.67) . . . "First, as long as a patriarchal society delegates the care of children exclusively to women in the private sphere, individual women are held accountable for the welfare of individual children. Second, as long as women serve almost exclusively as the caregivers of children, the question of allocation of resources to the care-giving function of society is a women's issue. Third, current child welfare policy practice are built on the oppression of several categories of women." (Hutchinson, 1992, p. 67 – 68)

Thus, as we review the history and examine the current systems of child welfare we need to recognize that concerns about families and children may to a large extent fall beyond the purview of "child welfare".

In the United States from its beginnings in colonial times up through the present "there is a strong belief that individuals and families serve as the primary social service system for all children" *(Hutchinson, 1992, p. 68).*

Key events and time periods highlight the development of child welfare below as follows:

Child Saving Movement 1600-1800

The origins of child saving go back to colonial days when poverty was a sin and work was the way to salvation. The power of "child savers" relied on the oversight of the poor and the power to intervene in parent-child relationships under laws of guardianship and the right to protect the child, the helpless and the incompetent. Children and women were integral parts of the economic life. Work was a form of discipline for children. Children might be "bound out" to work with families or businesses. Poor and orphan children were often imported to be bound out as laborers. A child could be removed from parents with a court order. The community was not interested in protecting children from hard labor or abuse; they were removed when there was fear that children would not grow up to become independent citizens. Fatherless children and illegitimate children were often removed on the grounds that the mothers could not care for them. As children were seen as "little adults" there was no concern about their development during these years.

Child Rescue Movement 1800–1900

In this period there was focus on increasing the rights of children through the application of the law. Judicial decisions were made in which courts overrode the rights of parents. This was done to protect the child from abuse. The most famous example of court intervention took place in 1874 in New York City and was known as the "Mary Ellen Case." In this case the Society for the Prevention of Cruelty to Animals went to court on behalf of Mary Ellen, an abused child. This step led to the development of chapters of Society to Prevent Cruelty to Children. Earlier developments in the century (1850's) included the establishment of the Children's Aid Society, which led to the development of foster care and adoption. Children's Aid also established the "Orphan Train" which took children "at risk" and transported them to the Midwest or the West for adoption by farmers or businessmen. The mid-century also saw the development and growth of orphanages that became a main feature of the child welfare system. In the last two decades of the century major reforms towards children occurred and included the development of public education, the passage of child labor laws and the establishment of juvenile courts.

Initial National Awareness of Children's Needs (1900–1930)

In 1908 there was the first White House Conference on Child Welfare which focused national attention on children. A report from the conference stated: "Home life is the highest and finest product of civilization...children should not be deprived of it except for urgent and compelling reasons... for children who for sufficient reasons and must be removed from their own homes, or who have no homes it is desirable that they should be cared for in families whenever practicable. The carefully selected foster home is for the normal child the best substitute for the natural home".

The recommendations from the White House Conference became critical to the movement in establishing programs for assisting mothers to care for their children in their own homes, efforts to keep delinquent and dependent children in their own homes,

to the development of adoption as a method for providing homes for homeless children,

to the increased use of the foster homes rather than the institution for the care of the

children, and to the development of a "cottage" type of institution for children instead of

the large, congregate type of institution. The White House Conference led to the

establishment of the Federal Children's Bureau (1912). It was the first area in which the

Federal Government showed interest in supporting social services. States began to follow

suit and began assuming selected roles regarding children e.g., paying for foster care.

Also, as a result the Child Welfare League of America was established in 1910 and

became an organized voice for children. It established standards for operations of

childcare agencies and became active in federal legislation. Also, in this time period

(1920's) child guidance clinics were established. They worked closely with schools,

communities and agencies. They offered mental health care aimed at preventing juvenile

delinquency.

The New Deal and the Two Decades After (1930–1960)

The Depression marked the near collapse of the American economy. In 1935, the

Social Security Act was passed and marked major federal intervention in social welfare.

The Act established basic income support systems in the United States (public

assistance and social insurance). As part of that act provisions were made to the states

to establish Child Welfare Services which were geared towards care of the homeless,

dependent, and neglected children. In the latter 1940's and 1950's there was growth in

child welfare services with respect to issues of neglect and abuse, delinquency and

physically and emotionally handicapped children. There was substantial growth in the use of foster care. Further, there was growth in special institutions for emotionally disturbed children.

The Great Society (the 1960's)

The 1960's marked a great growth in the social and human services and a rediscovery of the issues of poverty and social justice. There were many new programs that positively affected the growth of services and benefits for children and families. These include: *Food Stamps* (1961) – food benefits for poor families; *Social Services Amendment* (1962) – that reimbursed states up to 75% for social services given to welfare recipients including children and families; *CMHC Act* (1963) – established community mental health care including children's services; *Civil Right Act* (1964); *Economic Opportunity Act* (1964) – which included Jobs Corp Training, Neighborhood Youth Corps, Work Study, VISTA, Headstart, Upward Bound; *Medicaid* (1965) – medical benefits for poor individuals and families.

Child Protection (1970's through the present)

Towards the end of the 1960's there was the discovery of the "battered children syndrome" which led to the passage of federal and state legislation that focused on "child protection." It was media attention from that initial period through the present time that has shaped this "child protection system." The system focuses on mandated reporting and investigations and at present nearly 3,000,000 telephone calls are received a year by child abuse hotlines (in more than 50% of the cases the complaints are unsubstantiated; further, the reports to hotlines overwhelming consist of cases of neglect and much fewer findings of actual physical abuse, especially serious physical abuse). It is this system that in fact characterizes the present child welfare system.

Hutchinson describes the following philosophical perspective that governs child welfare at present:

> "The current child-protection movement focuses on policing family rather than enhancing the resources for family caregiving. The recent construction of child maltreatment inspired a child welfare system that relies on mandatory reporting laws as the case-finding method, emphasizes involuntary rather than voluntary services, and seeks solutions to cope with individual caregiver deficiencies. The continuing allegiance to the separate-spheres ideology ensures that women's deficiencies are likely to be noted in the child welfare system, and even when men are the perpetrators of maltreatment, women are held accountable for controlling the maltreatment behavior. In recent years, with the skyrocketing rates of reporting, increasing portions of child welfare budgets have gone toward the process of investigative disposition, with little left for services" (Hutchinson, 1992, p. 20).

Current Systems of Care

Defining child welfare is not a simple task. Various authors use different definitions; some of the definitions are broad and may include financial support while others in fact are much narrower and deal with a more limited concept usually related to selected services. The authors have chosen not to include the concept of a financial support system because operationally it doesn't fall under the purview of social work. In reviewing the presentations in our earlier sections we point out that the 1996 Welfare Reform Act reduced financial support for children and families. Public Assistance for poor children and families is no longer a federal mandated benefit and it is up to the states to establish individual systems. Further, financial support is now time limited (no more than five years of lifetime financial support) and includes quite rigorous requirements, e.g. work activities. When compared to other highly industrialized countries the present financial support system for families in the United States is "extremely weak."

For our purpose we consider child welfare as a range of services and programs to children and families. Whitelaw, Downs et al suggest that services to families and children can be classified into 4 major groups "supportive, protective, foster care and adoptive." They describe them as follows:

- Supportive services are available to families to support and strengthen family life, to promote the healthy development of children and adults, and to help families maintain connections with community institutions such as schools, welfare, and the workplace. Depending on the type of service offered, these services may be called therapeutic, preventive, or supportive.

- Protective services are for families who have fallen below a minimally sufficient level of child rearing and whose children therefore suffer from abuse or neglect. Services include investigation of the family's situation and help in improving family life so that the children can remain safely in the home.

- Foster care services are for families who temporarily cannot maintain a minimally sufficient child-rearing environment in the home. While children are in foster care, the focus is on helping parents to improve their life situation so those children can be returned to them safely. Children may be placed with relatives, called "kinship care," in a foster family, in a group home, or in children's institution. They are helped to cope with the separation and to adjust to their new living situation. Arranging visitation to help family members maintain connection with one another and planning for reunification as early as possible are important aspects of foster care services.

- Adoption services are available to children in need of a new, permanent family because their biological parents have relinquished them for adoption or had their parental rights permanently terminated in court. Helping the child (if older) grieve for the loss of his or her biological family and adjust to the new family are key adoption services. Adoption services provide support to the adoptive family and the biological family.

Supportive services differ from the other three service categories – protective services, foster care, and adoption – in a number of ways. Protective services, foster care, and adoption are traditionally considered the elements making up the domain of child welfare services. Government, through regulation, funding, and the legal system, defines much of the framework within which these services are offered. Families usually do not seek out protective services and foster care services voluntarily; the agencies, through their legally established mandates, require the family's participation when it's ability to maintain a minimally sufficient environment for children is in serious question. The families in these service systems come disproportionately from the poorest and most vulnerable segments of the population.

Supportive services, in contrast, are a loosely grouped category comprising a number of disparate programs and approaches offered in a variety of community settings. Family counseling, individual therapy for adults and children, and group work may all be used. Services are offered in mental health and family service agencies as well as community settings such as schools, community centers, and other neighborhood-based programs. They are available to families on a voluntary basis, to help them improve the quality of family life, weather a crisis, or find and use community resources. Traditionally, these services have fallen outside the child welfare system and were not closely linked to it.

Despite detailed conceptual models, the actual systems of child welfare in fact are replete with serious deficiencies and are frequently destructive and not supportive to children and families. Why? Services are often not comprehensive and often do not provide continuity. Services have a history of not being culturally responsive and some are actually destructive to the cultural values of various ethnic groups. Often child welfare did not unite families but actually separated families; part of the service system, e.g. foster care, is often quite harmful to children.

Most often the child welfare approach has in fact been too narrow and only concentrated on a small set of issues affecting children and families and not on their overall wellbeing. The following example portrays the types of problems confronting families in which the present response is inadequate.

Case Example: Susan and Family

Susan* had planned to leave for years and after every beating she prayed for the strength to do so. Though her husband threatened her life, her total financial dependency on him made it practically impossible for her to leave him. But finally she found the strength to turn him over to the authorities after he had chained her to a pole the day she returned from the hospital after giving birth. While chained to the pole, her husband beat her into a state of unconsciousness. She claims it was not until her hospital discharge that the medical staff gave a second thought to the possibility of domestic violence when they witnessed her crying hysterically. They advised Susan to turn in her husband – a decision that got him less prison time than when he stole a car.

This period for Susan was actually "psychologically worse than the beatings" she endured under her husband. She was repeatedly harassed by her husband in his frequent jail cell phone calls to her. In a particular phone call, he threatened: "You're dead. I can do this time in my sleep bitch. When I get out I will OJ you and [then] what will protect you – your stupid Order of Protection?"

She did not know the answer to that question. What would exactly protect her? When she called the police in prior instances they only stayed a few moments and left before the situation heated up. After the police left was when Susan had real hell to pay. Susan also claims that the child welfare workers assigned to her repeatedly made her feel like a criminal. They were always examining her parental abilities and making her feel that if she were to reveal her domestic situation she would in turn lose all those she loved and cared for. She had tried to hold down a job of her own through her difficult relationship, but between the number of harassing phone calls she received from her husband and days she missed as a result of it, she was soon fired from her job, thus leaving her totally financially dependent on her husband.

Her physical wounds were bandaged up during her visits to the emergency room but no such care was given to assuage the deeper psychological devastation caused by her partner or to clarify her perception that her husband is the root of her hardship. She had also lost all social support; people around her turned away from her because they "tired of her marital problems". She was truly alone. Susan felt as if she was to blame. She felt she was the one who did something wrong.

It was not until her husband came home high on drugs and struck her 12-year-old son that the client decided to leave. Here she faced yet another hurdle. The shelter that she was able to get into did not allow adolescent boys. This meant having to leave her 2 children behind. As a result of this drawback, Susan endured countless more bouts of physical abuse at home until she was able to find a relative willing to take her children in.

So in the middle of the night Susan fled to a shelter, leaving her two children, her home, her possessions and her identity behind. She claims it was the loneliest she ever was. She was told she would be in the shelter for 90 days, yet she was separated from her children for 9 months until housing became available.

The housing Susan received was the first four walls she had not been beaten under. Yet, her food was scarce, she knew none of her neighbors, and she had no idea where any area resources were located. It was apparent that she felt scared and alone. She had become accustomed to her shelter environment and had a pervasive feeling of fear of being on her own again. A fear that was so great that Susan actually considered calling her husband back. She needed support, yet she was scared of the system and distrustful of the people who were part of it.

The problems faced by Susan and her children and in other cases are not uncommon among the at risk populations of children and families. In working with children and families noted in these examples, it is important for us to have a broad understanding of issues and problems, societal inequities and the role of policy and program/practices in addressing these issues. Further, we need to have a conceptual framework for defining our work both in providing direct care or articulating and acting on improving the lives of these clients. In the information that follows we seek to provide approaches and knowledge useful for successful actions by social workers.

New Conceptual Models of Service

In thinking about resolving the inequities that impact on children and families and confronting some of the major issues that impact on populations most at risk, the authors suggest we need to conceptualize three levels of response. They are (1) a broad level of societal response that addresses physical, economic and social well being of families, (2) a strong model for comprehensive services that represents a continuum of care most needed but often not available, and (3) a philosophical approach to the provision of services that strengthens the resiliency of children and families and empowers them to become active participants in events that shape their lives. These three levels of approaches provide a scope of response broader than a narrow definition of "child welfare." They represent a more comprehensive response needed in social work.

A Broad Societal Response

The PEW PARTNERSHIP in (2001) published a monograph entitled "Wanted Solutions for America – What We Know Works" that provides for a basic conceptualization of a broad societal response. In their introduction to the monograph they quote from a work by Schorr, 1991 that establishes the overview for the model. The quote is as follows: "We know from documented research that the physical, economic and social well being of an entire family is crucial to creating positive futures for children and youth. Successful interventions for children see the child in the context of the family and the family in the context of its neighborhood and surroundings.

. . . We cannot separate aid and support for children and support of these families" *(PEW PARTNERSHIPS, 2001, p. 2).*

The conceptual framework they present involve 4 key elements, which are:

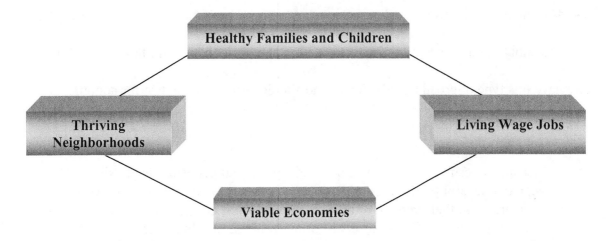

(1) **Healthy Families and Children**

With respect to creating healthy families and children they suggest building

extensive systems of support for children and families with comprehensive services and

programs which include parent education, early childhood development, prenatal care, youth

development, after school programs, addressing risky behaviors and stopping violence.

(2) **Thriving Neighborhoods**

The PEW Partnership describes the need for neighborhoods with decent and

affordable housing, that are safe and which provide for networks that provide social and

emotional support.

(3) **Living Wage Jobs**

The PEW Partnership calls for establishing meaningful jobs with future

opportunities that provide good wages and the chance for learning and growth.

(4) **Viable Economics**

A meaningful economic structure that stimulates job and growth for individuals

and communities is essential for families.

(PEW Partnership, 2001, p. 3-21)

This broad agenda requires significant mobilization. It is not an agenda for social work alone but social work needs to be involved in broad coalitions to pursue these goals. It is essential in our concern to promote social justice for children and families that in fact we have this type of broad agenda. It can and should serve as a catalyst for action.

The PEW Partnership notes:

> Change doesn't just happen. It demands gifted and persistent leadership. We must expand the ability of our communities to recognize and mobilize the wealth of leadership in their midst – of all ages and races, of all income levels and in all neighborhoods, and in all levels of organizations. Building a broad-based constituency for change is the key to implementing what works. In the words of Albert Einstein, "We cannot solve the problems that we have created with the same thinking that created them."
>
> *(PEW PARTNERSHIP, 2001, p. 37)*

(2)   A Conceptual Model for Services

In thinking about services to children and families we should operate from a strong conceptual model that describes a continuum of care available for children and families with differing levels of needs and emphasizes prevention and family employment and community development. These programs focus on broad based strategies of activities and if needed, the use of intensive services for the children most in need.

(3)   A Philosophical Approach to the Provision of Services

It is not sufficient that services exist, in addition it is crucial that they operationalize a philosophy that promotes the resiliency of children and families. Although there are numerous articles written on the subject, the authors have chosen to utilize some of the observations made by Paul Smokowski in his classic article

"Prevention and Intervention Strategies for Promoting Resilience in Disadvantaged

Children" (*Social Service Review,* Sept. 1998). He provides an important overview

toward understanding risk and resilience. He writes:

> Risk factors represent "any influence that increase the probability of onset,
> digression to a more serious state, or maintenance of a problem condition."
> There are several important mechanisms through which risk can be transmitted.
> Risk traits, on the one hand, are individual pre-dispositions that heighten
> vulnerability to negative outcomes. Temperament or family histories of
> depression or heart disease are examples of such traits. Contextual effects, on
> the other hand, are environmental correlates or conditions conducive to risk.
> These effects can be indirect (e.g. neighborhood poverty, high unemployment)
> or direct (e.g. inadequate parenting, peer pressure). Links between different risk
> variables often occur forming risk chains. Poverty, for example, commonly
> coincides with parental unemployment, single-parent households, high parental
> stress, lower educational attainment, and a complex array of other risk factors.
> This accumulation of risk and stress has been shown to have strong deleterious
> effects on children's development. Michael Rutter's investigation of family risk,
> for instance, showed that when two or more risk factors are present in a child's
> life, the probability of subsequent disorder is significantly bolstered.
> Resilience, in contrast, denotes positive adaptation and competence despite the
> presence of substantial risk. "Resilience factors" have been described by some
> authors as adaptive processes internal to the child while "protective factors"
> exist in the environment. "Resilience strings" are chains of factors that promote
> positive outcomes – the adaptation mobilizing a well-researched protective
> factor. Similar to mobilizing protective factors is attempting to foster
> "resilience strings" of beneficial behavior. An intervention that encourages
> academically successful students to tutor their less-accomplished peers is an
> example of such an approach. Beyond the benefits to the less-accomplished
> student, the successful child experiences a sense of mastery and also enhances
> his or her communication skills or social skills, which are useful protective
> factors in the social domain.

(Smokowski, 1998, p. 340)

Websites for More Information

The Annie E. Casey Foundation

www.aecf.org

Center for Youth Development and Policy Research,

Academy for Educational Development

www.aed.org/us/cyd

Chapin Hall Center for Children

www.chapin.uchicago.edu

Children's Aid Society

www.childrensaidsociety.org

Children's Defense Fund

www.childrensdefense.org

Family Resource Coalition of America

www.frca.org

Mott After-School Initiative

www.mott.org

The Search Institute

www.search-institute.org

U.S. Department of Justice, Justice for Kids and Youth

www.usdoj.gov/kidspage

NYU World Wide Web

Chapter 8 – Services to the Aged

One major demographic factor that has dramatic implications for social work and social welfare is the aging of American society. As this new century begins "unimagined numbers of people are growing to be very old in America." It has been noted that increases in the number and proportion of the population sixty-five and older represent the most dramatic demographic change in American society in the 20th century. In the last 30 years of the 20th century (1970–1999) the population aged 65 and older grew by 74% and increased from 20 to 35 million with the elderly representing 13% of the population as we entered the 21st century. Projections call for additional dramatic "graying of America well into the 21st century". The projected growth rate will increase further when the 76 million baby boomers reach age 65 between 2010–2030. In addition, the 85 and older population is the fastest growing segment of those 65 and older. The implications for policy and service delivery and for insuring social justice of this population should be of great concern to the student entering the field of social work. Rabbi Nachnun writes: "the prosperity of a country can be seen simply in how it treats its old people." And the elderly as a result of major policy action (e.g. Social Security, Medicare, the Older Americans Act) have achieved substantial economical and service benefits over the past half century in the United States. But, despite the gains, our society holds distinctly negative views of the elderly. Often we view the aged as sick, demented, frail, weak, disabled, powerless, sexless, passive, alone, unhappy and unable to learn – in short, a rapidly growing mass of irreversibly ill, irretrievable older Americans, and to many, the elderly are seen as a figurative ball and chain holding back society.

How will we address the key issues that are emerging with respect to this population? As the society ages will we be prepared to provide the needed supportive health and social services to the 90%+ of the elderly who wish to stay at home? Will the needed financial security systems, e.g. Social Security, Medicare, Medicaid, pensions, be maintained at levels to insure that large numbers of aging remain outside of poverty and have the necessary health and medical care available and accessible to support the population in need? Can we revamp our health, mental health and social service systems to better address the changing needs of this age group? Can we create growing productive job opportunities for seniors who want to work and remain economically self-sufficient? These and other questions are of major concern to a profession that only within the past decade or less has awakened to the challenges and opportunities to serve this population.

Key Facts About the Elderly
General Demographic Trends

As we noted above America is aging. An examination of the data from 1900 to projections for 2030 dramatically portrays this shift. Robert Hudson notes that in the 1900s the percentage of the population was 4%, in 1950 it was 8%, in 2000 it was 13% and by 2030 it is estimated that the percent over 65 will be 21% *(Hudson, 1999, p. 362)*. Life expectancy at birth in the United States has increased from 47 years to 76 years today and life expectancy at age 65 for the average American is now 17 years, a full five years longer than at the turn of the 20th century. While the entire population of the United States has tripled since the turn of the (20th) century, the absolute number of older persons, currently thirty five million has increased elevenfold and, as we have noted, the continued and increasing growth of this population is guaranteed through the aging of the "baby boomers". Beyond the general increase it needs to be indicated that the fastest growing segment of the elder population is the "old-old," those over 85 years. A number of years ago it was a rare experience for an individual to reach 100 years of age, now it is much more commonplace with an estimated 600,000 in that age category today. It is suggested that by 2010 just under six million Americans will be over 85 years of age.

Aging By Gender and Race

A major factor about aging is that women outlive men. In the United States women have a life expectancy of seven years more than men do. As population cohorts age there is, at every age, a preponderance of women. Additionally, there are major differences in aging by racial category, with white women on the average living six years longer than women of African-American decent, and white men living about eight years longer than African-American men. Those demographics have significant implications for social work practices.

Aging in Place

Contrary to myths that we have about aging, an overwhelming percentage of the elderly do not live in institutions, e.g. nursing homes. By type of residence, 89% of the elderly live in their own homes or apartments, 7% live in housing built for seniors and only 4% live in institutions. This fact is a reflection of the choice of the elderly; they want to live independently and remain within their own home or communities. This desire is reflected in study after study. Many of the elderly own their own homes. There are multiple reasons that the elderly want to remain at "home" (home can be a residence {apartment or house} that a person has occupied for several years, be it rented or owned). The benefits of a home are, according to observers are related to independence, such as privacy and control over the physical environment, to the familiarity of a particular home environment, are related to residence in a specific neighborhood including a social network of friends and neighbors, are related to the activities of home maintenance as a source of meaning, are related to the home as a place to entertain friends and family, to reciprocate hospitality and to pursue vocational activities, and are related to the home as a locus of meaning – the rite of important and memorable events. Further, from an economical perspective their home may be their largest single financial asset.

The Economic Well Being of the Elderly

What is the economic or financial health of the elderly? The fact is that the financial well being of the elderly has improved markedly over the past 4 decades. The elderly have progressed from being a largely poor population to that of being more affluent with a significant percentage still poor. The economic benefits that have assisted the poor have come more from government action specifically in the form of social welfare benefit and entitlement programs, e.g. social security, Medicare. It is interesting to note that contrary to conservative social welfare ideology, the elderly do clearly represent a group that has benefited dramatically from government interventions that have occurred.

Health and Mental Health Perspectives

The myths about the health and cognitive functioning of the elderly are quite commonplace. To be an elderly person in the United States today is still to be seen as physically and cognitively impaired. Rowe and Khan cite two commonly held beliefs: "to be old is to be sick" and "the lights may be on but the voltage is low" *(Rowe and Khan, 1998)*. Rubin writes:

> "Funny things happen on the way to old age . . . For one thing, everyone – the clerk in the store, the bank teller, your new dentist – they all seem so young to you. And maybe because they are so young, they begin to treat you as if you're so old. They call you "ma'am" as if you were their grandmother; they talk louder as if you can't hear; they speak condescendingly to you as if you were a child; they explain the obvious that needs no explanation."
> *(Readings Satow, Roberta 2001, p. 18)*

Research does indicate that elder Americans are becoming healthier than their counterparts of earlier times. Within the past two decades it has been found that there are significant reductions in arthritis, diabetes, hypertension, stroke and emphysema and a dramatic decrease in the number of diseases an older person has. At 65, American men have 15 more years of life expectancy, 12 are likely to be spent fully independently and healthy. For woman at 65 with an average 19 more years of life expectancy, at least fourteen will be as independent and healthy. Rowe and Kahn (1998, p. 16) observe that:

> ". . . . most older Americans are free of disability. Of those aged 65 – 74 in 1994, a full 89% reported no disability whatsoever. While the proportion of elderly who are fully functioning and robust declines with advancing age, between the age 75 – 84, 73% still report no disability and even after age 85, 40% of the population is still fully functional."

Thus, age 85 is often when health starts to deteriorate.

What about cognitive functioning e.g. Alzheimer's Disease? Rowe and Khan write:

> "current estimates are no more than 10% of all elderly people, aged 65 to 100 or more, are Alzheimer's patients. In fact, even among those aged 74 – 81, a full half show no mental decline whatsoever over the following seven years."
> *(Rowe and Khan, 1998, p. 19)*

It is for the population over 85 that the risk of Alzheimer's becomes more pronounced with the prevalence rates of 30 – 45%. However, our discussion about the health status of the elderly needs to include a discussion of mental health issues. Approximately 20% of the elderly experience mental health disorders that are not a normal part of the aging process. The rates of mental disorders are underreported. The most common disorders are: depression, anxiety, psychosomatic disorders, adjustment to aging and schizophrenia. The elderly have major issues around depression and between 8 – 20% of the elderly suffer from it. The rate of suicide in this group is the highest of any age group. For those over 85 the rates of suicide are the highest (two times the national average). Depression often leads to physical symptoms and an overuse of medical services.

Alcohol and substance abuse can also be a major problem for the aged. Heavy drinking occurs in 3 – 9% of the elderly and men are four times more likely to be heavy drinkers than women. Substance abuse normally takes the form of misuse/overuse of prescription drugs and is more common among women than men.

The elderly use fewer mental health services than any other adult age group. They use less than 50% of services compared to their percentage of the population. Only 50% who acknowledge mental health problems receive care from any health care provider and only 3% get specialty mental health care. Over 50% get their mental health care from primary care physicians. The elderly also rarely seek help for alcohol and substance abuse problems.

Political Power

The political power of the elderly has increased significantly over the past several decades. They vote in the highest percentage of any age group. They also have an extremely effective lobbying organization, the American Association of Retired Persons (AARP). Through the exercise of political power many of the elderly's gains in the form of entitlements and benefits have been institutionalized. In November 2003 the power of AARP helped pass new Medicare legislation that added drug benefits to the law. But are we beginning to witness backlashes and efforts to reduce social and economic support provided by the government and are other age groups increasingly concerned about the political power of the elderly?

Issues Impacting the Elderly

As we look ahead for the first two decades of the 21st century, advocates, policy makers and practitioners have identified five major issues with relevance to social welfare and social justice that have/are emerging. They are (1) independent living, (2) elder abuse, (3) income security, (4) health and mental health issues/medical care and (5) age discrimination.

(1) Independent Living

As we noted, the overwhelming percentage of elderly desire to live independently and in their own homes or apartments. Yet for so many, especially the "old-old" and others in this age group with significant physical or cognitive disabilities, this is not a simple task. Although some positive strides have been made on local, state and federal levels to facilitate this goal, there is still a great deal to be done. In fact, support systems for the elderly like other social welfare/social service support systems for other populations have in this society been inadequate. As we noted throughout this text, we often do not provide comprehensive service resources for populations most in need.

Support for the elderly to remain in their own homes most often falls to family members who serve as primary caregivers. This burden of caregiving usually falls on women, e.g. daughters. AARP describes "typical" caregiving as follows:

> "A snapshot of the typical caregiver shows a woman about
> 45, married, working full time who has been looking after
> a parent with a chronic condition for four or five years. A
> quarter of caregivers are in their 50s or 60s, and there are

> many of them: more than 22 million households have a
> caregiver (mostly a family member) . . . . Caregivers may
> give occasional or constant help with simple daily activities
> like dressing and bathing or with more strategic or
> instrumental activities like grocery shopping, managing
> money or cooking meals. Nearly half or all caregivers
> spend up to eight hours a week on care. About one in five
> spends up to 20 hours and nearly another fifth are giving
> constant care to a frail relative, most often a parent."
>
> *(AARP, AARP on the Issues of Caregiving, p. 1, 2001).*

Caregiving by family members often comes with a great price – physical,

emotional and financial. Frequently, women are caring for their own parent(s) while

caring for their own children and working. The term "sandwich generation" has been

coined to describe this phenomenon which is growing due to the aging of society and the

fact that women more frequently have their own children later in life. Psychologically,

this role is made harder by the fact that within this society there are expectations that

daughters/children will care for their parents. Further, if child power is not enough to

provide caregiving, families and the elderly on their own have to pay for caregiving. This

itself can have a major negative impact on the finances of the elderly person or on their

children or their children's families. Further, paying for caregiving by others does not

guarantee good caregiving and may inadvertently cause the elderly individual to be put at

risk.

Another major factor about maintaining the independence of the elderly relates to

their housing accommodations. As we noted earlier only 7% of seniors live in housing

designed for their needs and 4% live in nursing homes. Thus, 89% live in homes that,

especially for the old or the elderly with physical infirmities, are not designed for their

needs. The physical conditions within their homes, e.g. lack of ramps, safety rails, kitchen design, may not only be not helpful but in fact harmful. Falls are a major problem for the elderly and can lead to devastating injuries. Injuries, e.g. broken hips, not only are costly but can begin the cycle leading to deteriorating health or mental health care perhaps ultimately to institutionalization or untimely death.

Given these two factors – caregiving and housing structure – how do we as a society begin to develop programs and services that facilitate independent living? How do we as social workers advocate to further steps in this direction?

(2) Elder Abuse

Elder abuse can be physical, psychological and financial and the American Medical Association estimates that one older person in four experiences some form of abuse or neglect. The harm done to older people may come at home from relatives including spouses, children, friends, caregivers or institutioners and in institutions. Further, elder abuse is often hidden and is grossly underreported. Over two million older persons are victims of abuse and yet for every case of elder abuse it is estimated that five cases are not reported. Most of the abuse against the elderly occurs in their own home and much of it is perpetrated by family members. Abuse by spouse, family member or a caregiver is often not reported because the elderly person is being provided with care by the abuser. This is a growing issue. The author, as part of a project on the Victims of Mentally Ill Offenders conducted for the Office of Victims of Crime of the U.S. Department of Justice, found that the elderly are at high risk of being abused by their untreated mentally ill children or grandchildren. New studies suggest that up to 75% of accused elder abusers are in fact mentally ill children/grandchildren. Spousal abuse is quite prevalent. Physical and financial abuse in institutionalized settings, e.g. nursing homes, are another problem. For the "captive and disabled populations" in these settings they are most often unable to speak out. They are dependent on government agencies that monitor these facilities to act. Clearly abuse against elderly can impact on their health, mental health, income security and ability to live independently.

How can/should social work respond to elder abuse? What program or policy action should/must we champion?

(3) Income Security

Over the past half-century, especially over the past 30 years, the economic well being of seniors has improved markedly. Pensions and retirement savings have been a major source of income. Social security represents an average of 40% of the incomes for the elderly. We also indicated that a source of great concern is rising health care costs — — that of prescription drugs poses as significant threat. Finally we indicated that more elderly are increasingly dependent on job income to support themselves. The income security questions are extremely important to preserve the economic well being of the elderly. These are very significant questions for social workers from a social justice perspective.

With respect to Social Security there are numerous issues that have arisen. Although most experts believe that social security is on a sound financial footing, President George Bush's Social Security Commission in a July 2001 report stated "Social security faced demographic pressures that would overwhelm its ability to pay full benefits if no changes were made". (*New York Times July 25, 2001. P.A14*). There is a raging debate within that Commission about when the Social Security Trust Fund could run into trouble, 2016, earlier or later. Further, there are groups and individuals that espouse individual investment accounts, raising the retirement age and reducing cost of living increases for beneficiaries. Changes in Social Security could in the short term or even long term negatively impact on services for the elderly. The potential of Social Security not being able to meet its benefit obligations could be devastating to the elderly. Finally, as these questions are debated, how does the media report the effect on an elderly individual's belief that he or she will be in good financial straits in the later years?

We noted earlier the issue of pensions is also a significant and growing concern. About 1/3 of the elderly have pension income but this has become riskier with a greater emphasis on 401K plans. The stock market has recently been very volatile and may dramatically impact on individual investment accounts. Thus this represents another major issue in income security.

As further noted, rising health care costs are a continuing and growing threat to the elderly. As the availability of company retiree health insurance plans declines, more of the aged population is at greater risk of rising health care costs. Further, with the continued growth in prescription drugs prices many of the elderly, who are highly dependent on these drugs, are being placed at greater financial risk and even with the passage of new Medicaid legislation in November 2003 many within this population are still at risk.

Will the elder's growth in income security be slowed or stopped? Will more of the aged be driven into poverty? What will individual elderly costs be for healthcare? Will there be areas of positive growth in social welfare benefits for this population?

(4) Health and Mental Health Issues

Although the aging population is healthier than previous generations, the need for health and mental health services, especially for the old-old or those impacted by physical or mental illness before 80, is significant. Among the major issues we will discuss is not only the availability of care but also the nature of care and the financing of that care.

The elderly are major consumers of health care services. Despite these high levels of consumption there are a number of key issues that need to be raised. Who provides health care? How is it provided? To what degree is preventive care available? There are a number of crucial issues that need to be raised, e.g., the number of gerontologists contrasted to the number of the elderly population is quite small. Further, the number of medical students interested in becoming gerontologists is also small. Thus the elderly are most often seen by general practitioners or internists. Their degree of knowledge about the special needs of the elderly may be limited; further, personal attitudes, especially "patience", are not a guarantee. A growing number of the elderly are securing services from managed care organizations. For service recipients, the receipt of managed care can be confusing and frightening. Additionally, as we witnessed there are major public debates in the United States about managed care in general. A continuing concern is whether or not the managed care companies discourage the use of needed medical services to insure their profitability. It should be noted that over the past 2 or 3 years managed care companies in selected states have given up on their contracts to service the elderly because they do not make profits. AARP in their position paper on managed care states: ". . . . AARP believes that standards and regulations must promote the delivery of high quality care at a moderate price . . . and not encourage less care or inadequate care. We believe that good health and the good practice of medicine must take precedence over profitability". *(AARP, 2000).* Given the provisions of the new Medicare legislation in November 2003 are more of the elderly population going to be negatively impacted by managed care?

Additionally, there are continuing concerns about the payment sources for health care costs. Medicare and Medicaid are key financial mechanisms to assist the elderly in meeting their health care costs. Yet, Medicare is on occasion in financial difficulty. AARP reports that in 1997 there was a major crisis with respect to the financial stability of Medicare PART A (hospital insurance that was projected to be insolvent by 2001). Only emergency budget changes saved PART A until 2010. As part of these changes the monthly charges to consumers was increased by 50%. Medicaid, which provides health cost coverage for the poor elderly, is also under intense financial pressure. Finally, as we noted earlier the cost of prescription medication for some elderly is extremely high and paying these costs has negative impacts on the economic well being of seniors. Federal legislation was passed in 2003 to assist the elderly with the cost of these bills, the answer may be far from adequate as drug costs continue to rise.

As we note earlier the mental health (depression) and cognitive issues, e.g., Alzheimer's Disease, are major problems with respect to the elderly. Although depression is a significant factor it often does unrecognized and untreated. In fact, the elderly are very low users of mental health services and often avoid them due to stigma and shame. The elderly receive fewer mental health services than other age groups. Mental health professionals including social workers have up until recently largely ignored the elderly.

Further, few social workers are choosing careers in geriatrics. With the growth in the old-old populations there will be need for major increases in Alzheimer's care programs. New approaches to closing significant program gaps in providing mental health care for seniors are also necessary.

(5) Age Discrimination

Age discrimination is another big issue. In light of the need and desire of many older persons to continue working after the traditional retirement age, discrimination by age is a major issue.

AARP writes:

"Age discrimination specially in hiring is prevalent in the work place ——— because many employers don't question existing stereotypes about declining abilities of older workers. They wrongly assume that older workers are more costly to train, and more likely to leave soon.
More over, many older workers don't know how to pursue their rights and protect their jobs . . . Its is important to add that proving age discrimination is difficult"
(AARP, 2000 "Age Discrimination in Employment" p.1)

AARP also notes that:

"We also believe that denying work to older people squanders the nation's productivity and does damage to our prospect for economic growth" *(AARP, 2000. "Age Discrimination in Employment. P.2)*

Historical Background – Social Welfare and The Elderly

Policy and programs aimed at addressing the lives and needs of the elderly have undergone a radical evolution. The story of social welfare, public policy and the elderly tells of how one segment of society went from being among the poorest to one of the most financially well off segments within the general population. While not all elderly individuals share in the current prosperity of the elderly and many needs remain unaddressed, the historical development of programs and policies have effected many

beneficial changes in the welfare of the elderly as a group. This transformation is more

remarkable when one considers that the majority of programmatic and political

developments have occurred in roughly the last one hundred years. This section will

examine the process by which the elderly went from being a poor and relatively

powerless segment of the population to being one of the most financially secure and

politically powerful groups in the country.

The Period Preceding the Great Depression

The period before the full-scale development of industrialism was one of relative

security for the aged when compared to the later period of industrialization and

urbanization. Perhaps, foremost among these reasons, was that there were fewer

individuals living to be elderly. Within the predominantly agricultural systems of the

time, the elderly were able to remain active and productive as they performed necessary

yet less physically demanding tasks on the farm or in the home. Within agricultural

systems, the fact that many elderly remained in possession of their land helped to ensure

that family members would provide for their security until their death, at which time the

land would be given to the family. Due to the relatively few numbers of elderly

individuals and their place in society, elders tended to be revered during this period,

according to Price. Family members' tendencies to assume responsibility for their aging

parents and grandparents was formally established as early as the English Poor Law of

1601, which decreed this system of care. Furthermore, though public aid was

rudimentary during this period, those that did receive aid tended to be older and

widowed. Thus, they tended to fall into the category of being "worthy" of assistance.

The subsequent period of industrialization and urbanization brought many changes for the elderly. As families broke up and dispersed in the quest for employment in the cities, families were less able to provide for extended family members, especially in the more crowded conditions of city living. Within the city, there was often the lack of a concerned community that would care for the elderly. During this period, characterized by the growth of industry and wage labor, elders came to be seen as less productive and often lost jobs to younger, more capable workers. By the second decade of the 20th century, if not before, most Americans were affirming the obsolescence of old age.

As more and more elderly individuals were adversely affected by these trends, one wonders what happened to these people. With families less able to care for them and being viewed as liabilities in the industrial workforce, how were these individuals' needs met? The answer may be found in the developing almshouses, poorhouses, and county institutions of the period. While developed for the poor and needy in general, these institutions often came to house the elderly, though often as a last resort. While the elderly were usually housed with all types of the poor and needy, the elderly came to comprise a large percentage within these institutions. Even as late as 1923, fifty-four percent of almshouse residents in the United States were sixty-five or older. As poorhouses slowly transformed themselves into old-age homes, the association with public relief often remained, as did the attached stigma. In his study of the Erie County Poorhouse in New York, Katz (1983) discovered that elderly residents often tended to stay in the poorhouse for extended periods of time, often until they died. He also found that within this particular poorhouse, there were more elderly male residents than elderly females residents. Katz offers several possible reasons for this. Due to social conditions, values, and attitudes, children may have taken in their mothers more readily than their fathers. Another reason might be found in the fact that outdoor relief was more frequently given to women than to men. Interestingly, the lack of family and children has determined to be a primary determinant in placement in a poorhouse during this period *(Katz, 1983)*.

The period after the Civil War saw the beginning of pensions as many veterans of the conflict received funds in return for their service to the country, beginning in 1862. After 1890, any veteran who had served for ninety days or more and who could no longer perform manual labor was eligible for benefits; coverage was expanded to include dependents, as well. (In 1906, the age at which these men could no longer perform manual labor was automatically set at sixty-two, whether they could or could not perform such tasks.) Pensions such as these were usually viewed as a form of social insurance, as beneficiaries had "earned" their pensions.

Additional advances for the elderly – though embryonic and rudimentary in nature – were advanced during the Progressive Era. Some states began to initiate state pension programs during this period. Most of these plans, however, were ineffective and covered a small percentage of workers. These plans also served as a means by which elders could be coerced out of the workforce. This era also saw preliminary interest in creating a national old-age pension plan. President Hoover himself, often known for his conservative laissez-faire policies, even supported such a plan until the Great Depression presented more immediate issues to deal with . The Progressive Era also saw the development of many private institutions for the aged; these were often run by religious, fraternal or ethic groups or by unions. These private institutions were the forerunners of today's nursing homes.

The Great Depression before the Social Security Act of 1935

The elderly, like the rest of the general population, were adversely affected by the Great Depression. In fact, many of the nation's elderly had been facing economic hardship and marginalization before 1929. Between 1920 and 1934, the population of the United States had increased by twenty percent, while the number of industrial jobs decreased by approximately twenty-five percent during this same period. This trend was paired with a declining death rate as individuals lived longer. The process through which elderly individuals were excluded, especially men, from the industrial workforce was heightened by these paired trends. As the families of elderly individuals learned to survive on less during the Depression, they possessed fewer resources to support elderly family members *(Abramowitz, 1996)*.

Several political mass movements arose from the social, political and economic turmoil of the early Depression years. Perhaps the most popular movement was that led by Dr. Francis E. Townsend. Townsend, who attracted large numbers of seniors to his movement, proposed a universal pension of $200 per month for all U.S. citizens aged sixty and older. Receipt of this monthly pension was to be contingent upon two stipulations: those sixty or older would have to withdraw from the labor force and would be required to spend the full $200 within one month of its receipt. The ideas behind such a plan would be that by forcing elderly individuals out of the work force, more jobs would be available for younger workers; at the same time, the requirement that beneficiaries would have to spend the full $200 within one month would be good for businesses with increases in purchases. The number of members within this movement was widely disputed. Many of the figures being in the millions; one particular petition pressing for old age insurance had over twenty-five million signatures, although the number of actual members was probably significantly less than this. Though the Townsendites failed in achieving their proposed universal pension plan – it was deemed to be unfeasible by the U.S. Congress – the pressures put upon politicians by the Townsendites and other groups helped to bring about the formation of the Committee on Economic Security in 1934 and the Social Security Act of 1935.

The Social Security Act of 1935 and Later Amendments

The landmark legislation which eventually gained passage as the Social Security Act of 1935 included two basic types of assistance for adults aged sixty-five or older. The first type of assistance, known as Old Age Insurance (OAI), consisted of a social insurance program for retired workers regardless of economic need *(Abramowitz, 1996)*. Those eligible for the program were paid in monthly cash payments, and the level of benefits varied depending on the amount that workers had earned and contributed during their employment. The federally administered OAI program would be funded by a mandatory payroll tax, which was levied on both the employer and the employee; this type of system was regressive in structure, as those that earned more over their occupational history received a higher level of monthly payments. This initial legislation had many shortcomings, however. For one's employment to count toward one's level of benefits, the individual had to work in a covered occupation. Many popular occupations were excluded from the program, including agricultural workers, domestic workers in private homes, casual laborers, government workers, those working for non-profit organizations, and others *(Abramiwitz, 1996)*. The initial exclusion of certain occupations – traditionally the domains of women – combined with the fact that women had more sporadic employment histories due to childbearing and other family issues, meant that women were frequently excluded from the program in its original form. Furthermore, women's retirement income was less likely to include separate individual pension plans *(Abramowitz, 1996).*

The second type of assistance provided for the elderly in the Social Security Act of 1935 was Old-Age Assistance (OAA). This means tested program provided public assistance to poor elderly individuals. This program tended to cover those not eligible for OAI and those that were still in need after receiving their OAI benefits. The OAA program was administered by the states in conjunction with the federal government. This created several problems however. As the individual states determined both eligibility requirements and benefit levels, there was a relatively wide variance in the distribution of benefits from state to state. Many southern and rural states enacted restrictive eligibility rules and low levels of support for those needing assistance. The OAA program was eventually phased out after passage of legislation establishing Supplementary Security Income (SSI) in 1972.

Over the years, there have been subsequent changes to the original Social Security legislation that have extended the benefits of the program to more elderly individuals. The 1939 Amendments to the Old Age Insurance (OAI) program, for instance, extended coverage to dependents and survivors of covered workers and provided for supplemental grants to be given to the dependent families of deceased workers. Many of the eligibility requirements of the original program were loosened, as well *(Abramowitz, 1996).* The nature of the program's funding also changed over time. Whereas the original plan was similar to a self-sustaining pension program in which the amount paid in equaled the amount one got back with additional interest, the political pressures to raise benefit levels divorced the link between what one paid in to the amount one received in return. In the original plan, a worker paid into the system, assuming that he or she would receive that amount when one retired plus the additional interest. As pressure mounted to increase benefit levels from time to time, the politicians conceded. Therefore, there is little correlation today between the amount a worker pays in and the amount that same worker gets back in return. The benefit levels currently paid are dictated by the amount that current workers can afford to pay in order to support those retired workers currently receiving benefits. Incidentally, once benefit levels are raised, it is politically difficult (if not impossible, given the current collective political power of the elderly) to lower levels. Thus, it is difficult to lower benefit levels in times of economic downturns after they have been raised during periods of relative financial prosperity. Another change in the original program occurred with the passage of a cost-of-living-adjustment (COLA) clause in 1972. This clause stipulates that benefit levels will automatically increase when the Consumer Price Index increases by three percent or more.

The Social Security program has benefited both the elderly and their families. Within one generation, the elderly went from being one of the poorest and vulnerable groups to one of the wealthiest. This was largely due to periodic increases and COLA adjustments to Social Security benefits for retired workers . As the elderly have benefited, their families have benefited indirectly, as they are able to expend their financial resources on their own children and immediate families instead of supporting their parents and grandparents. Some might counter this, however, by pointing out that younger family members are supporting their elders by way of increased taxes, which thereby diminishes the amount that they could directly spend on themselves and their own children.

Medicare

The Kerr-Mills Act of 1960 was the forerunner of Medicare. This original act proscribed a health insurance plan for poor seniors along the lines of a public assistance program. The system was funded by federal grants which were given to the states on a matching basis. This program was relatively unsuccessful as the individual states had the option to participate in the program and, like the original Old-Age Assistance (OAA) program, coverage varied greatly between those states that chose to participate.

Medicare established a more comprehensive and expanded program that addressed the medical needs of a greater number of elderly individuals – both poor and non-poor alike. The Medicare amendments to the Social Security Act were signed into law by President Johnson in 1965 and consisted of two parts. The first part, Part A, consisted of a system of compulsory hospital insurance, which was financed by increases in Social Security taxes. The second part of the plan, called Part B, provided for optional enrollment in a medical insurance plan, paid for by minimal monthly premiums and by general tax revenues. Coverage under Part B included physician's services and helped to pay for diagnostic test, medical test, and prescription drugs.

Although the merits of the Medicare program have been debated in the past and continue to be debated presently, Medicare has generally benefited the elderly in several ways. Medicare has, since its inception, allowed many seniors to access medical and hospital care that they would not have been able to afford without falling back upon the stigmatized system of public relief, and this without the stigmatizing means test. By assisting with the economic cost of health care for elderly individuals, Medicare has prevented many from depleting their financial resources on increasingly high medical and hospital bills, thus keeping them off of the welfare rolls. It was found that Medicare also appeared to have increased the elderly poor's use of medical services. In November 2003 Medicare was changed to add payments for prescription drug expenses. However, the very complex legislation doesn't cover all of the elderly population or all expenses. It has also increased the role of managed care organizations.

Older Americans Act

The Older Americans Act, originally passed in 1965, attempted to address the needs of the increasing number of elderly individuals in the United States. The Act established the Administration on Aging (AoA) within the U.S. Department of Health and Human Services. One of the primary functions of the AoA is to work in conjunction with the other federal agencies, organizations and businesses to advocate on behalf of the needs of their elderly constituents. The AoA also serves to educate these groups and the public at large about issues pertaining to the elderly. The AoA also administers several components of federal level programs established under the Older Americans Act that include supportive services for vulnerable seniors living in the community, as well as programs designed to improve health and encourage employment and volunteerism among the elderly *(Administration on Aging, 1997)*. The federal AoA works with an established network of fifty-seven State Units on Aging and roughly 660 local or Area Agencies on Aging (AAAs) to coordinate state and locally-based programs to address needs of elderly clients, utilizing the services of more then 27,000 public and private provider agencies *(AoA, 1997)*. Funding is allocated to the individual states in proportion to the number of elderly individuals living in the state *(AoA, 1997).* Services provided include assistance with access to services and transportation, in-home services, community services (which includes senior centers, nursing home ombudsman services, elder abuse preventive services, legal services, and other programs) caregiver services (such as respite care and counseling), nutritional services and training programs *(AoA, 1997).*

Under the Older Americans Act, any individual aged sixty or over is entitled to its benefits. As a result of this universal, non-means tested policy, the Act has frequently been highly scrutinized. AoA has a relatively humble position within the hierarchy of the Department of Human Services has limited its influence in other federal agencies and furthermore, a low level of funding has forced AoA and its service network to focus on those with the greatest socioeconomic needs. The final verdict on the Older Americans Act remains to be seen. As an increasing proportion of Americans joint the ranks of the elderly, the Act may be strengthened to reflect the growing needs of a diverse elderly population.

Developing and Implementing New Comprehensive Service Models to Support the Elderly in the Community

There is a significant need to provide support for seniors who live at home and in their own communities. Many of the existing models of care are too limited in scope and their activities/services are not responding to the needs of the elderly focused on living independently. Until recently social work has not been focused on seniors and on providing needed support. As this changes social workers need to focus on developing these new models. One approach to developing a new model built on a sound conceptual basis is the work of Ronald and Jacqueline Angel. Using this conceptual basis, we then examine the development and experiences of providing comprehensive service support

programs to seniors at NORC's (Natural Occurring Retirement Communities) and it's

potential to serve as a model.

(a)   Conceptual Model

Angel and Angel describe a model as follows:

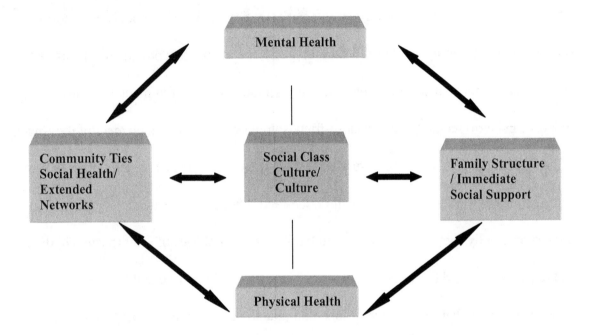

The model identifies key four factors in the lives of seniors – physical health, mental

health, community ties (social health/ extended networks) and family structure or immediate

social support. The importance of physical health and mental health was discussed earlier in

this chapter. However, we need to stress that physical and mental health is substantially

linked in this age group. The linkage between the physical and mental health issues is

known as "co- morbidity". Angel and Angel made the point that single or multiple physical

symptoms often leads to reduced functioning which is likely to impact on mental health.

Further, they also highlight the impact of emotional distress, e.g. depression, on physical

health and symptomology. Angel and Angel further note the importance of community ties/extended networks and family or other sources of social support. Activities in the community and the availability of immediate social support are crucially important to insure the quality of life of seniors and continuing supports. These community ties and activities are often crucial to seniors in providing opportunities for interacting with the broader world and finding meaningful experiences, e.g. volunteer or paid job activities, links with religious, fraternal or community groups, social activities. Family or immediate support is very important. If family and/or friendship networks are strong they provide mechanisms for practical and emotional support. Note, for many seniors the lack of immediate family support can be overcome through a close-friendship network. A crucial element of the Angel and Angel model is its focus on culture and social class issues. They note the importance of culture in many ways, e.g. defining health issues and reflecting responses to symptomology. Most significantly, they point out that culture often affects linkages of seniors with children and relatives. Selected groups, e.g. Hispanics, are more likely to have children remain in close contact with their elderly parents and continue to provide ongoing support. Further, Angel and Angel indicate that poverty and low social-economic status are associated with higher rate mortality and morbidity.

(a) The NORC Supportive Services Program Model

Is it possible to design programs that effectively implement the elements of the Angel and Angel model? Over the past decade to serve seniors in natural occurring retirement communities a supportive services program (SSP) model has developed. This SSP model is not developed yet universally through out the country. Rather it has had it's most extensive implementation in New York City and New York State (with 30+ programs) and selected programs have been developed in other locations, e.g. Cleveland, Philadelphia, Pittsburgh, Chicago.

The reason for its extensive development in New York State / City is related to the work by advocates to have state and city government funding available for started up and continuing programming. The other factor which needs highlighting is that the programs were created experimentally and the key elements/principles were identified over time and finally a model resulted.

The principles of the NORC SSP are as follows:

- Collaborative partnerships

- Comprehensive services (on site)

- Services well and frail seniors 60 years and older

- Housing entitles most contribute resources

- Resident participation in program development

The core service components are identified as follows:

Social Services	Activity Programming	Nursing Services	Ancillary Services
- Assessment - Information and referral - Case Management - Counseling	- Wellness - Education - Creative arts - Socialization - Volunteer experience	- Health screenings - In home assessments - Chronic symptoms management - Medication Management	- Transportation - On site medical care - Onsite mental health service - Financial Management as - Shopping - Transportation assistance - Escorts - Laundry service - Social adult day care - Support groups - Intergenerational programming

Vladeck, UHF (2000)

Resident participation in program development and decision making is seen as crucial; it is this participation that enables residents to develop programs that are culturally relevant and reflect other specific needs of the community.

What is described above represents the ideal model; operationally, the programs developed have shown substantial variation from the elements defined in the model. Operationally, steps to develop programs that effectively implement the model means addressing key issues: can the program obtain needed governmental and non-governmental resources? Can effective and meaningful partnerships be developed among agencies (many of which may have histories of competing and not cooperating)? Can the program give effective roles to residents in planning and program development (considering the fact that residents may not have experience with their roles?) Can programs recruit highly motivated and experienced staffs (confronting the reality that social work, as a profession has tended to ignore the elderly)? How do you develop culturally relevant programming? How do you respond to changes in the demography of communities, e.g. the growth of young families with children? There are crucial issues that do need to be addressed but they do not undermine the value of the model. The model offers an important direction especially for social work developing comprehensive program for seniors.

Examples of NORC Programs in Operation

Big Six

This program is run by Self-Help Community Services Inc. who already had a relationship with Big Six apartments in Queens, New York through their housing management company. In March of 1997 they were given very accommodating office space at the site. A needs assessment was conducted at the start of the program after an explanation of the purpose of the program was shared with residents. After the needs assessment the NORC Advisory Council was set up. Members were initially appointed by the Board as a sub-committee but didn't really participate in the NORC-SSP. Some of the Council members now volunteer. At the start the program it provided case management, information/referrals, and programming including recreational activities including classes, trips (dinner theaters, Montauk, local places, etc.). Later, other needs were identified and met by providing transportation to the doctor (program pays half the cost), a staff housekeeper, and a staff member who helped in interviewing for a part-time home health aid. They also have a personal emergency response system available to older residents.

Staff includes two full-time social workers, one full-time housekeeper, a part-time bookkeeper, and a part-time office worker. Staff is recruited through advertisements in papers but don't usually mention "NORC" as most people don't know what they are.

They advertise for experience with seniors, programming, group work, and other relevant experience. They also put up postings at schools and get some people through their school placements.

There is a very strong volunteer base for the program, mostly 60 and over. Also, some teenagers provide computer tutoring. Self-Help employs the staff of the SSP and there are regular meetings with the NORC Advisory Council, which is comprised of members of the Board and the program director. There are nine Board members and the NORC Advisory Council is comprised entirely of 60 and older residents.

Big Six has a very trusting environment. Caseworkers go to residents' apartments for case management to ensure privacy. They receive partial funding from the housing entity as the law requires. A regular newsletter is published and distributed with monthly event calendars, which are also posted in all buildings.

Residents are mostly of European descent and English speaking. The program has brought many people together for social interaction through program. New money has also provided funds for more space as they are outgrowing current space. The program maintains good relationships with local elected officials and it has received some local grants for funding.

Some of the current outstanding needs have been identified as support groups for bereavement, contracts with local hospital for psychiatric help (trying to get more onsite work for psychiatrist), and transport for the handicapped. Resistance can come from residents who are under 60 in terms of questioning why funds should go towards programs for the seniors. A focus has been placed on intergenerational programming and also on fixing up the playground and providing funds for expenditures which benefit other age groups as well.

Queensview

This program is also run by Self-Help Community Services, Inc. It started as a request from the community (neighbor to neighbor program). It's a bigger operation than Big Six but had the same type of programming at the beginning. The same person directs both programs. It has two full-time social workers and 1 part-time social worker. There is also a home health aid, housekeeper in the works, and a psychiatrist who goes on site. Self-Help has contracted with VNS for nurses to provide screening and home care. There are office hours set at both sites so people can check in. The

resident population is mostly retired professionals with a large percentage of Jewish

residents.

There are two Boards of Directors and two management companies who meet

monthly with Director's Committee (budgetary role), 4 members from each side. The

NORC Advisory Council role is primarily programming and needs assessment. The

two separate entities were a challenge at first since they didn't do much together and

are physically separated by a major road but they have gradually come together. There

are two office spaces on each side of the road as some frail elders couldn't get across

the road when there was only one office. The program has also received some

dedicated DFTA space. There are some retired social workers and a psychiatrist

involved in the program.

It took at least a year at both Queensview/Big Six for the programs to become

integrated with the community but both programs have proven to be very successful

and effective in their settings.

Co-op Village (Senior Care)

The program has been in existence for 12 years. Over 4,000 seniors live in the

housing complex. 95% are Jewish and while the program has done outreach to

Catholic and Episcopal churches it is still mostly identified with the Jewish

population. There are three housing developments that make up Co-op Village. A

fourth housing complex was not part of it but the program did not deny services to

seniors there and then they became part of the program recently. There was a UJA study in the summer of 1992 with a survey to all of the cooperators and there was a focus group through 1993 that served as a needs assessment. UJA originated the project. Services involved groups (exercise, computer classes, dancing, games), nursing, social work/case management and transportation for medical services. Later a companion program was started and then came mental health services. Visiting Nurse Service comes in with the equivalent of a half-time worker and there is a half-time program nurse on staff.

With DFTA funding came an expansion of the social work staff. There is a satellite office that serves some of the residents who find it challenging to get to the main office. There are about 10 – 12 staff members all together and volunteers run the programs. There are 4 Boards that are elected in the housing entities, there is a NORC planning committee that is made up of some members from each Board (usually the Presidents), an Education Alliance rep, and a UJA rep. They meet four times a year. Advisory Committee made up of senior residents and volunteers and meet every 6 weeks. There is an annual flea market to raise funding for NORC-SSP. There is a raffle as well.

Outreach consists of events every Thursday afternoon, bulletin board announcements, monthly newsletter for group members ($15/yr. for group programs) and a newsletter go to social work and nursing clients every other month. It costs a non-member $1 to come to an event. There are about 300 registered members and it seems to be increasing every year.

Spokane County, Washington Model

The goals of Elderly Services are to decrease nursing home residence by increasing home care, identify marginalized elderly who may be high risk and without a support system, and the integration of a solid mental health component to all home are services. In an effort to broaden the scope of elderly services, provide more comprehensive and appropriate services, and reduce the number of elderly receiving residential care, Elderly Services has designed a multi-pronged approach that includes outreach together with integrated and specialized services.

Across Spokane County six interdisciplinary teams composed of 18 clinical case managers, six team leaders, several registered nurses, one psychiatrist, a family physician and a clinical coordinator provide in home evaluation, care provides a 24- hour crisis response telephone number as well as an information line for high-functioning elderly.

Perhaps the most innovative element of Elderly Services is the Gatekeeper program. Designed as a dynamic outreach and identification procedure, the Gatekeeper program systematically trains community members who would have natural interactions with elderly residents. Often holding these are proactive supermarket employees, librarians, apartment managers, bank tellers, building inspectors, ambulance employees, fuel company clerks and mail carriers.

These individuals act as feelers in the community and are careful observers of elderly residents' status. For the truly isolated elderly who have no family to advocate for them, a Gatekeeper may be the only individual with the knowledge, skills and desire to refer them to services. Gatekeepers often act as the main links between elderly people who don't possess full control of their mental or physical faculties and have no family, with the home care or residential services they need.

PACE (Program of All-Inclusive Care for the Elderly)

Program of All-inclusive Care for the Elderly (PACE) programs provide comprehensive health services for individuals age 55 and over who are sufficiently frail to be categorized as "nursing home eligible" by their state's Medicaid program. Services include primary and specialty medical care, nursing, social services, therapies (occupational, physical, speech, recreation, etc), phamaceuticals, day health center services, home care, health-related transportation, minor modification to the home to accommodate disabilities, and anything else the program determines is medically necessary to maximize a member's health.

PACE programs are managed care programs — they are reimbursed on a fixed per member per month rate (or capitation payment) and, in return for this fixed payment, they are responsible for providing 100% of the health services their members require.

Because PACE programs enroll only those individuals who are very frail and incapacitated, they are exactly the patient population for whom prevention and health promotion makes a difference. Most PACE patients have multiple diagnosis, with an average of over 7 diagnoses per member. Among the most common are cardiac problems, diabetes, hypertension, and vascular disease. PACE programs have strong incentives to help keep their members as healthy as possible — their patients, if left without care, are likely to require a hospital stay, which is very expensive. So PACE programs tend to provide high levels of preventive services, such as very frequent check ups, exercise programs, dietary monitoring, programs to increase strength and balance, etc.

PACE programs also focus on "PACE Centers". These Centers tend to have a Day Health Center, physician' offices, nursing, social services and rehabilitation services, along with administrative staff, all in one site. Members may attend centers from rarely to 7 days a week, depending on their care plans. Care planning is done with the member, his or her care team, and appropriate family members. Because most members attend about 2 days per week, staff gets to know the patient extremely well — their concerns, their moods and their condition. This means that staff of the Centers can quickly determine when a Member does not seem herself on any given day. In that case, the Member will be sent to see the nurse or the physician down the hall, where the clinician can intervene quickly to prevent exacerbation of the problem. As of March 2007, 38 PACE and 8 Pre-PACE programs operate in 23 states. The largest of these has more than 2,000 frail elderly enrollees, but most serve a few hundred. More information about PACE programs can be obtained from the National PACE Association, based in Virginia.

Social Work and the Elderly - Future Considerations

In this chapter, we have reviewed demographic factors influencing the aging of America's Society, highlighted outstanding policy and program issues and suggested new program models to provide comprehensive services. Yet, as the reader thinks about that population it needs to be acknowledged that social work has tended to ignore this population. This is no longer possible. Geriatric services offer important new opportunities for social workers. Students should consider opportunities in this field.

Chapter 9 –Mental Health

Social workers are the primary providers of mental health care in the United States. As the primary providers, it is important to understand the consequences of mental health policies on the ability social workers have to deliver key services. This chapter (a) explores the definitions of mental health and mental illness; (b) presents an overview of the prevalence and incidence of mental illness; (c) briefly describes the impact of mental illness; (d) describes the history of mental health care in the United States; (e) provides an overview of the present mental health delivery system; (f) examines, key issues in the present mental health system, e.g., gaps in services for youth, minorities, for the aged, criminalization of mental illness; (g) discusses emerging directives and (h) outlines advocacy for change.

As a professional who practices in social work settings, you may sometimes feel frustrated because you want your clients to get all the services they need. Yet, it may be difficult, on occasion, to find an appropriate mental health service. You may hear that, "the system doesn't work," or, "the system is fragmented", or that care cannot be provided because the client is in a managed care company that does not provide coverage for mental health services, or that the person has no insurance at all. In order to help understand why mental health services are "fragmented" and why many cannot access appropriate mental health services we need to understand how mental illness is defined and measured, and how the history of care for mentally ill persons and past policies affects our current programs and policies.

(A)   What is Mental Health? What is Mental Illness?

Mental health is critical to health and human functions. Mental health is considered a state of effective performance of mental function, resulting in productive activities, fulfilling relationships with other people, and the ability to adapt to challenge

and cope with adversity (DHHS, 1999). From early childhood until death, mental health

is the backbone of thinking and communicating, learning, emotional growth, resilience,

and self-esteem (DHHS, 1999). The Surgeon General's report notes that:

> **Mental health is fundamental to health.** The qualities of mental health are
> essential to leading a healthy life. Americans assign high priority to preventing
> disease and promoting personal well-being and public health; so too must we
> assign priority to the task of promoting mental health and preventing mental
> disorders. Nonetheless, mental disorders occur and, thus, treatment and mental
> health services are critical to the Nations health.

(Surgeon General's Report, 2001)

Yet, as we will see, mental disorders or mental illness impacts on significant

numbers of the youth and adult populations in the United States. The Surgeon General's

report also notes that mental health and mental illness are actually points on a

continuum. The report also suggests that mental health is not easy to define and is very

much influenced by cultural and value judgments. The same, to a significant degree, is

true about mental illness and it is therefore incumbent on the social work practitioners to

be aware of the effects of values and cultures.

Example:

An elderly Haitian woman is brought by her family to the psychiatric emergency room

of a major New York City hospital. Her husband of forty years has died within the last

year. At the emergency room she is examined by a psychiatric resident who was educated and trained in the United States. The woman reports "talking to her husband". The resident immediately decides she is "psychotic" and there is a need to hospitalize her. Yet, the resident is totally unaware that in the Haitian culture it is not uncommon for individuals to "communicate" with recently departed loved ones. What is really going on with the woman and what needs to be done?

What is Mental Illness?

Mental Illness refers collectively to all diagnosable mental disorders. Mental disorders are health conditions that are characterized by alterations in thinking, mood, or behavior (or some combination thereof) associated with distress and/or impaired functioning. Alzheimer's disease exemplifies a mental disorder largely marked by alterations in mood. Attention-deficit/hyperactivity disorder exemplifies a mental disorder largely marked by alterations in behavior (overt activity) and/or thinking (inability to concentrate). Alterations in thinking, mood, or behavior spawn a host of problems—patient distress, impaired functioning or heightened risk of death, pain or disability and loss of freedom. To assist clinicians, especially psychiatrists, a guidebook and statistical manual in the United States (DSM) has been developed to "categorize" symptoms into specific disorders. Many social work practitioners or students either from their work in mental health programs or via training are aware of these diagnostic categories. However, prior to reviewing information about the prevalence of mental illness, it is important to highlight the tendency over the past two decades to medicalize or give diagnoses to everyday problems. Welch, Schwartz, and Woloshin (2007) in a provocative web article entitled "What's Making Us Sick is an Epidemic of Diagnoses" write this is "the medicalization of everyday life. Most of us experience physical or emotional sensations we don't like and in the past this was considered part of life. Increasingly, however, such sensations are considered symptoms of disease. Everyday experiences like insomnia, sadness, twitching legs and impaired sex drive have become symptoms . . . " With respect to mental illness the broadening of labeling has become an important issue to observe.

The Epidemiology of Mental Disorders

The term *epidemiology* refers to the study of "how much" mental illness is present in the general population. Epidemiologists study the distribution of illness in a population, the causes of the illness as well as how interventions can modify risk factors to prevent the illness or modify its causes. Although a relatively new science in mental health, there are now studies that can give us a good base for estimating "how much" mental illness exists in the population as a whole. While this chapter will not detail the methods psychiatric epidemiologists utilize, it will present data from some recent studies. Results from the National Comorbidity Study, reported in 1994, by Kessler and others, are the standards that guide what we know about the prevalence of mental disorders. Since these studies were carried out in the early 1990's, diagnostic categories refer to categories in DSM-III and DSM III-R. The most commonly assesses disorders are mood disorders, anxiety disorders, addictive disorders and non-affective psychoses (Kessler, Abelson and Zhao, 1998). The National Comorbidity study was a nationally representative study, based on 8,098 household respondents. Perhaps the most astounding finding from this study is that almost 50 percent of the population reported a lifetime history of at least one of the mental disorders noted in the study. This is considerably higher than the previous studies.

It should be noted that the national major study conducted in the late 1980s and known as the Epidemiology Catchment Area Study (ECA study) was the first major national scientific study of mental illness in the U.S. While less than 1 percent of the respondents in the National Comorbidity Study reported a lifetime prevalence of a non-affective psychosis, almost 20 percent reported a lifetime prevalence of any mood disorder, almost 29 percent reported a lifetime prevalence of any anxiety disorder and more than 26 percent reported a lifetime prevalence of any addictive disorder (Kessler, et al., 1998). When we consider what this means in terms of the need for mental health services, the prevalence of any mental disorder in the population is astounding.

Another way of looking at how mental illness affects us is to look at the burden mental illness imposes on health and productivity in society. In a study of the Global Burden of Disease which was conducted by the World Health Organization, the World Bank and Harvard University, it was noted that mental illness ranks *second* in the burden of disease in market economies. The term "burden of disease" is calculated using a measure called "Disability Adjusted Life Years (DALYs). This measure is a measure of the lost years of healthy and productive life, whether the lost years are due to death or disability. A way of interpreting the significance of this finding is that the percent of total DALYs due to mental illness represents 15.4 percent, while the percent of DALY for all cardiovascular condition was 18.6 percent and of all malignant diseases was 15.0 percent. (Mental Health, A Report of the Surgeon General, 1999 p 4) What do these percents mean to social workers? They mean that many clients will be seen who are suffering from a variety of conditions, including mental illness. They mean that for families already burdened by poverty, lack of opportunity, or who represent cultures in which it is improper to talk about feelings to strangers, there still may be significant

problems which the social worker needs to understand, assess and intervene with

knowledge and empathy. These data also mean that for social workers working in

schools, community centers, substance abuse programs, shelters for the homeless,

domestic violence programs, jails, prisons and schools, it is important to understand that

a person's emotional condition should not be overlooked, even in the case where the

agency is not a "mental health" agency.

Causes of Mental Illness

Areas of considerable controversy are the causes of mental illness. Despite much

attention, in the last decade to biological causes, it can only be demonstrated that

biological causes such as in cases of schizophrenia can only be definitively determined in

less than 2% of all cases. Multiple other factors e.g. neurochemicals, genetic,

psychological, trauma, stress, social or environment and others have a large role in

creating mental illness. Frequently, the causation can be related to multiple factors. For

the practicing social worker, causation should not be a focus but rather the focus needs to

be insuring clients get the services they need and for advocating for more effective

systems of care.

Stigma and Discrimination

Stigma and discrimination towards the mentally ill are still major problems in our

society. Historically the mentally ill were seen as "possessed" and although this stigma

has decreased the mentally ill are too commonly seen as violent. The media, in the form

of movies, TV and newspapers, often picture the mentally ill as violent. This negatively affects our society's willingness to enact the needed changes or fund programs they need.

Further, stigma and discrimination often lead the mentally ill not to seek treatment.

The Impact of Mental Illness

Mental Illness has a significant impact on the lives of the person affected, his/her

family and the community/society. For the individuals impacted, depending on the

severity of the illness, the disorder can lead to a lifetime of pain and anguish seeking to

get relief. It can lead to a loss of employment, a disconnection from families and friends

and even homelessness. For family members, the pain of dealing with a relative suffering

from those disorders, the results are often traumatic. Jay Neugeborne, in his book

Imagining Robert, in which he recorded the 30 year history of dealing with his mentally

ill brother Robert, writes:

"the major fact of mental illness is it's larger devastation (is shaped by) it's

generally long-term character and with a condition which is insidious, unpredictable in

nature and course, tears families apart, and for which condition, most of the time, there

are no solutions, long or short term." (*Imaging Robert*, p. 19)

Further, although not discussed in this chapter, stigma and discrimination are

constant companions for the affected individuals and their families. Stigma and

discrimination, although less severe than, 30 or 40 years ago, are still significant.

Unfortunately, this stigma and discrimination does impact on our policy and program

response to the issue and causes limitations on our financing. Lastly, mental illness

involves a cost to society in terms of low productivity, e.g., it is estimated that the cost of

worker absences due to depression may exceed $150 billion per year and in the cost of

paying for mental health services is in excess of 70 billion dollars annually.

History of Mental Health Care in the United States

Beginnings through the 1800's

Mental Health Care in the United States—
An Historical Overview

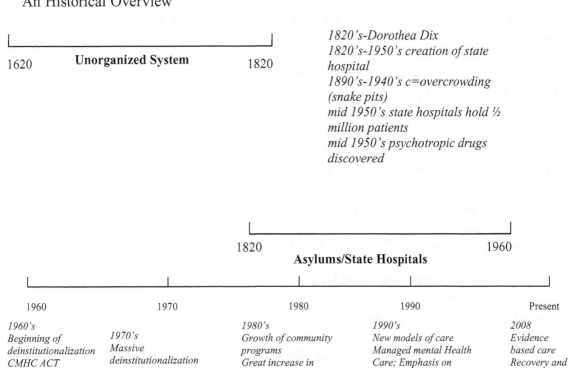

1620   **Unorganized System**   1820

1820's-Dorothea Dix
1820's-1950's creation of state
hospital
1890's-1940's c=overcrowding
(snake pits)
mid 1950's state hospitals hold ½
million patients
mid 1950's psychotropic drugs
discovered

1820   **Asylums/State Hospitals**   1960

1960	1970	1980	1990	Present
1960's Beginning of deinstitutionalization CMHC ACT	*1970's Massive deinstitutionalization Growth of community programs with emphasis on chronic patients*	*1980's Growth of community programs Great increase in homelessness of MI "criminalization of MI"*	*1990's New models of care Managed mental Health Care; Emphasis on biological mental health care*	*2008 Evidence based care Recovery and consumer operated programs*

Mental health care in the United States has shifted between the community and

institutions since the country's founding. In the 18th century, the "insane" were often

supported by families, in their own home except when they were considered

"uncontrollable" or threatening to others safety. Almshouses which served general

welfare functions did not discriminate between the mentally ill, the physically ill, the

orphaned, the aged and the debilitated. Certain almshouses provided excellent medical

care, and such institutions as Bellevue Hospital Center (New York), Kings County

Hospital Center (Brooklyn, New York) and Baltimore City Hospital, which had begun as

almshouses, became the first public hospitals.

The philosophy of "moral treatment" for the mentally ill began in England and in France, as a humanitarian effort. One of the key ideas behind moral treatment, as espoused by the French psychiatrist Phillipe Pinel, was that the symptoms of severe mental illness could be alleviated if patients were treated with kindness, and if they were permitted to live a healthy life in a setting conducive to their growth and development. This was in stark contrast to the prevailing idea that the mentally ill were dangerous. It was an attempt to "medicalize" the treatment of the mentally ill. The concept was carried to the United States, where Pinel's ideas influenced American psychiatry. While moral treatment was practiced in the United States in the 19th century, a two-tiered system of care was forming and moral treatment was available to more wealthy citizens. For the most part, the indigent who suffered from mental illness were still subject to poor conditions in county run almshouses.

In the mid 19th century, Dorothea Dix was a crusader on behalf of the indigent mentally ill. She advocated for the development of centralized state hospitals, reasoning that state resources could be more efficiently and effectively utilized and a higher caliber of staff could be hired. She effectively lobbied Congress to have the Federal government assume responsibility for the development of state institutions for the mentally ill by allocating federal land to the states for this purpose. While Congress passed legislation in 1854 that would allow this to occur, President Franklin Pierce vetoed the measure and indicated that the Federal government should bear no responsibility for the social welfare of the nation. Despite Pierce's veto, state institutions for the care of the mentally ill multiplied at a rapid rate during the latter part of the 19th century. One reason for the growth of these institutions was that the forces of immigration, and industrialization were powerful, yet many new immigrants were not able to adapt to the new conditions.

As a result, communities often sent those who were not able to work and who exhibited

"bizarre" behavior to these institutions. In addition, as family structure changed from

large families to smaller units, disabled family members were also sent to these state

institutions when the family could no longer care for them. Due to changing patterns of

disease and the increase of dementia, chronicity and hopelessness increased, and with it,

the growth of the state institutions.

Shifting Responsibilities

In 1890 New York state passed the New York State Care Act which shifted full

financial responsibility for the care of the mentally ill to the state. As a result of this

legislation, all local responsibility for the care of the mentally ill ceased. With this

development, localities began to send even more elderly and senile individuals to the

state institutions, as well as continuing to send the acutely mentally ill. This resulted in a

different "case mix" in the state institutions: the elderly were mixed in with those

individuals who exhibited symptoms of serious mental illness. The facilities were usually

built in rural areas, far from population centers. One reason for this was based on the

philosophy of "moral treatment", that is, to allow the patients opportunities to participate

in the maintenance of the hospital, and to live a life free of the stresses of urban areas.

Another reason was surely to keep those with bizarre behaviors "out of sight and out of

mind." As was true in general terms with respect to social welfare, the American public

generally was prone to beliefs that those in need were a "drain" on society and should

not be supported by public institutions. While Pierce's veto of legislation that would give some financial responsibility for the mentally ill was based on his interpretation that the federal government should not interfere with social welfare institutions, Congress, in 1882, enacted legislation which made it unlawful for those with mental illness to enter the country as new immigrants. Thus, the federal government actively denied entry into the country, thus taking a stand against those with mental illness.

Shortly after New York state passed the state passed the New York State Care Act, other states followed suit and between 1903 and 1950 the number of patients at these state facilities increased by 242 percent (Morrissey and Goldman, 1985). As the number of patients increased, what was to be "humane" treatment deteriorated into custodial care, and resources decreased significantly. David Mechanic reviews the history of the first state mental institution, Worcester State Hospital in Massachusetts, established in 1830 (Mechanic). He notes that "enlightened reformers" were responsible for the hospital initially and that the institution practiced "moral treatment." However he notes that, as industrialization and urbanization led to increasing numbers of patients, and as there was less tolerance for deviance, the philosophy of the institution became one of custodial care: a process that was occurring throughout the country during the latter part of the 19th century.

While these state institutions were increasing, ideas about providing some kind of "aftercare" were beginning to develop. In 1905, the concept was discussed at the National Conference of Charities and Correction. The first aftercare workers were social workers hired by the New York State Charities Aid Association who, according to Trattner, investigated what happened to patients who had been discharged from Manhattan State Hospital. The investigation, which showed that many of the patients were not cured (and many could not be found) led to the development of an aftercare system. The major focus of the aftercare workers was on the acute patients, not the elderly and senile patients. It should be noted that the development of aftercare occurred as a result of widespread interest in the voluntary sector; and that social work played a significant role in this process.

The Second "Revolution" in Mental Health

Moral treatment has been called the "first revolution" in mental health care. The "second revolution" began with Clifford Beers. Beers had been a patient in both public and private institutions for three years and had experienced deprivation and cruelty at the hands of staff. In 1908, with the assistance of Adolf Meyer who was a leading psychiatrist, Beers published *A Mind that Found Itself:* an expose of conditions in the mental institutions of the day. He also founded the Connecticut Society for Mental Hygiene which became the model for a new mental health movement and the organization known today as the Mental Health Association. The main purpose of the new "movement" was to promote mental health and to prevent mental illness. This was to be accomplished in a variety of ways, including developing educational campaigns to target families, physicians, schools and the general public about the need for early diagnosis and treatment. One component of this new model of mental illness was to target the environment as an important component in understanding mental illness, thus addressing the issue of responsibility for becoming mentally ill. As a result of the new emphasis on early identification and the importance of the family, child guidance centers were opened in many communities. The child guidance center was to be a place where families could go for counseling and assistance when it was felt there might be a problem. In this way, child guidance centers foreshadowed the emphasis that would be placed on early identification in the decades of the 1960's and 1970's.

The Community Mental Health Movement and Deinstitutionalization

The so-called "third revolution" in mental health care is the most significant one. This was the development of the community mental health movement in the 1960's and its corollary, deinstitutionalization. The beginnings of this movement have roots in a combination of factors. While the Mental Hygiene Movement played a small role, it was a confluence of several other factors that led to the community mental health movement. One major influence was World War II. Psychiatrists played a major role in World War II by participating in the screening process for draftees. To a surprising degree, many draftees were rejected from service as a result of being diagnosed with psychiatric symptoms. While one may question the adequacy of the screening process employed, the high rejection level did serve to alert and alarm the country about the "problem" of mental illness in a general population. Military psychiatrists also began to experiment with shorter term interventions and group interventions with soldiers, thus opening the way for newer treatment modalities.

In 1946 Congress passed the Mental Health Act, creating the National Institute of Mental Health. This landmark decision acknowledged that the Federal government had responsibility for research into mental illness and the care of the mentally ill. The threefold purpose of the National Institute of Mental Health (NIMH) was to improve mental health services through research, training and practice. The Institute encouraged states to designate one agency to serve as the state mental health authority, holding all responsibility for the mentally ill in its hands. Grant-in-aid programs were established to assist the state authorities to improve the quality of community-based clinics. More funding for the training of mental health professionals was appropriated, and research programs were encouraged through the efforts of the National Institute for Mental Health.

The Joint Commission on Mental Illness and Health and The Community Mental Health Movement

In 1955, the Mental Health Study Act established the Joint Commission on Mental Illness and Health. The purpose of the Joint Commission was to investigate care at state mental health facilities and to develop recommendations that would lead to a national mental health policy (Morrissey and Goldman, 1985). It was becoming increasingly clear to many American psychiatrists and other mental health workers, as well as to journalists and others, that conditions in the state facilities were abominable, with dirty wards, little to no treatment or the use of interventions such as lobotomies to keep patients manageable. It was also becoming increasingly clear that large state institutions could not effectively deal with mental illness and that these institutions were becoming increasingly costly to maintain.

A significant development at the state level one year before the creation of the Joint Commission occurred in New York state with the passing of the Community Mental Health Services Act in 1954. This landmark legislation authorized localities to develop mental health authorities which were to be responsible for planning, developing and monitoring mental health services at the local level. Thus we see the beginning of the transfer back to communities for some responsibility for mental health services.

However the state was still to maintain the primary responsibility to coordinate and monitor services at a statewide level. Local plans were to pass an approval process by the state. A major innovation of the Act was that localities would be eligible to receive fifty percent of funding for the development and maintenance of services from the state. The remaining fifty percent was to come from tax-levy monies raised by the locality. Thus there would be a cost-sharing mechanism between the state and its localities. Additionally, the local governments would set up Community Mental Health Boards which would have the primary responsibility, at the local level, for developing mental health services and maintaining them. The focus of the localities was to be on outpatient services and the provisions of the Act were not seen to be a substitute for the state mental hospitals which continued to have the responsibility of serving the severely mentally ill on a long term, inpatient basis. Many states followed the model developed in New York, and developed similar policies.

Additionally, by the late 1950s the first psychotropic drugs "began to be utilized to control the behaviors of the mentally ill." From that period to the present the use of drugs became a major tool for treating the mentally ill. Meanwhile, members of the Joint Commission were investigating the conditions of the mentally ill in state institutions around the country. In 1961 the members issued their report, *Action for Mental Health*, to a new President, John F. Kennedy. While making a host of recommendations in many areas, including calling for more research, increased expenditures in mental health and better training programs, *Action for Mental Health* is most notably remembered for its arguments in favor of new mental health clinics in the community.

As we have noted in other sections, policy is made in response to social, economic and political factors, and based on a value system held by the majority of those who are in a position to influence policy. President Kennedy was sensitive to

mental health issues, in part because of a sister who was institutionalized. In addition,

the country was in good economic shape, and was beginning to move toward more

dynamic social change. With respect to psychiatry, in addition to the factors mentioned,

there were significant advances in developing psychotropic medications during the

1950's. These medications, beginning with chlorpromazine, were to lead to significant

changes in the understanding and treatment of mental illness. While chlorpromazine and

the medications developed subsequently could not (and still do not) cure mental illness,

they alleviate the most severe symptomatology if taken consistently. These factors which

included the development of the psychotropic medications, developments and

refinements in psychotherapeutic techniques, the criticisms of the conditions in the state

psychiatric hospitals and the strong economy, in addition to the interest of the President,

converged to initiate the third "revolution" in mental health care: the community mental

health movement. While deinstitutionalization did not follow immediately, the

community mental health movement was necessary, if not sufficient, to promote

deinstitutionalization a few years later.

The Legislation which inaugurated the community mental health movement was

passed in 1963 and signed by President Kennedy. The Act, called **The Mental**

Retardation Facilities and Community Mental Health Centers Construction Act

(commonly referred to as the Community Mental Health Centers Act) contributed toward

a major ideological shift in the treatment of the mentally ill with the focus on treatment

in the community for the majority of those needing mental health services. The

legislation provided "seed money" in order to establish a national network of community

based facilities. Five essential services were mandated by the legislation: inpatient care (which was to be acute care, provided on a short term basis and in a hospital in the community); outpatient services; partial hospitalization; emergency services and consultation and education. Many of these services, such as partial hospitalization, emergency services and consultation and education were new developments. The focus was to be on prevention, rather than long term care, and services were to be organized on a geographic basis in order to ensure that all who resided in a designated "catchments area" would be served. In addition, there was to be input by local citizens into the planning process for these services. There was also supposed to be a plan for ensuring the "continuity" of services and services coordination. In theory, then, services were to be seamless: when a person was transitioned from one service to another, communication between services would occur, there would be no duplication of services and the individual would receive the proper care. These concepts represented a new focus for services.

Problems soon arose with the new community mental health centers. The 1963 legislation allowed no new money for programs and new staff; the federal money that was allocated was meant only for construction of facilities. In addition, the federal money was to go to a locality, deliberately bypassing the State Mental Health Authority. Further, the money was given directly to a locality on a decreasing basis, over the course of ten years. Ultimately, it was the intention of the legislation that localities would assume the full burden of the cost of the centers. In addition it was soon recognized that money was certainly needed for programs and staff, especially as there were to be these new services. It was also recognized fairly early that the five original services needed to be expanded to include services for children, the elderly, alcohol abusers and others.

A series of amendments over the course of time were passed to deal with these issues. However the concept of the community mental health center as being the focal point in the community for mental health services was never really fulfilled.

Several other factors were responsible for the failure of the community mental health center concept to become the reality that had been envisioned. These included that localities were often reluctant to assume the cost of subsidizing the centers with the knowledge that they would be fully responsible for their cost, as well as the "built-in" lack of coordination with the State mental health authority. Thus, while persons in the community experiencing an acute episode of mental illness could go to the community mental health center, those who had been hospitalized in the reviled state institutions and were beginning to be discharged into the community did not have the same access. Thus dual systems of care were frequently created: a "community" mental health center for some and a state "after care" service for those discharged from state hospitals. Occasionally these facilities would even be located in the same building, with little to no communication between the two programs. As a result there was little continuity of care or, in fact, communication, between the "community" center and the state center.

Deinstitutionalization

At the end of the 1950s there were nearly 500,000 residents in state hospitals and long lengths of stays e.g. 5+ years were quite common. State hospitals, because of their size were costly to run. Thus, the community mental health movement on the discovery of useful antipsychotic drugs and the costs were the background for deinstitutionalization.

Other developments at the Federal level were to have a significant impact on mental health care. In 1965 the Medical Assistance Program (Medicaid) and Medicare Bills were passed, thus creating new financing and reimbursement mechanisms for service delivery. With this legislation, it became clear to states that were increasingly facing large expenditures that it would be less costly to release patients into the community, rather than maintain them in state facilities which are costly to run. The Medicaid funding allowed this to occur because Medicaid is shared funding between the states and the Federal government, and unlike this shared funding, states bear the entire cost of maintaining a person in a state hospital. Thus costs could be transferred from the state to these federally subsidized programs, an attractive proposition to the states. As a result, patients began to be shifted to the community: many of them were sent to nursing homes, others to families who would care for them and others simply discharged, without adequate preparation, to the community to fend for themselves. While the term "deinstitutionalization" was not used until 1975, the effect of transferring patients to communities without adequate preparation was beginning to take a serious toll. It should be stated that there was a naïve optimism that was behind the trend to release patients from the state facilities, in addition to the budgetary concerns of politicians. While the framework for the development of the community mental health movement was based on a public health view of mental health, including the view that mental illness could be prevented by early identification and treatment in the community setting, there were no provisions made to support persons who had been institutionalized for many years and who thus, had lost any skills they may have once had to enable them to live in the community. There were also extremely limited funds to develop a host of community-based services, thus ensuring that those released would go untreated and unsupervised.

Another significant factor that has impacted mental health services occurred in the early 1970's. Concurrent with the policy emphasis on "civil rights", several judicial decisions regarding mental health treatment occurred which stressed the right to treatment in the "least restrictive setting" (See, for example, Wyatt v. Stickney, 1972 and O'Conner v. Donaldson, 1975). These decisions reinforced the concept that mental patients should be treated in the less restrictive community-based settings, rather than the more restrictive hospitals. The focus on civil rights, and rights to treatment in the least restrictive setting, further encouraged the wholesale discharge of patients from hospital to community. While there had been much progress during the 1960's and early 1970's in the care of the mentally ill, much remained to be accomplished. The locus of care had dramatically shifted, from the inpatient state psychiatric hospital to the community setting. Newer forms of therapy and new medications were being developed, and many patients were treated quickly in community settings. However problems were also beginning to emerge.

The Uninstitutionalized Population

While there were clearly developing problems noted by the mid 1970's with the policy of deinstitutionalization, it did not help matters that, during Nixon's presidency, there was an "anti" mental health mind set. This resulted in loss of monies for research, training and manpower, further diminishing the ability of mental health professionals to serve those in need. In addition, by the late 1970's it was becoming increasingly clear that the population most in need, those with severe mental illness, were not receiving adequate services. Community mental health centers tended to serve those with less severe problems, while the needs of the most severely ill were not being met. While more people were being treated in the community, the readmission rates at state psychiatric hospitals dramatically rose. Other unforeseen consequences of deinstitutionalization were beginning to emerge. In the early 1980s others identified an emerging population, the "young adult chronic" was identified. This population was described as an "uninstitutionalized" generation as a result of the higher standards for admission to state facilities and other issues. The population was characterized as being "difficult to treat"; extremely mobile; substance abusers; and often came into contact with the criminal justice system. Many mental health professionals were uncomfortable treating a population who was so resistant to keeping appointments. There were other influences on American society that were having an impact on those who needed mental health care including the increasing mobility of the general population, and of the generation that was approaching adulthood in particular, was somewhat disconcerting. A young person, who had an appointment at a specific treatment facility, might suddenly "disappear", to wind up several thousand miles away on the date of the appointment. The "baby boomers" were at an age when schizophrenia was likely to occur, thus the at-risk population had increased enormously, by percent. The generation that came of age in the 1960's and 1970's were much more comfortable using drugs such as marijuana and other drugs, thus often exacerbating symptoms of mental illness. Further, it was becoming increasingly difficult to hospitalize an individual for any length of time.

In 1976, Jimmy Carter became President of the United States. President Carter's wife, Rosalyn, was a proponent of better mental health care, and an active advocate on behalf of the mentally ill. In response to concerns from the professional mental health community, as well as a result of Mrs. Carter's interest, no doubt, President Carter established a Presidential Commission on Mental Health in 1977. The goal of the commission was to review the mental health needs of the nation and to make recommendations for improvement in care. By the time the Commission was established, it had been noted that there were many problems in the delivery of community-based services; it was the role of the Commission to make note of the problems and recommend new solutions. The Commissioners reported to the President in 1978. In a broad based report they focused on the need to develop a better system of financing and delivering community based services. They were also concerned with the development of a more appropriate measure of mental illness in the general population. Until the early 1980's, in fact, the measurement of the prevalence of mental illness in the general population was an underdeveloped science. In the early 1980s when Ronald Regan was president the CMHC legislation was repealed and he attempted to eliminate the mentally ill from SSDI roles. As a result of deinstitutionalization we witnessed a major growth in the value of mentally ill who were homeless and the beginnings of the criminalization or mental illness.

The 1980's and the 1990's saw (a) the continued decline in the numbers of patients in state hospitals and the actual closure, in most states, of many of the state hospitals and (b) the continued growth of community based mental health services of various types and the emergence of managed care. During this time the community mental health movement increasingly focused on services to the seriously and persistently mentally ill and forced a reduction in services for non-seriously ill populations.

The decline in state hospital census can be seen in the fact that from its peak in 1955, state hospital census of 550,000 to it's current level of *60,000*. In many states, numbers of state hospitals were closed. In New York State, the number of state hospital beds for adults was reduced from 93,000 to 6,000. As a result, the "case mix" in the state hospitals has changed from patients with acute and chronic conditions, to a "hard core" of persons with the most severe mental illness, many of whom also have histories of involvement with the criminal justice system.

With respect to community based mental health services which traditionally from the 1960's onward consisted of outpatient services; day treatment, rehabilitation services and residential services have expanded. For example, in the 1990s and to the present we have seen the growth of a variety of care management programs including Intensive Case Management. Case management provides staff members, either professional or non-professional or even a peer (a counselor who is a former mental health client). Case managers assist clients with their reality tasks—housing, benefits, keeping appointments, etc. and serve to enhance the ability of clients to adhere to treatment. We have recently seen the growth of Assertive Community Treatment teams (ACT) which consist of small, multiple disciplinary teams that provide high risk clients with intensive 24 hour, 7 day a week service. As a result of the criminalization of mental health, we have seen the modest growth of specialized programs geared to serve the mentally ill with extensive histories of using the criminal justice system. We also witnessed the growth of managed care programs explained in greater detail below and from the later 1990s to the present we have seen evidence based mental health services and the development of the recovery model and consumer operated services which are discussed in more detail below

Newer Developments in Mental Health

Managed Care- What is it and how does it work? Mechanic in his book *Mental Health and Social Policy* (1999) describes managed care in these general terms:

> Managed care is a general term that refers to a variety of organizational and financial structures, processes, and strategies designed to monitor and influence treatment decisions so as to provide care in the most cost-effective way. As it is used generally, the term is confusing because it covers approaches that vary in their incentives, processes and effects and that combine in a multitude of ways. Although

there is a great deal of discussion about whether managed care is good or bad for mental health, such debate is not informative because the answer depends on the specific arrangements in the place. Many of the complaints about managed care from psychiatrists and other mental health professionals reflect their anxieties about how these new developments will affect their patient flow, incomes, and clinical discretion. Some reflect concern that service changes being put in place are more motivated by cost-reduction than by a desire to improve services and that the changes will have damaging effects on access to care and the quality of service. With growing competition and many more profit-oriented enterprises, there is little trust that managed care approaches will bring benefits to patients or their caretakers.

(Mechanic, 1999, p. 101)

The extent that mental health clients fall under a managed care plan varies markedly by state, county or city and therefore, too difficult to define for this text. The use of managed care to serve mental health populations, although a fact, raises some controversy for clients and practitioners. For some observers, policy makers and others, managed care imposes standards/consistency on a field—mental health which is extremely individualistic, fragmented and not standardized managed care represents a positive step. For mental health organizations and practitioners, managed care can be seen as too rigid and bureaucratic. For some mental health clients managed care removes choices in terms of agency and/or practitioners. Despite these issues it is important for students to understand the role of managed care in mental health.

Evidence Based Interventions

What is evidence based intervention?

In 2004, the Millbank Memorial Fund issued a report on evidenced based mental health services they identified an intervention as evidenced based if:

- A substantial body of outcomes research supports the efficacy of a wide range of mental health treatments

- Mental health services can be expected to provide evidence-based practices in order to yield good outcomes

- Mental health service authorities and providers should be held accountable for providing services consistent with evidence-based practices

- Measures of "program fidelity" have been developed that permit monitoring and accountability

- Outcomes should be monitored regularly by clinicians as a part of good practice

- The wide array of effective treatments should be available within a community, because even when treatments are equally effective on average, many of them are not equally effective for significant subgroups

- Treatment choice and wide selection are essential in order to maximize treatment response and adherence to treatment

- Access to evidence-based practices is necessary but not sufficient to ensure a quality mental health service system

The evidence based interventions that SAMSHA and Robert Wood Johnson Foundation identify as being effective for seriously mentally ill population are:

-ANTIPSYCHOTIC MEDICATIONS

-FAMILY EDUCATION & SUPPORT

-ILLNESS SPECIFIC COUNSELING

-ASSERTIVE COMMUNITY TREATMENT

-SUPPORTED EMPLOYMENT

They further write these findings have significant relevance for mental health treatment for the coming years.

"A significant approach to increasing the value gained from the expenditure of health care dollars is adoption of evidence-based practices; that is, the purchase of treatments and services that have been scientifically confirmed to improve outcomes. With respect to treatment for persons with severe mental illnesses the news is both good and bad. The good news is that solid scientific evidence suggests that many potentially available treatments and services are *efficacious*; substantial gains in the form of improved symptoms and functioning are possible with the right treatment. The bad news is that there are substantial gaps between what science tells us to do and what we do in actual practice, despite the significant investment of public resources. These gaps exist for several reasons:

- The knowledge and skills of practitioners, as well as state of mental health authorities, lag substantially behind the evidence. Hence, practitioners and service systems often continue to provide some interventions that either are unsupported by evidence or have been shown to be ineffective.

- Policies related to the expenditure of public mental health dollars often do not hold practitioners or public mental health authorities accountable to provide evidence-based practices and to eliminate practices that do not help people. Monitoring program fidelity and outcomes is essential for ensuring this accountability.

- Public funding for mental health services in various instances is often inadequate, or is constrained in such ways as to make support for certain evidence-based practices difficult (for example, the awkward and multiple funding streams needed to support certain employment rehabilitation services), or is poorly invested for other reasons.

Recovery Movement

The recovery movement is a recent development in mental health. Driven primarily by consumers the recovery concepts represent a major challenge to the traditional mental health paradigm. In this paradigm mental illness was seen as a lifelong illness and that without professional intervention improvement is not possible. Recovery is a set of beliefs adopted by people with mental illness. The beliefs, seen as a key to a mentally ill person, wellness are as follows:

A) That their identity will not be defined by their illness

B) To have choice of treatment and the right to choose no treatment

C) That stigma must be eradicated

D) That social support and resources are necessary for recovery

E) That they must mobilize their own resources in whatever way they can

F) They have made a decision that they must meet challenges head on

David Gonzalez, a consumer describes the principles of recovery as including hope, self direction, resiliency, nonlinear, holistic, wellness oriented, and contrasts the traditional models to recovery values as follows:

From Restraints to Recovery

Traditional Practices	vs.	Emerging Practices
• Harsh Restraint Methods • Sheltered Workshops • Long Term Hospitalization • Staff Directed Treatment • Overuse of Medications • Custodial Care		• Elimination of Restraints • Meaningful Employment • Community-Based Services • Recipient Directed Treatment • Informed Choice • Recovery-focused Services

The federal government, many studies and advocacy organizations have actively been promoting the recovery paradigm. Yet, the question for most practitioners is there are no specific programs or directions that are readily available to pursue. Recovery, most importantly, is a philosophy that should be utilized in providing service.

Policy Making In Mental Health

The diagram below illustrates the structure of how mental health policy is made. The key role is played by the studies; each of the *fifty* states has a state mental health department or its equivalent. The states have the primary agency in making policy, in planning, in budget development, in establishing rules and regulations and in oversight of programs and services. Secondary roles are played by counties or large localities in areas of program development and funding. The federal government is *not* a primary player in the mental health system except in financing research and supporting pilot programs. Sources of political pressure include the media, advocacy groups and politicians.

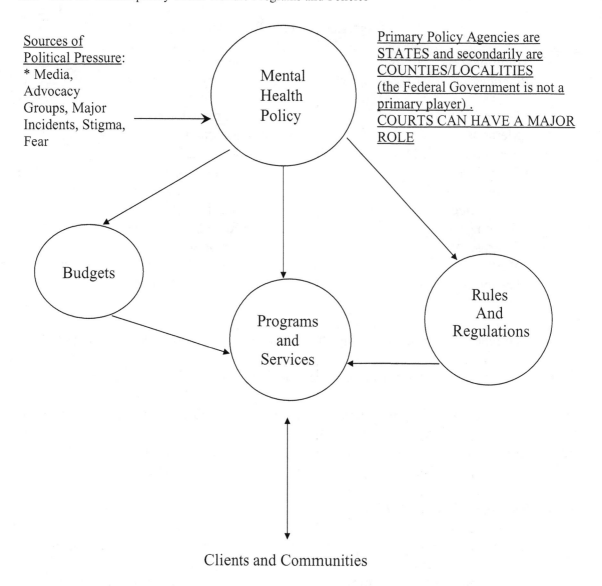

Sources of
Political Pressure:
* Media,
Advocacy
Groups, Major
Incidents, Stigma,
Fear

Mental
Health
Policy

Primary Policy Agencies are
STATES and secondarily are
COUNTIES/LOCALITIES
(the Federal Government is not a
primary player) .
COURTS CAN HAVE A MAJOR
ROLE

Budgets

Programs
and
Services

Rules
And
Regulations

Clients and Communities

The Present State of the Mental Health System and Its Shortfalls

The present "mental health system" can more accurately be labeled a "nonsystem"

or rather a maze of programs in which programs often don't work. The National Mental

Health Association in its newsletter noted that in the interim 2002 report of the Presidents

Freedom Commission on Mental Health the public mental health system is in "shambles".

The Executive Summary of the Freedom's Commission report noted:

> "While many people are given good care and manage to recover, the reality is
> that about one out of every two people who needs mental health treatment does
> not receive it". It also suggests that the individual who reaches care may find that

many treatments and services are simply unavailable, especially in rural areas. Also, the quality of care may be inadequate. Further, it finds that a diagnosis may sometimes be missed, the dose of medication may be insufficient, or the length of treatment too short. For ethnic and racial minorities, the rate of treatment is even lower than that of the general population, and the quality of care is poorer. After thorough study of the problem, the Surgeon General's report concluded that minorities, in comparison to whites, bear a greater burden from unmet mental health needs and thus suffer a greater loss to their overall health and productivity

President,
(Freedom Commission, 2003, p.3)

The report further states:

The mental health services system defies easy description. Loosely defined, the system collectively refers to the array of programs for anyone with mental illness. The programs deliver and pay for treatments, services, or any other types of supports, such as disability, housing, or employment. These programs are found at every level of government and in the private sector. They have varying missions, settings, and financing. The mission could be to offer treatment in the form of medication, psychotherapy, substance abuse treatment, or counseling. Or it could be to offer rehabilitation support. The setting could be a hospital, a community clinic, a private office, or in a school or business. The financing of care, which amounts to at least $80 billion annually, could come from at least one of a myriad of sources-Medicaid, Medicare, a state agency, a local agency, a foundation, or private insurance. Each funding source has its own complex, sometimes contradictory, set of rules. Taken as a whole, the system is supposed to function in a coordinated manner; it is supposed to deliver the best possible treatments, services, and supports-but it often falls short.
(Freedom Commission, 2003, p.5)

The reality is that the mental health system looks more like a maze than a

coordinated system of care. When the system fails to deliver the right types and

combination of care, the results can be disastrous for our entire Nation: school failure,

substance abuse, homelessness, minor crime, and incarceration. While there are 40,000

beds in state psychiatric hospitals today, there are hundreds of thousands of people with

serious mental illness in other settings, in nursing homes and homeless shelters, not

tailored to meet their needs. US jails and prisons hold over 700,000 mentally ill

everyday. The rates of serious mental illness among incarcerated persons are about three to four times those of the general U.S. population. Something is terribly wrong, terribly amiss, with the mental health system.

In fact, the Alliance for the Mentally Ill which has become a major advocacy group, has in its assessment of mental health services in the United States given the system an overall grade of D. The unmet needs are likely to deepen with the aging of the population and the demographic growth of minority populations. Fulfilling even the existing unmet needs means addressing fragmentation, as well as inadequate capacity to train personnel, monitor quality of care, and give information to consumers, families, and providers about best practices.

Let us begin by looking in more detail at its failures with respect to four populations-children and adolescents, minorities, the dually diagnosed and the elderly and also review the issues associated with the criminalization of mental illness.

Children and Adolescents with Serious Mental Illness

The President's Freedom Commission described the inadequacies for youth in need of mental health care in highly negative terms. They wrote "mental health maze" is more complex and more inadequate for children than for adults. The most seriously affected children are defined, under Federal regulations, as having "serious emotional disturbance." Which means that they have a diagnosable disorder that severely disrupts social, academic, and emotion functioning. About 7-9 percent of all children (ages 9 to 17) have serious emotional disturbance, or SED (DHHS, 1999). *That means one or two kids with serious emotional problems are in virtually every classroom.* The Commission heard from families whose children could not get an accurate diagnosis for years and for whom the maze of "helping" programs is "opaque," in the words of a father from Chicago. The potential sources of help may include teachers, school counselors, pediatricians, family physicians, psychiatrists, clinics, psychologists, and courts. Families do not know where to turn, and the first choices may not be able to help. The service systems in many communities is *more fragmented* for children than that for adults, with even more uncoordinated funding streams and differing eligibility requirements. This problem is partly the unintended streams and differing eligibility requirements. This problem is partly the unintended result of good intentions: there are more programs set up to serve children than adults.

But this leaves coordination up to families who are coping with their children's behavioral problems and who may not have the knowledge to navigate the maze. All of the problems are disproportionately worse for children who are ethnic and racial minorities (President's Freedom Commission, 2003, p.7) A recent report suggests that only 20% of children who have mental health problems receive mental health care. 80% do not get care.

The failures of effective mental health programming have had profound and continuing effects. Numerous children are frequently doomed to academic failure or placement in special education classes, and incarceration juvenile justice facilities often have 75% of their populations filled with children and adolescents with diagnosed or often undiagnosed mental disorders. The costs to families and to the broader society are enormous. One newspaper, the New York Times, ran a series of articles on parents who gave up their children to child welfare departments to insure they got more adequate mental health treatment.

Minorities

Minorities are badly shortchanged by the mental health system. The Surgeon General in a supplement to his Report on Mental Health issued entitled "Mental Health; Culture, Race and Ethnicity" concluded:

> Minorities have less access to, and availability of, mental health services. Minorities are less likely to receive needed mental health services. Minorities in treatment often receive a poorer quality of mental health care. Minorities are underrepresented in mental health research.
>
> More is known about the disparities than the reasons behind them. A constellation of barriers deters minorities from reaching treatment. Many of these barriers operate for all Americans: cost, fragmentation of services, lack of availability of services, and societal stigma toward mental illness (DHHS, 1999). But additional barriers deter racial and ethnic minorities; mistrust and fear of treatment, racism and discrimination, and difference in language and communication. The ability for consumers and providers to communicate with one another is essential for all aspects of health care, yet it carries special significance in the area of mental health because mental disorders affect thought, moods, and the highest integrative aspects of behavior. The diagnosis and treatment of mental disorders greatly depend on verbal communication between patient and clinician. More broadly, mental health care disparities may also stem from minorities' historical and present day struggles with racism and discrimination, which affect their mental health and contribute to their lower economic, social, and political status. The cumulative weight and interplay of all barriers to care, not any single one alone, is likely responsible for mental health disparities.

(Supplement Report—Surgeon General, 2001, p. 5)

The continuing failures of the mental health system mean long lasting and dramatic impacts on minority populations. The lack of treatment often shows up in longer term disability, loss of possible work experiences, increased likelihood of homelessness and increased likelihood of incarceration.

The Dually Diagnosed—Mentally Ill with Substance Abuse Problems

Within the past 20-25 years it is increasingly being recognized that a growing percentage of those in need of mental health treatment are dually diagnosed and while suffering from mental illness they also suffer from drugs and alcohol abuse. The percentage of dually diagnosed clients now exceeds better than 50% of those in need. Further, in some urban centers emergency rooms estimate that over 75% of those seeking psychiatric care suffer from a dual diagnosis. Further research indicates that the dually diagnosed are likely to have negative outcomes—high rates of relapse, hospitalization, violence, incarceration, homelessness and serious infections—HIV and Hepatitis. Most alarming is that treatment sources for this population are fragmented and provide inadequate care. Most often they are excluded from either the mental health of substance abuse or both. How many mental health programs employ a drug specialist? How many drug programs employ a mental health counselor? This population often suffers the enormous consequences from these system failures.

The Mentally Ill and the Aging Population

The elderly, as we noted in an earlier section, are the fastest growing age group in America. It is the population 85 years of age and older that are growing at exceptionally high rates. Contrary to stereotypes, the overwhelming percentage of elderly live in the community and normal aging is *not* characterized by mental or cognitive disorders. However, stressful life events including declining health, loss of family members or close friends can have a major impact on the mental health of the elderly. Although the needs for mental health services are evident the elderly are grossly underserved by the present care system. The elderly often don't seek care due to the stigma about mental illness. Further, mental health professionals often, due to stereotypes of aging, do not want to serve this age group. Primary care physicians who do treat the aging population often fail to diagnose mental health condition and do not refer them to the specified services they need. A major task that exists for the field of mental health is to begin to more effectively serve this population and the time to do it is now and not later.

Criminalization of Mental Illness

Within the past two decades we have witnessed the criminalization of mental illness. With downsizing of state hospitals, deinstitutionalizing and the lack of community resources including housing for the mentally ill, jails and prisons have become the new asylums. The Criminal Justice/Mental Health Consensus Project coordinated by the Council of State Government in their 2002 report described the problem as follows: "People with mental illness are significantly overrepresented among the segment of the population in contact with the criminal justice system. Approximately 5-10 percent of the U.S. population has a serious mental illness. The U.S. Department of Justice reported in 1999, however, that about 16 percent of the population in prison or jail has a serious mental illness. Recent estimates suggest that this percentage may actually be higher. Of the 2.2 million Americans currently in jail or prison at least 700,000 had a serious mental illness; approximately three-quarters of those individuals had a co-occurring substance abuse disorder. A study conducted in New York State found that men involved in the public mental health system over a five-year period were four times as likely to be incarcerated as men in the general population; for women, the ratio was six to one."(Consensus Project Report, 2002, p.2)

The project report also emphasizes the impact of the problem as follows:

"The current situation not only exacts a significant toll on the lives of people with mental illness, their families, and the community in general, it also threatens to overwhelm the criminal justice system. Police departments dedicate thousands of hours each year transporting people with mental illness to hospitals and community mental health centers where staff often are unable to admit the individual or quickly return him to the streets. Judges, prosecutors, and defense attorneys' race through backlogged dockets, disposing of most cases in minutes, with mental illness who appear in their courtrooms cannot be processed as quickly. On any given day, the Los Angeles County jail holds as many as 3,300 individuals with mental illness – more than any state hospital or mental health institution in the United States. Without adequate planning to transition inmates with mental illness back into the community, many will quickly return to jail or prison; recidivism rates for inmates with mental illness can reach over 70 percent in some jurisdictions."

(Consensus Project Report, 2002, p.4)

Although there have been actions to remedy the project through the development of models of care and establishing a selected number of new and affective programs, the mental response compared to the need of the number of those affected is insufficient. The problem needs to be addressed with a greater priority.

Concluding Observations

The mental health system is in difficult straits and the needs of the mentally ill, children, adults and the aged often go unmet. These unmet needs have major negative consequences of the mentally ill individual, their families, the community and the society as a whole. Social workers, given their primary role in the mental health system need to become advocates for needed changes.

Advocating for Change

In the last section of the text we discuss advocacy in great detail however, a fitting approach to end this section is to discuss the need for advocacy to change the mental health system. As you have read in the preceding materials, the mental health system is very much in need of change. Social work students are strongly urged to explore these opportunities to participate in change actions. This can be done by exploring the advocacy work in this area being done by the Mental Health Association, the Alliance for the Mentally Ill, Local NASW chapters, and other groups.

Chapter 10–Poverty/Economic Insecurity

Introduction

America has been seen as a very wealthy country having among the highest standards of living in the world. Yet, the poor represent a significant percentage of its overall population. Further, important key groups such as minorities, immigrants, unmarried women, children and the elderly have significantly higher rates of poverty than other groups. Further, recent economic events in the United States have "pushed" the country into a recession with unemployment and economic insecurity expanding rapidly. For social workers, a profession built upon a concern for social justice, recognizing and seeking to address these economic concerns and their psychological, health and well being is crucial. Social workers must strive to assist impacted individuals, families and communities.

What is poverty? According to Dolgoff and Feldstein (2009) poverty can be seen in the following terms:

> There is a social minimum which can be understood as a basic requirement for living a human life. Poverty means, essentially, that one has "insufficient and uncertain access to food, water, clothing, shelter, basic health care, and elementary education." There are those who believe the poor have a moral right to be assisted in achieving the basic necessities of life. The social work profession, according to its Code of Ethics, "seeks to ensure that all people have equal access to the resources, employment, services, and opportunities they require to meet their basic human needs, and to develop fully" (NASW Code, 6.04.a).

> This human right is included in the Universal Declaration of Human Rights, which was created under the leadership of Eleanor Roosevelt, widow of President Franklin D. Roosevelt, when she served on the United Nations Commission of Human Rights. Article 25 of the Declaration states that everyone has the right to a standard of living adequate to the health and well-being of himself and of his family, including food, clothing, housing, and medical care.

266

Understanding Poverty

There are different perspectives, complexities, and problems associated with the concept and definition of poverty. However, for our purposes, poverty is economic deprivation, a lack of economic resources by which to obtain the goods and services necessary for a minimally adequate standard of living. There are several ways in which poverty is defined. Basically, they fit into three categories: (1) Poverty means a person or family has less than an objectively defined minimum; (2) they have less than others in society; or (3) they feel they do not have enough to get along. Decisions about the choice of definition to be used are made on pragmatic grounds (What data are available?), political grounds (Which groups favor one definition or another?), and historical grounds (What has been our experience with particular definitions?).

(Dolgoff & Feldstein 162-163)

The impact of poverty nationally is dramatically portrayed by their table entitled

Poverty Rates for Selected Groups (2006)

These authors further elaborate on poverty in the United States by noting:

Of the 36.9 million poor in 2006, just over 80 percent of the poor lived in metropolitan areas, including 15.9 million residing in central cities. We can observe that there were 12.3 million poor children under 18 years of age, including 4.7 million under 6 years of age living in poor families, many of whom lived in families headed by the four million female householders with no spouses present.

We can focus directly on the well-being of people with the lowest incomes by examining the poverty rate. Throughout the 1960s and the early 1970s, the poverty rate fell dramatically, from more than 22 percent to just over 11 percent in 1973. The overall poverty rated increased generally until it reached 15.1 percent by 1993. By 2006, it stood at 12.3 percent. In table 8.3 we can observe that groups experience poverty at different rates. Note that all poor persons constituted 12.3 percent (one in eight persons) of the total population. But the differential rates among groups form a pattern. For example, two-parent couple families have much lower rates than female-householder families with no husband present. White and Asian and Pacific Islander families have lower poverty rates than African American families. Children, persons living in central cities and those residing outside metropolitan areas have higher poverty rates, as do those residing in the South; residence (central cities or rural areas, region in the United States), education (less than high school education completed), as well as employment are among other factors. Some major groups overrepresented among the poor are persons in families with a female head of household, children under 18 years of age (and especially very young children), African Americans and Latinos. Trends confirm earlier predictions that the poverty population will be composed primarily of women and their children.

One serious misconception about the poor is the belief they do not work. In fact, the poor work more than is generally believed. Employment plays an important part in determining whether or not one is living at the poverty level, but employment does not explain everything. Having a job, even a full-time job, does not guarantee an escape from poverty. In 2006, 2.3 million poor persons worked *full-time year-round*. The implication of these figures is that many jobs pay less than is needed to lift families out of poverty.

For those who lack education and skills, employment opportunities are difficult to find. Manufacturing jobs have grown scarcer. Technology is used in place of people where possible. Where potential jobs exist in the service area, they are usually lower-paying and without benefits such as health insurance and pensions. Furthermore, technology has begun to affect the service sector as well. Another phenomenon affects employment opportunities: A "contingent workforce" has developed. These persons have no direct ties to a corporation. They are part-timers, temporary full-timers, and contract workers. Furthermore, globalization, outsourcing, and competition influence the number, types of jobs, and pay scales.

But poverty is not simply a matter of unemployment or underemployment. In 2006, the median earnings for year-round, full-time employed males was $42,261 whereas the median earnings for year-round, full-time employed females was $32,515. Thus, the average woman working full-time and year-round earned 77 percent of what a man doing comparable work earned. This ratio, though up from 60 percent since 1980, indicated there is still a significant gap between the earnings of men and women. The gain by women is partially explained by the earnings of men, which have been lagging.

(Dolgoff & Feldstein, 168/170)

Poverty is also a major problem in New York City and through these series of maps from a recent publication by the Community Service Society and the United Way entitled "Mapping Poverty in New York City Pinpointing the Impact of Poverty, Community by Community" we get a graphic picture of the problem.

Mapping Poverty in New York City

Pinpointing the Impact of Poverty, community by community

United Way of New York City

United Way of New York City creates, leads, and supports strategic initiatives that address the root causes of critical human care problems in order to achieve measurable improvement in the lives of the city's most vulnerable residents and communities. Throughout our work, we partner with neighborhood agencies, government, business, foundations, volunteers, and others so that collectively we can achieve more than any one organization working alone.

The Community Service Society of New York

The mission of the Community Service Society is to identify problems which create a permanent poverty class in New York City and to advocate the systemic changes required to eliminate such problems. CSS will focus on enabling, empowering, and promoting opportunities for poor families and individuals to develop their full potential, to contribute to society, and to realize social, economic, and political opportunities.

Figure 1: Public Use Microdata Areas.

The United States Census Bureau's 2005 American Community Survey makes it possible to examine economic and demographic patterns on a fairly fine geographic scale. Most of the maps are based on geographic areas called PUMAs (Public Use Microdata Areas), which have been defined by the Census Bureau. They are the smallest areas that can be described using data from the 2005 ACS. Each PUMA usually has a

A City of Neighborhoods

population of at least 100,000 people, and each usually contains several generally recognized neighborhoods. The PUMAs also closely resemble New York City's Community Planning Districts. This map shows the names of one or two neighborhoods for each PUMA.

Poverty and Low Incomes Are Highly Concentrated

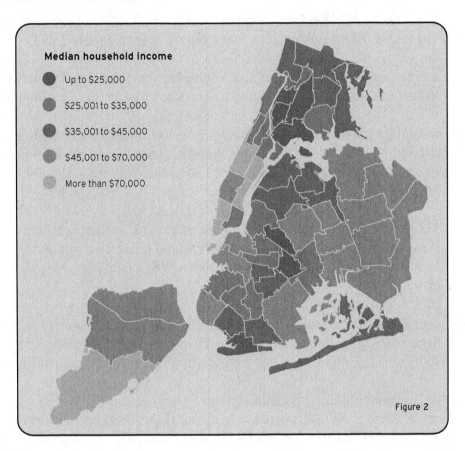

Figure 2: Income and poverty.

All of the variables we mapped are related in some way to income and poverty. These maps present the median income and the absolute number of poor people for each PUMA using a color scale. The data come from the 2005 ACS. Not surprisingly, the poorest areas are also the ones with the lowest median incomes. They are concentrated in Upper Manhattan, the South Bronx, and Central Brooklyn.

In the sections of this chapter that follow we have sought to provide social work students with different perspective on poverty and economic insecurity by utilizing materials from very current sources. These include the following:

- an article by Dr. Robert Hawkins of the McSilver Institute on poverty of the Silver School of Social Work at NYU entitled "More than Money: The Causes, Consequences and Challenges of Poverty"

- an article by Michael Luo from the November 12, 2009 of the New York Times entitled "Job Woes Exacting a Heavy Toll on Family Life,"

- another article from the New York Times on November 17, 2009 written by Jason DeParle entitled "49 Million Americans Report a Lack of Food."

- we add a view of a topic that often goes unexamined; this is the link between poverty, minority status and imprisonment. Here we add the introductery of an article by David Cole which appeared in the November 19, 2009 issue of the New York Review of Books.

- Spriggs, William, "The Changing Face of Poverty in America- Why are so many women, children and racial and cultural minorities still poor?" *http://www.prospect.org/cs/articles?article=the_changing_face_of_poverty_in_america*

- Greenberg, Mark, "Building a National Effort to Address Poverty" in NFG Reports *Bridging the Gap: Reshaping Poverty Policy in America.* 3(15), Fall 2008. pp 6–13. *http://www.nfg.org/index.php?ht=a/GetDocumentAction/i/3571*

- Levin-Epstein, Jodie. "Sustaining Anti Poverty Solutions: Keeping an Eye on the Prize in NFG Reports *Bridging the Gap: Reshaping Poverty Policy in America.* 3(15), Fall 2008. pp 19–21. *http://www.nfg.org/index.php?ht=a/GetDocumentAction/i/3571*

- Limbacker, Spence, "Community Organizing, Public Policy and Building a Vibrant Democracy in NFG Reports *Bridging the Gap: Reshaping Poverty Policy in America.* 3(15), Fall 2008. pp 22-25. *http://www.nfg.org/index.php?ht=a/GetDocumentAction/i/3571*

Additional Resources: (Taken from Dr. Robert Hawkins' Ending Poverty Syllabus)

Edwards, J., Crain, M., & Kalleberg, A. K. (2007). *Ending Poverty in America: How to restore the American Dream.* The New Press: New York.

Handler, J. F. Hasenfeld, Y. (2007.). *Blame Welfare: Ignore poverty and inequality.* Cambridge University Press: New York.

Wilson, W. J. (2009). *More than Just Race: Being Black and Poor in the Inner City.* W.W. Norton & Co: New York.

Bowles, S., Ginntis, H., & Groves, M. O. (2005). *Unequal Chances: Family background and economic success*. Russell Sage Foundation: New York

Farmer, P. (2004). *Pathologies of Power: Health, Human Rights, and the New War on the Poor*. University of California Press.

Oliver, M. L., & Shapiro, T. M. (2006). *Black wealth/white wealth: A new perspective on racial inequality (Tenth Anniversary Edition)*. New York: Routledge.

Newman, K. S., & Chan, V. T. (2007). *The Missing Class: Portraits of the Near Poor in America*. Beacon Press: Boston.

New York Times (2005). *Class Matters*. New York: New York Times Press.

Hawkins, R. L. (2005). From self-sufficiency to personal and family sustainability: A new paradigm for social policy. *Journal of Sociology & Social Welfare, 32*(4), pp. 77–92.

Edwards, Crain, & Kalleberg (2007). Introduction, *Ending Poverty in America*, pp. 3–22.

Handler & Hasenfeld, The State of Poverty, Chapter 3, pp. 70–149.

Handler & Hasenfeld, Chapter 2, The State of Poverty, pp. 17–69.

Wilson, Chapters 1 and 2, Structural and Cultural Forces that Contribute to Racial Inequality, pp. 1–24. And The Forces Shaping Concentrated Poverty, pp. 25–61.

Handler & Hasenfeld, Chapter 4, Demonizing the Single Mother, pp. 150–185.

Ending Poverty in America:

Shipler, D. K., Connecting the Dots, pp. 13–23.

Bernstein, J. Economic Mobility in the United States: How much is there and how does it matter? pp. 23–37.

McLanahan. S. Single Mothers, Fragile Families, pp. 77–87.

Oliver, M. L., & Shapiro, T. M., Chapter 11, Reducing Wealth Disparities Through Asset Ownership. pp. 139–143.

Sherraden, M., Chapter 12, Assets for All: Toward Universal, Progressive, Lifelong Accounts pp. 151–164. (Including Orszag)

Stegman, M. A., Chapter 13, An affordable Homeownership Strategy that Promotes Savings Rather than Risk, pp. 165–178 (Including Eakes).

Newman, K. S., Chapter 8, When the working poor are poor no more, pp. 101–113.

Orthner, D. Chapter 17, Public Schools: Building Capacity for Hope and Opportunity, pp. 218–229.

Brown-Graham, A. Chapter 18: Top-down meets bottom-up: Local job creation in rural America, pp. 230–243, including Seaman & Ferber.

Blackwell, A. G. Chapter 19: Fighting poverty with equitable development, pp. 244–255.

Sawhill, I. V. (2003). The behavioral aspects of poverty. The Public Interest, Fall. Available at: *http://www.brookings.edu/views/articles/sawhill/2003fall.htm*

Shapiro, T. (2003). The Cost of Being Black and the Advantage of Being White. In *The Hidden Costs of Being African American.* Oxford University Press, pp. 41–43.

Levitt, A. J., Cullhane, D. DeGenova, J., O'Quinn, P., Bainbridge, J. 2009 Health and social characteristics of homeless adults and social characteristics of homeless adults in Manhattan who were chronically or not chronically unsheltered. *Psychiatric Services, 60*(7), pp. 978–981.

Treadwell, H. M., Ro, M. (2008). Poverty, Race, and the Invisible Men. *American Journal of Public Health, 98*, pp. 142–145.

Onolemhemhen, D. N. (2009). Meeting the challenges of urban aging: Narratives of poor elderly women of Detroit, Michigan. *Journal of Gerontological Social Work, 52*(7), pp. 729–743.

Edin, K. & Reed, J. (2005). Why Don't They Just Get Married? Barriers to Marriage among the Disadvantaged. The Future of Children. *http://www.futureofchildren.org/ information2826/information_show.htm?doc_id=290932*

Wilson, Chapter 3, The economic plight of inner-city black males, pp. 62–94. Chapter 4; The fragmentation of the poor black family, pp. 95–132.

Mincy, B. & Pouncy, H. Why we should be concerned about young, less educated black men, *Ending Poverty in America,* pp. 191–204.

Ellwood, D. T. & Jencks, C. (2004). The Spread of Single Parent Families in the United States since 1960, John F. Kennedy School of Government, Working Paper RWP04-008 Available at: *http://ssrn.com/abstract=517662*

Wilkerson, I. (2005). Angela Whitaker's climb: Up from the projects, a journey never easy, never over. In *New York Times,* Class Matters, pp. 202–233.

Egan, T. (2005). No degree and no way back to the middle, In *New York Times*, Class Matters, pp. 105–110.

Handler, J. F. & Hasenfeld, Y. Work and the low-wage labor market: Mothers and Children, pp. 238–281.

Leonhardt, L. (2005). The college dropout boom: Working class and staying that way. In *New York Times*, Class Matters, pp. 87–104.

The Urban Institute (2005). Low-Income Working Families: Facts and Figures. *http://www.urban.org/url.cfm?ID=900832*

Keels, M., Duncan, G., DeLuca, S., Mendenhall, R., Rosenbaum, J. E. (2003). Fifteen Years Later: Can Residential Mobility Programs Provide A Permanent Escape from Neighborhood Segregation, Crime, and Poverty? JCPR Working Paper 330 03-18-2003 Available at: *http://www.jcpr.org/wp/WPprofile.cfm?ID=388*

Eyrich-Garg, K. M., Cacciola, J. S., Carise, P., Lynch, K. G., McLellan, A. T. (2008). Individual characteristics of the literally homeless, marginally housed, and impoverished in a US substance abuse treatment-seeking sample. *Social Psychiatry and Psychiatric Epidemiology, 43*(10), pp. 831–931.

Harris, R. P. & Zimmerman, J. N. (2003). Children and Poverty in the Rural South. Southern Rural Development Center Policy Series, November, No. 2, Available: *http://srdc.msstate.edu/publications/srdcpolicy/harris_zimmerman.pdf*

Edwards, J. Conclusion: Ending Poverty in America, pp. 256–267.

Handler & Hansenfeld, Chapter 7, Welfare Reform and Moral Entrepreneurship, pp. 282–315.

Handler & Hansenfeld, Chapter 8, Addressing Poverty and Inequality, pp. 316–348.

Wilson, Chapter 5, Framing the issues: Uniting structure and culture, pp. 133–155.

issues and action

More Than Money: The Causes, Consequences, and Challenges of Poverty

Robert L. Hawkins, McSilver Assistant Professor in Poverty Studies

Poverty is both a cause and a consequence. To understand this statement, however, one has to consider the circular and cumulative nature of poverty, how it stems from structural failings — a lack of education, chronic joblessness and under employment, serious health problems, poor neighborhoods — and a host of other social problems. But poverty also feeds on itself. Neighborhoods with low-quality housing are often the only place low-income residents can afford to live; these are often the communities with the worst schools and high unemployment. When there is little work and few options for opportunities, families break up, increasing the number of single-family households, and become easy targets for crime. Poverty also takes a psychological toll, increasing stress in families, contributing to teen pregnancy, crime, and substance abuse. Not having enough money to sufficiently survive is usually only one problem related to poverty.

While most researchers understand that poverty is more than an economic issue, policymakers tend to gauge poverty based on measures developed in the early 1960s. The federal poverty measure, which solely included the cost of food, has never been updated to reflect current spending habits, and excludes consideration of the costs of other family necessities, such as shelter, clothing, health care, and utilities. Although the federal poverty measure does not tell the entire story, a national poverty rate of 13.2% is compelling (DeNavas-Walt, Proctor, & Smith, 2009). That, according to the U.S. Census Bureau, means that nearly 40 million people lived in poverty in 2008. The rate increased slightly for non-Hispanic whites from 8.2% in 2007 to 8.6% in 2008. Members of minority groups saw larger increases in poverty from 2007 to 2008. The Latino poverty rate rose from 21.5% in 2007 to 23.2% in 2008; Asians increased from 10.2% in 2007 to 11.8% in 2008, and the African American poverty rate for 2008 was statistically unchanged at 24.7% (DeNavas-Walt et al., 2009).

Unemployment is often linked to poverty and during the recent economic recession, all groups were placed at risk of economic hardship because of unemployment. Among Latinos, the unemployment rate rose to 9.3% in the first quarter of 2009 from 6.4% in the first quarter of 2008; among Asians, joblessness rose from 5.5% in the first quarter of 2008 to 7.1% in 2009. Whites also experienced an increase, from 3.0% to 3.7%, while African Americans' unemployment nearly tripled, increasing from 5.7% to 14.7%.

In New York City, while all groups saw on average a 72% increase in unemployment between the first quarters in 2008 and 2009, Blacks and African Americans in the city saw an increase of 167% (Office of the New York City Comptroller, 2009). According to the U.S. Census Bureau's American Community Survey (2009), poverty in New York City remains well above the national average and has been that way over the past ten years. While income nationally saw a slight decline in 2008, New York City's median family income rose to $56,553 from $54,846. Yet, New York City's poverty rate sits at 18.2%, 5 percentage points higher than the national average. Communities in New York City also have high rates of concentrated poverty, in which the percentage of the poor reaches or exceeds 40% (Lang, 2007). Bronx County consistently measures the highest percentage of family poverty at 25%; when only female-headed households are counted, the poverty level is 46%. Manhattan, Brooklyn, and Staten Island also have poverty levels for single mothers of nearly 40% as well with Queens being the only borough whose poverty rate for single-mother lead households is just under 30% (American Community Survey, 2009).

How Poverty Affects Life Chances

Poverty is also not constant, except for a few. Families experience poverty spells, drifting in and out of poverty, according to the federal government's guidelines, yet continue to experience economic hardship. While most families that are new to poverty leave in under two years, more than half of individuals who are currently poor are likely to be experiencing a poverty spell that will last a decade or more (Lang, 2007; Bane & Ellwood, 1986). It is these families that use the most resources and continue experiencing economic hardship even when no longer consider "poor" by the federal government. These are often the families who see the life-long effects of being poor.

The cumulative effect of poverty that starts in neighborhoods and ends up in the brain is little acknowledged in policy research. Brain researchers consistently find that poverty and other forms of economic hardship negatively affect neurocognitive development, which in turn affects IQ, mental health, and school achievement (Farah et. al., 2006; Aber, Jones, & Cohen, 2005; Shonkoff, 2003; Brooks-Gunn, Duncan, & Maritato, 1997). Economic disadvantages have a long-term effect on the development of children, negatively affecting their life chances. The research suggests that poverty constrains development in a way that forces low-income children in a limited box while non-poor children develop in a spacious playground. As children age, it becomes more and more difficult to get out of that developmental box. By the time that poor children reach adolescence, they are more likely than their non-poor counterparts to experience school failure, become the victim or perpetrator of crime, and have other behavioral and developmental problems (Aber et al., 2005; Shonkoff, 2003).

One major barrier for low-income families is that they often live in poorer and more dangerous neighborhoods than the general population, with limited resources (Friis, Wittchen, Pfister, & Lieb, 2002). In these neighborhoods, low-income residents are more likely to be charged with and convicted of a crime than their middle- and upper-income cohorts (Reiman, 2007). Neighborhoods often predict school quality. Indeed, low-income children attend worse schools than middle-class children (McLeod & Nonnemaker, 2000; Brooks-Gunn et al., 1997). Further, they experience school failure more often than their middle-class counterparts, and are more likely to drop out of school (Brook-Gunn et al, 1997; McLeod & Nonnemaker, 2000). All of these issues affect future educational opportunities and employment.

The generally accepted argument on structural poverty stems from the view that while low-income residents existed in communities, long-term persistent poverty came about when industries that could provide living-wage jobs moved out of the inner city (Wilson 1996; Rank, Yoon, & Hirschl, 2003). This out-migration had a devastating and long-term effect on cities and their residents. The middle class followed the industry out of the inner city, taking their resources, social and cultural capital, and opportunities with them. What they left behind were racial minorities, unemployment, poor schools, high levels of crime and an underground economy, substance abuse, and single parent-lead households trapped in communities where governments, banks, and businesses no longer invested. This phenomenon, together with a steady decline in real wages, has created what Wilson (1996) refers to as a permanent "underclass" in urban communities. In the United States, rural poverty follows a similar pattern, in which large industries and farms closed, social and class isolation is common, lack of transportation limits access, children fail in schools, white and middle class families have left mixed-race schools and neighborhoods, and a history of racism has limited opportunities for many (Weber, Jensen, Miller, Mosley, & Fisher, 2005).

These real structural issues have psychological consequences as well. Poverty takes an emotional and mental health toll, creating stress and anxiety, affecting decisions, weakening self-esteem and self-efficacy, and promoting clinical depression (Coiro, 2001; Seeman & Crimmins, 2001). The stress of unemployment and low-income is well documented, with several studies finding that income and socio-economic environment are highly correlated (Dashiff, DiMicco, Myers, & Sheppard, 2009; Gresenz, Sturm, & Tang, 2001). Together with the structural barriers, the stress of growing up and living in poverty also affects health and life expectancy. Because health operates on a social gradient, the higher your socio-economic status, the better your health, as we go down the gradient, the lower your social position, the greater your chances of poor health and an early death (Adler & Rehkopf, 2008; Marmot, Kogevinas, & Elston, 1987).

Research tells us that race is a factor as well. Even when controlling for income, racism emerges as a major source of stress for minority populations. African Americans, for example, are more likely to have one of the top three fatal conditions, and die at an earlier age than whites. These differences have been directly linked to racism and discrimination (Lantz, House, Mero, & Williams, 2005; Din-Dzietham, Nembhard, Collins, & Davis, 2004). Adding poverty to the mix only makes matters worse, as racism and discrimination carry their own life- and health-threatening stressors (Williams, 2005; Lantz et. al., 2005).

Connecting the Pieces of Poverty to Find Solutions

One approach in which to start to address the complexities of poverty is to examine where the issues connect and overlap. Research on poverty causes, consequences, and interventions suggest that we can find these connections across overlapping areas related to family and social structure, human capital development, work and employment, wealth and asset development, and psychosocial factors, including mental health and socio-demographic factors such as race and gender (Hawkins, 2005; Lang, 2007). Addressing family and social structure, for example, would allow for an exploration of the increase in low-income single parent households, neighborhood quality, little bridging social capital or positive role models found in low-income communities (Hawkins, 2005; Shonkoff, 2003; Wilson, 1996). Understanding human capital as the education, training, and skills development that facilitate productive activities (Becker, 1983) is also a keystone in poverty reduction. As human capital develops, employment should follow, but work alone may still not be enough to sustain a better way of life (Lang, 2007).

Psychosocial factors matters as well, as race and culture limit access to resources. And despite the correlation of psychological issues to poverty, mental health factors are largely ignored at the policy level (Aber et al., 2005; Coiro, 2001). Likewise, wealth and asset development is almost entirely absent from poverty-reduction policies, yet research evidence suggests that wealth accumulation is related to sustaining economic security in low-income minority populations, just as it has done historically for middle and upper income families (Lui, et. al., 2006; Rank et al., 2003).

The Social Work Response to Poverty

Poverty operates on different levels and within a structural, psychological, and cultural system. Social workers are trained to examine and work within systems; they are prepared to operate from the nexus of the "person-in-environment." This perspective is important in work to reduce poverty. Yet, more research is needed in order to help practitioners and policymakers move beyond traditional understandings of poverty in the United States. The McSilver Institute on Poverty Policy and Research at the NYU Silver School of Social Work will examine the multifaceted systems that create poverty and will seek a more nuanced assessment of its causes and consequences through collaboration and partnership. The Institute is exploring multiple routes by which to collaborate with community agencies, including joint grant-making efforts, program development, or research projects. The goal of these collaborations is to ensure an integrative approach by which the development of comprehensive intervention and preventative measures, at both the policy and practice levels, to achieve sustainable positive change will ensue. Our understanding of poverty tells us that it is grounded in a social-ecological system. Poverty did not begin as a simple problem, it will take a complex approach that includes the collaboration and knowledge of many to solve.

Job Woes Exacting a Toll on Family Life

By MICHAEL LUO
Published: November 11, 2009, New York Times

THE WOODLANDS, Tex.—Paul Bachmuth's 9-year-old daughter, Rebecca, began pulling out strands of her hair over the summer. His older child, Hannah, 12, has become noticeably angrier, more prone to throwing tantrums.

Initially, Mr. Bachmuth, 45, did not think his children were terribly affected when he lost his job nearly a year ago. But now he cannot ignore the mounting evidence.

"I'm starting to think it's all my fault," Mr. Bachmuth said.

As the months have worn on, his job search travails have consumed the family, even though the Bachmuths were outwardly holding up on unemployment benefits, their savings and the income from the part-time job held by Mr. Bachmuth's wife, Amanda. But beneath the surface, they have been a family on the brink. They have watched their children struggle with behavioral issues and a stress-induced disorder. He finally got a job offer last week, but not before the couple began seeing a therapist to save their marriage.

For many families across the country, the greatest damage inflicted by this recession has not necessarily been financial, but emotional and psychological. Children, especially, have become hidden casualties, often absorbing more than their parents are fully aware of. Several academic studies have linked parental job loss—especially that of fathers—to adverse impacts in areas like school performance and self-esteem.

"I've heard a lot of people who are out of work say it's kind of been a blessing, that you have more time to spend with your family," Mr. Bachmuth said. "I love my family and my family comes first, and my family means more than anything to me, but it hasn't been that way for me."

A recent study at the University of California, Davis, found that children in families where the head of the household had lost a job were 15 percent more likely to repeat a grade. Ariel Kalil, a University of Chicago professor of public policy, and Kathleen M. Ziól-Guest, of the Institute for Children and Poverty in New York, found in an earlier study that adolescent children of low-income single mothers who endured unemployment had an increased chance of dropping out of school and showed declines in emotional well-being.

In the long term, children whose parents were laid off have been found to have lower annual earnings as adults than those whose parents remained employed, a phenomenon Peter R. Orszag, director of the White House Office of Management and Budget, mentioned in a speech last week at New York University.

A variety of studies have tied drops in family income to negative effects on children's development. But Dr. Kalil, a developmental psychologist and director of the university's Center for Human Potential and Public Policy, said the more important factor, especially in middle-class households, appeared to be changes in family dynamics from job loss.

"The extent that job losers are stressed and emotionally disengaged or withdrawn, this really matters for kids," she said. "The other thing that matters is parental conflict. That has been shown repeatedly in psychological studies to be a bad family dynamic."

Dr. Kalil said her research indicated that the repercussions were more pronounced in children when fathers experience unemployment, rather than mothers.

She theorized that the reasons have to do with the importance of working to the male self-image, or the extra time that unemployed female breadwinners seem to spend with their children, mitigating the impact on them.

Certainly, some of the more than a dozen families interviewed that were dealing with long-term unemployment said the period had been helpful in certain ways for their families.

Denise Stoll, 39, and her husband, Larry, 47, both lost their positions at a bank in San Antonio in October 2008 when it changed hands. Mrs. Stoll, a vice president who managed a technology group, earned significantly more than her husband, who worked as a district loan origination manager.

Nevertheless, Mr. Stoll took unemployment much harder than she did and struggled to keep his spirits up, before he landed a new job within several months in the Kansas City area, where the family had moved to be closer to relatives. He had to take a sizable pay cut but was grateful to be working again.

Mrs. Stoll is still looking but has also tried to make the most of the additional time with the couple's 5-year-old triplets, seeking to instill new lessons on the importance of thrift.

"Being a corporate mom, you work a lot of hours, you feed them dinner—maybe," she said. "This morning, we baked cookies together. I have time to help them with homework. I'm attending church. The house is managed by me. Just a lot more homemaker-type stuff, which I think is more nurturing to them."

Other families, however, reported unmistakable ill effects.

Hunger in U.S. at a 14-Year High

By JASON DePARLE
Published: November 16, 2009

WASHINGTON—The number of Americans who lived in households that lacked consistent access to adequate food soared last year, to 49 million, the highest since the government began tracking what it calls "food insecurity" 14 years ago, the Department of Agriculture reported Monday.

The increase, of 13 million Americans, was much larger than even the most pessimistic observers of hunger trends had expected and cast an alarming light on the daily hardships caused by the recession's punishing effect on jobs and wages.

About a third of these struggling households had what the researchers called "very low food security," meaning lack of money forced members to skip meals, cut portions or otherwise forgo food at some point in the year.

The other two-thirds typically had enough to eat, but only by eating cheaper or less varied foods, relying on government aid like food stamps, or visiting food pantries and soup kitchens.

"These numbers are a wake-up call for the country," said Agriculture Secretary Tom Vilsack.

One figure that drew officials' attention was the number of households, 506,000, in which children faced "very low food security": up from 323,000 the previous year. President Obama, who has pledged to end childhood hunger by 2015, released a statement while traveling in Asia that called the finding "particularly troubling."

The ungainly phrase "food insecurity" stems from years of political and academic wrangling over how to measure adequate access to food. In the 1980s, when officials of the Reagan administration denied there was hunger in the United States, the Food Research and Action Center, a Washington advocacy group, began a survey that concluded otherwise. Over time, Congress had the Agriculture Department oversee a similar survey, which the Census Bureau administers.

Though researchers at the Agriculture Department do not use the word "hunger," Mr. Obama did. "Hunger rose significantly last year," he said.

Analysts said the main reason for the growth was the rise in the unemployment rate, to 7.2 percent at the end of 2008 from 4.9 percent a year earlier. And since it now stands at 10.2 percent, the survery might in fact understate the number of Americans struggling to get adequate food.

Rising food prices, too, might have played a role.

The food stamp rolls have expanded to record levels, with 36 million Americans now collecting aid, an increase of nearly 40 percent from two years ago. And the American Recovery and Reinvestment Act, passed last winter, raised the average monthly food stamp benefit per person by about 17 percent, to $133. Many states have made it easier for those eligible to apply, but rising applications and staffing cuts have also brought long delays.

Problems gaining access to food were highest in households with children headed by single mothers. About 37 percent of them reported some form of food insecurity compared with 14 percent of married households with children. About 29 percent of Hispanic households reported food insecurity, compared with 27 percent of black households and 12 percent of white households. Serious problems were most prevalent in the South, followed equally by the West and Midwest.

Some conservatives have attacked the survey's methodology, saying it is hard to define what it measures. The 18-item questionnaire asks about skipped meals and hunger pangs, but also whether people had worries about getting food. It ranks the severity of their condition by the number of answers that indicate a problem.

"Very few of these people are hungry," said Robert Rector, an analyst at the conservative Heritage Foundation. "When they lose jobs, they constrain the kind of food they buy. That is regrettable, but it's a far cry from a hunger crisis."

The report measures the number of households that experienced problems at any point in the year. Only a "small fraction" were facing the problem at a given moment. Among those with "very low food security," for instance, most experienced the condition for several days in each of seven or eight months.

James Weill, the director of the food center that pioneered the report, called it a careful look at an underappreciated condition.

"Many people are outright hungry, skipping meals," he said. "Others say they have enough to eat but only because they're going to food pantries or using food stamps. We describe it as 'households struggling with hunger.'"

Can Our Shameful Prisons Be Reformed?

The New York Review of Books

By *David Cole*

Race, Incarceration, and American Values
by Glenn C. Loury, with Pamela S. Karlan, Tommie Shelby, and Loïc Wacquant
Boston Review/MIT Press, 86 pp., $14.95

Let's Get Free: A Hip-Hop Theory of Justice
by Paul Butler
New Press, 214 pp., $25.95

Releasing Prisoners, Redeeming Communities: Reentry, Race, and Politics
by Anthony C. Thompson
New York University Press, 262 pp., $39.00; $21.00 (paper)

With approximately 2.3 million people in prison or jail, the United States incarcerates more people than any other country in the world—by far. Our per capita rate is six times greater than Canada's, eight times greater than France's, and twelve times greater than Japan's. Here, at least, we are an undisputed world leader; we have a 40 percent lead on our closest competitors—Russia and Belarus.

Even so, the imprisoned make up only two thirds of one percent of the nation's

general population. And most of those imprisoned are poor and uneducated,

disproportionately drawn from the margins of society. For the vast majority of us, in other

words, the idea that we might find ourselves in jail or prison is simply not a genuine concern.

For one group in particular, however, these figures have concrete and deep-rooted

implications —African-Americans, especially young black men, and especially poor

young black men. African-Americans are 13 percent of the general population, but over

50 percent of the prison population. Blacks are incarcerated at a rate eight times higher

than that of whites—a disparity that dwarfs other racial disparities. (Black—white

disparities in unemployment, for example, are 2–1; in nonmarital childbirth, 3–1; in

infant mortality, 2–1; and in net worth, 1–5[1]).

In the 1950s, when segregation was still legal, African-Americans comprised 30

percent of the prison population. Sixty years later, African-Americans and Latinos make up

70 percent of the incarcerated population, and that population has skyrocketed. The

disparities are greatest where race and class intersect—nearly 60 percent of all young black

men born between 1965 and 1969 who dropped out of high school went to prison at least

once on a felony conviction before they turned thirty-five. And the incarceration rate for

this group—black male high school dropouts—is nearly fifty times the national average.[2]

These disparities in turn have extraordinary ripple effects. For an entire cohort of

young black men in America's inner cities, incarceration has become the more-likely-

than-not norm, not the unthinkable exception. And in part because prisons today offer

inmates little or nothing in the way of job training, education, or counseling regarding

their return to society, ex-offenders' prospects for employment, housing, and marriage

upon release drop precipitously from their already low levels before incarceration.

That in turn makes it far more likely that these ex-offenders will return to criminal behavior—and then to prison. Meanwhile, the incarceration of so many young men means more single-parent households, and more children whose fathers are in prison. Children with parents in prison are in turn seven times more likely to be imprisoned at some point in their lives than other children. As Brown professor Glenn Loury puts it in *Race, Incarceration, and American Values*, we are "creating a racially defined pariah class in the middle of our great cities."

The most dramatic effects of this incarceration are concentrated on the most disadvantaged—those who are not only African-American or Latino, but also poor, uneducated, and living in highly segregated ghettos. While roughly 60 percent of black high school dropouts have spent time in prison, only 5 percent of college-educated African-Americans have done so. The indirect consequences of such disparities, however, extend much further. Many people cannot tell whether an African-American is a dropout or college-educated—or, more relevant, a burglar or a college professor, as Harvard professor Henry Louis Gates found in July 2009, when he was arrested after trying to get into his own house. The correlation of race and crime in the public's mind reinforces prejudice that affects every African-American.

How do we escape the self-defeating cycle of crime and punishment? Anthony Thompson suggests that we focus on the neediest—the 700,000 or so prisoners who are released each year. Before the incarceration boom, the avowed purpose of criminal sentencing in America was rehabilitation. Prison sentences were often open-ended, with the idea being that a successful course of rehabilitation would warrant an earlier release. In the 1970s, however, the nation began to sour on rehabilitation, and over the next two decades state and federal authorities eliminated most efforts to educate, train, and counsel prisoners with a view toward preparing them for their return to society.

Thompson argues that when 700,000 prisoners are being released each year, we ignore at our peril their reintegration into our society. A stable home, job, and health are strong predictors of law-abiding behavior. But incarceration makes stability much more difficult to obtain in all these respects. Public housing laws often bar offenders, and private landlords routinely discriminate against them. Federal and state laws broadly prohibit ex-offenders from hundreds of jobs, often without any rational justification, and even where no bar exists, private employers are less than eager to hire them. Prisoners who enter prison without physical and mental illnesses often develop them while inside. Yet as Thompson demonstrates, society does virtually nothing to help ex-offenders find homes, jobs, or health care—thereby virtually guaranteeing a cycle of recidivism.

The Changing Face of Poverty in America

Why are so many women, children, and racial and cultural minorities still poor?

WILLIAM E. SPRIGGS | *April 22, 2007*

"Water, water everywhere, nor any drop to drink."
— Samuel Taylor Coleridge, *The Rime of the Ancient Mariner*

in 1960 American workers produced a gross domestic Product of $13,847 (in year 2000 dollars) for every man, woman, and child in the country. By 1969, GDP per capita rose to $18,578. In that period, the poverty rate for American children dropped almost by half, from 26.5 percent to 13.8 percent. The most recent data, for 2005, show child

poverty has risen again, to 17.1 percent, while the GDP per capita stood at $37,246,

roughly double the value in 1969. How did the nation become twice as wealthy but its

children become poorer?

In 2000, the number of poor Americans reached an 11-year low at 31.6 million,

and the poverty rate stood at a 26-year low at 11.3 percent. While the nation again

became richer after the post-2001 recovery, more than 5 million Americans fell into

poverty, and the latest figures put the number of poor Americans at 36.9 million people.

To put a face on American poverty, it is important to first put that poverty in

context—to understand not just who is poor today but to examine how poverty changes

over time. With that perspective, we can appreciate that in a nation as wealthy as the

United States, poverty is not intractable.

"The federal government declared war on poverty, and poverty won."

— Ronald Reagan

That line from President Reagan's 1988 state of the Union address, was used to

ridicule Lyndon Johnson's efforts to fight poverty. President Johnson launched that fight

in March 1964, submitting the Economic Opportunity Act to Congress and saying these

words: "Because it is right, because it is wise, and because, for the first time in our

history, it is possible to conquer poverty?"

Johnson believed that a wealthy nation produces enough for each individual

citizen to live above poverty. This was a question of political and moral will, not an

economic constraint. So, he differentiated between the day's global struggle to end

poverty in countries like Mali and Haiti, where there was a real economic constraint to be overcome, and the situation in America, a land that was not poor in resources but that lacked moral conviction. The Johnson legacy chart on the following page shows the path of poverty for black children, a primary beneficiary of LBJ's programs. In 1965, almost 66 percent of black children lived below the poverty line. In four short years, that share was cut to 39.6 percent, a tremendous accomplishment. By contrast, the Reagan legacy chart shows the path of poverty for black children from 1981 to 1989, the era of Reagan and George Bush Senior. In 1980, 42.1 percent of black children lived below the poverty line; and by 1988 that share had risen to 42.8 percent. Yes, poverty won.

How Policy Influences Poverty

The face of poverty in America is the result of policy choices, of political will, and of moral conviction — or its absence. The incidence of poverty is heavily concentrated in the United States across the South and the Southwest. The legacy of slavery is part of that story. Forty percent of America's poor live in the South. Four of today's five poorest states were ones that existed in the old Confederacy. Of the onetime Confederate states, only two—Florida and Virginia — do not rank in the current 20 states with highest poverty levels.

Why do some people lack the income to rise above poverty? For many, the reason is that they do not work; for others, the reason is that they work but do not earn enough money. Nonworkers include the elderly, the disabled, and children, as well as the unemployed. And public policy treats different groups differently.

The Social Security old-age program insures virtually all retired workers against the risk of outliving their savings. The old-age benefit formula is tied to the rising productivity of current workers, indexing the benefits to the average national wage. The shared risk, and the insured shared prosperity, explain why the poverty rate for those over 65 has declined from more than 28 percent in 1966 (nearly double the national poverty rate of 14.7 percent) to 10.1 percent today (below the national rate of 12.6 percent). In 1974, the poverty rate for the Census category of white non-Hispanic seniors, at 12.5 percent, was double the poverty rate for working-age (18–64) white non-Hispanics, at 5.9 percent. Today, the poverty rate for the two age groups is virtually equal, at 7.9 percent for seniors and 7.8 percent for working-age white non-Hispanics.

Another group of people who do not work, by law, are children. But their income is derived mostly from their parents. The rise in child poverty, therefore, reflects the rise in the inequality of their parents' earnings. So, while 9.8 percent of the poor are seniors, 33.5 percent of the poor are children. Children make up a much higher share of the poor among blacks (41.9 percent of poor blacks) and Hispanics (42.6 percent of poor Hispanics) than among whites (24.5 percent of poor whites). And while the poverty rate of seniors has shown a steady trend downward as national income has risen, child poverty rates are as intractable as the growing inequality in working families' earnings.

The wide divergence in how public policy treats different groups was not Congress' original intent. The Social Security Act of 1935 sought to protect the incomes of those who did not work because of age or a poor economy by establishing a federal framework for unemployment insurance, old-age benefits, and assistance to women with dependent children. In 1939, the old-age benefit structure was fully federalized to produce consistent benefits. But, Aid to Families with Dependent Children (AFDC) and the unemployment-insurance system were put in state hands. And in the 1990s, AFDC

was transformed from its Social Security Act roots into a state block grant. The mostly

state-run unemployment-insurance system, meanwhile, is strained by the transformation

of the economy from one in which workers could expect to be laid off in recessions and

then rehired into one based on the structural creation and destruction of whole industries

and occupations.

Children in our antipoverty system are oddly split. Today, more children receive a

check from the Old Age, Survivors and Disability Insurance (OASDI) Program than are

helped by the new Temporary Assistance for Needy Families (TANF) program that

replaced AFDC. Some children, therefore, enjoy their parents' protection against the loss

of income from disability, untimely death, or old age, and receive benefits that are based

on the same formula used for the old-age benefit. Low-income black children are

especially helped by the disability benefits their parents receive, or by the survivor

benefits that the child receives—because the benefit formula is national and intended to

alleviate poverty.

By contrast, children receiving TANF aid are subject to the whim of their state. In

2004, a widowed mother and two children, on average, received a monthly OASDI

survivors' benefit of $1,952. Those two children would live above the federal poverty

line. The TANF benefit for the same family, however, could range from $170 a month in

Mississippi to $215 in Alabama to $240 in Louisiana to $625 in New Hampshire, leaving

children in all of those states far below the poverty line. Adjusting for inflation, the

survivors' benefit has been increasing since 1970, while the average benefit under AFDC

(and now TANF) has been falling. While the OASDI benefit level is set by a federal formula, policy-makers in states with higher shares of black TANF recipients choose lower benefit levels.

Like TANF recipients, unemployed workers are also at the mercy of their state; the average weekly benefit can range from $179 a week in Mississippi to $320 in New Jersey. In the 1950s, close to half of the nation's unemployed workers received benefits; today, only about 35 percent do. This varies widely by state, from 21 percent in Wyoming to 24 percent in Texas to 58 percent in Pennsylvania to 71 percent in New Jersey. And the percentage of earned income replaced by unemployment benefits has steadily fallen as well.

Diligent and Still Poor

An ongoing topic of debate is the relationship of child poverty and parents' income to the increase in single-parent households. Other things being equal, two parents in a household usually earn more than one, but they are not assured of earning their family's way out of poverty. Hispanic and black children have roughly similar levels of poverty—33.2 percent for black children, and 27.7 percent for Hispanic children. Yet 41 percent of black families with children are married, whereas 68 percent of Hispanic families with children are married. In 1974, when the poverty rate among black children was at 39.6 percent, 56 percent of black families with children were married. Two-income families today are less likely to be poor, but much is at work besides family structure.

To be poor is to lack income, so the core issue is earnings. In 1962, on the eve of the March on Washington for Jobs and Justice in 1963, the median income of black men was below the poverty threshold for a family of three, but by 1967 it was above that level (not until 1995 did it get above the poverty level for a family of four). Because of the rise in the earnings of black women, poverty among black children fell in the 1990s, just as the rise in the earnings of black men helped lower black children's poverty level in the 1960s. By 1997, the median income of black women rose above the poverty level for a family of three.

Among the poor, 11.4 percent work full time, year-round. These 2.9 million Americans are directly hurt by minimum-wage laws that have lagged behind costs of living. This problem is especially acute for Asians and Hispanics, where 18 percent of the working poor worked full time, year-round.

Recent immigrants who are not citizens have a poverty rate of 20.4 percent. Like all groups, noncitizen immigrants had falling poverty rates in the 1990s as the labor market expanded: Their poverty rate fell from 28.7 percent in 1993 to a low of 19.2 percent in 2000. Then, following the national trend; their poverty rate started to climb. During the Reagan administration, the United States suffered its highest national unemployment rates since the Great Depression. In the black community, the effects were devastating: The unemployment rate for adult (over age 20) black men peaked at more than 20 percent in December 1982; during the entire Reagan presidency, the unemployment rate for adult black men remained in double digits. The highest recorded unemployment rate for adult white men was 9 percent in November and December 1982. But for black men, the unemployment rate remained above that mark for 182 straight months (15 years), from October 1979 to November 1994. Because children do not work and need working adults to support them, it is hardly surprising that during that period, black child poverty rates remained intractable above 40 percent.

Poverty for women is disproportionately higher than for men, 14.1 percent compared to 11.1 (in 2005), primarily because of higher rates of poverty among female-headed households, gaps in poverty for the elderly (7.3 percent for men over age 65 compared to 12.3 percent for women in 2005), and for single women (24.1 percent) compared to single men (17.9 percent) living alone. The gap reflects persistent gaps in earnings between men and women, though that gap is falling. White non-Hispanic men, age 25 and over, with a high-school diploma have a median income of $35,679, while women, age 25 and over, need a college degree to have a similar median income ($36,532 in 2005). And, while the median income of white males has been above the poverty line for a family of five since 1959, the median income for women only broke above the poverty line for a family of three in 1990. The persistent gap is best reflected in differences in poverty among the elderly, where the life-long earnings of women mean they have lower assets in Social Security benefits than do men, despite the progressive structure of the benefit formula. The gap among the elderly also reflects issues of access to jobs with pensions for women.

Women who are the single head of household face the extra burden of earning enough to raise dependent children out of poverty. This risk a woman faces of helping non-working dependents is not shared by society, as would be a woman's efforts to care for her elderly parents. The result is that female-headed households, harmed by the significant earnings gap between men and women, have a poverty rate of 31.1 percent compared to male-headed households (with no wife present) of 13.4 percent, while the overall poverty rate for families is 10.8 percent.

Full Employment and its Limits

It took the presidency of Bill Clinton, with its expansive labor market and increases in the minimum wage and the Earned Income Tax Credit, to dramatically improve the incomes of poor and minority families. As job creation reached a record pace, the unemployment rate for black men plummeted, reaching a recorded low of 6 percent in March 1999. With work comes income, and poverty for black families fell. This history suggests something about the proper way to view responsibility and poor people as agents in their own fate: Usually they are not victims of themselves, but of bad economic policies and barriers to opportunity.

Under Reagan, who ridiculed antipoverty efforts, the number of black children living below the poverty line increased by 200,000, from 3.9 million in 1980 to 4.1 million in 1988. During the Clinton years, the black child poverty rate fell steadily, from 46.3 percent to a record-low 30 percent, lifting about 1.6 million black children out of poverty. For all children, the poverty rate fell annually during the Clinton presidency, reaching a 30-year low of 15.6 percent when he left office. But those reduced poverty rates may be the best we can achieve simply by getting jobs for parents. While lower than during the Reagan years, they do not equal the lows America has achieved for its senior citizens, or the general population. And those gains reversed course when George W. Bush became president.

Because of record job creation in the 1990s, the number of people who worked and were poor declined from 10.1 million in 1993 to 8.5 million by 2000; greatly increased working hours and higher wages meant higher incomes. But during the current expansion, a record 48 months was required to get payroll employment back to the level preceding the employment downturn that began in late 2000, a lag not matched since Herbert Hoover. So while full employment is necessary to alleviate poverty, it is far from sufficient.

In short, America knows how to address poverty. Its great success in lowering the poverty level of those over 65 has changed the face of poverty. But for those subject to the whims of state differences and the correlation of race with state policies to address poverty, there have been great intractable issues that have left the face of poverty disproportionately young, black, Hispanic, and female. Growing inequality in the labor market, moreover, has increased the share of the poor who are of working age, and stagnant federal minimum-wage laws have increased the oxymoron of full-time, year-round working poor people.

In a nation with a per capita GDP above the poverty line for a family of four, it is appalling that almost 3 million people work full time, year-round and are poor, and that more than 12 million American children are living in poverty. Lyndon Johnson proposed to fight poverty "because it is right, because it is wise." In a land of vast wealth, twice as rich as America in the 1960s, can today's leaders to rise to the occasion?

William E. Spriggs chairs the department of economics at Howard University. He is a senior fellow at the Economic Policy Institute and former executive director of the National Urban League Institute for Opportunity and Equality.

Building a National Effort to Address Poverty

by Mark Greenberg

New data from the Census Bureau tells us that one in eight Americans–37.3 million people–had an income that was below the official federal poverty line in 2007.

Because the official poverty line is inadequate in many ways, that number does not reflect the far greater number of Americans struggling to make ends meet. There have been dramatic periods of poverty reduction in the nation's history, but the period since 2000 is not one of them. Instead, there were 5.7 million more poor Americans in 2007 than in 2000, even before the financial disruptions of this year.

Persistent poverty is bad for people, communities and the nation. It impairs the life chances of children and weakens mobility in America. It makes communities less desirable places to live and work, and increases the difficulty of ensuring that there are good schools educating children to meet their own and the nation's future needs. And it hurts the U.S. economy. Research by Harry Holzer and colleagues has estimated that the cost to the national economy of children growing up in persistent poverty is in the range of $500 billion a year–about 4 percent of the gross domestic product–as a result of lower productivity, increased health-related costs and increased crime costs.

The official poverty numbers tell us that poverty in America is experienced by all ages, both sexes, and across racial and ethnic groups, though it is far more severe for some than others. Under the official measure ($21,203 for a family of four), children are the poorest group (18 percent poor in the latest Census numbers), but 23 percent of the elderly have incomes at or below 150 percent of the federal poverty line. Women remain far more likely than men to be poor (14 percent of females versus 11 percent of males). African-Americans and Hispanics are twice as likely as whites to be poor (24.5 and 21.5 percent, respectively, versus 10.5 percent for white.) Overall in 2007, nearly one-third of Americans (30.5 percent) had incomes below twice the official poverty line, which is often used as a measure of low-income status.

In the past several years, there has been a notable increase in attention to poverty both within and outside of government. At least 10 states have created executive or legislative commissions or task forces charged with developing state strategies. In the presidential election, Senator Barack Obama has declared his support for a national goal of cutting poverty in half, and Senator John McCain has stated that poverty eradication will be a top priority of his administration. A national campaign effort, Half in Ten (*www.halfinten.org*), seeks to elevate attention to the need for a national goal, and there has been extensive engagement by a broad range of faith-based groups to bring more attention to addressing poverty. New developments are prominently highlighted at a website created by a set of foundations, Spotlight on Poverty and Opportunity (*www.spotlightonpoverty.org*).

In some respects, the developing crisis in the nation's financial, credit and housing markets makes it a more challenging time to encourage a national effort to address poverty; in others, it makes it more essential. On the one hand, it now seems possible that the first domestic and economic challenge for the next president will involve stabilizing the volatile and declining markets, and that the urgency of doing so will leave little room for addressing other issues. But while the President's economic strategy will need to deal with the immediate crises, it will also have to establish the conditions for long-run growth and shared prosperity–and one component of the overall strategy must be a plan for reducing poverty.

In 2006-07, I directed a task force on poverty for the Center for American Progress. The task force's report, *From Poverty to Prosperity: A National Strategy to Cut Poverty in Half* (*http://www.americanprogress.org/issues/2007/04/poverty report.html*), called for a national goal of cutting poverty in half in 10 years, and proposed a strategy for reaching that goal. We called for a national goal because such a goal would provide a clear, concrete, measurable and attainable target. U.S. history suggests that a goal of a 50 percent reduction in 10 years would be ambitious but attainable. And the experience of the United Kingdom, where there is a national goal of ending child poverty by 2020, suggests that adopting such a goal can become an important statement of priorities, promote accountability, and shift the political debate to one in which parties agree on the aspiration despite disagreeing on how to reach the target.

A goal of this magnitude cannot be accomplished with a single or narrow set of policies. Our task force made a dozen recommendations and identified a number of other important areas for action, with an overall approach grounded in four principles:

- **Promote Decent Work:** People should work and work should pay enough to ensure that workers and their families can avoid poverty, meet basic needs and save for the future.

- **Provide Opportunity for All:** Children should grow up in conditions that maximize their opportunities for success; adults should have opportunities throughout their lives to connect to work, get more education, live in a good neighborhood and move up in the workforce.

- **Ensure Economic Security:** Americans should not fall into poverty in times when they cannot work or work is unavailable, unstable, or pays too little to make ends meet.

- **Help People Build Wealth:** All Americans should have assets that allow them to weather periods of flux and volatility and to have the resources that may be essential for upward economic mobility.

As part of our effort, we commissioned the Urban Institute to model the impacts of one set of recommendations: raising the minimum wage to 50 percent of the average wage; expanding the Earned Income Tax Credit, particularly for adults without custodial children; making the child tax credit fully refundable so that all low-income children could benefit from it; and making child care assistance available to all low-income families, while broadening tax-based child-care assistance for an even larger group of families. The Urban Institute estimated that fully implementing these policies would reduce poverty by 26 percent and child poverty by 42 percent, using a definition of poverty that draws from recommendations of the National Academy of Sciences.

While the modeled policies are important, they are only one part of an overall strategy. Among others, we highlighted the importance of supporting unionization efforts to improve the conditions of work; broadening access to higher education; promoting housing mobility and equitable development strategies so that low-income communities can benefit from regional growth; removing the barriers that restrict access to unemployment insurance for low-wage workers; taking other steps to modernize the public benefits system, including eliminating prohibitions on assistance that affects legal immigrants; and promoting and supporting labor force participation by disconnected youth and individuals leaving prisons and jails.

Further, while the federal government has a crucial role to play, an overall effort cannot be just about the federal government. It must also include the active engagement of states, cities and local communities, along with the business community, the voluntary sector and individuals. That is one reason why the emergence of state and city commissions and task forces is a critical development, because such efforts are uniquely suited to identify the state and local policies and practices that can make the biggest

contributions to poverty-reduction efforts based on the conditions they face.

The challenge for the next administration is not that we do not know what to do.

While we can always benefit from additional research, there is already ample research

and experience from which to develop a comprehensive strategy. Nor is the challenge

that the public would object to a well-structured poverty-reduction effort. There is little

doubt that the public wishes there was less poverty in America. While poverty is rarely

listed among the top two or three issues facing the nation, large majorities view it as

problem. At the same time, the public is split on whether the principal reason people are

poor is related to individual decisions or social conditions. And whatever the underlying

reasons might be, a significant share of the public doubts whether government could act

effectively to reduce poverty even if it sought to do so. Thus, it is essential that an

effective strategy must balance individual and social responsibility, and must be

grounded in knowledge gained from strategies that worked in the past.

In particular, we can learn much from the 1990s, when poverty fell by 25 percent

as it declined for seven consecutive years. During that period, a near-full-employment

economy was combined with programs and policies that sought to both promote work and

reduce the poverty of those who worked: welfare reform, expansion of the Earned Income

Tax Credit, expansion of child care, an increased minimum wage, broadening health care

coverage, and others. We can draw from that experience the importance of macroeconomic

strategies to promote full employment, along with strategies to expand work opportunities

for under-employed populations and ensure that work is an effective route out of poverty.

At the same time, it's important to appreciate that poor adults in the United States

already work more than their counterparts in a number of other nations with lower poverty rates than ours, but the market results in higher levels of poverty here, while tax and transfer policies do less to reduce market-based poverty. Moreover, the experience of the 1990s underscores that even the most effective employment strategies will not be enough to address the poverty of groups such as the elderly and those individuals and families with the most severe barriers to employment.

Foundations have a key role to play in efforts to encourage and support federal, state and local poverty-reduction efforts. First and foremost, advocacy matters. Advocacy efforts in states and localities have played central roles in advancing minimum wage campaigns; promoting expanded Earned Income Tax Credits and reduction of regressive state taxes; addressing predatory lending practices; improving unemployment insurance access; advancing green jobs campaigns; and others. The highest-quality policy analysis and development can only be effective when there is energetic advocacy to advance it.

Second, foundations can play a key role in spurring and supporting the development of coordinated, integrated poverty-reduction strategies. Often, state and local commissions and task forces have little or no budget for staffing, research, meetings, seeking input from those directly affected by poverty, gaining access to lessons from other states and localities, modeling different approaches, and other components of developing effective strategies. Foundations can encourage state and local actors to come together, provide the resources that spur the creation of a commission or task force, and provide the resources and technical assistance that can make a key difference in the effectiveness of such efforts.

It is often particularly helpful for cities and states to learn from the experience of others, gaining insight about what has been tried, what has and hasn't worked, and what lessons from one jurisdiction can be transferred to another. Foundations can play an important role in fostering communication among communities, cities and states, and in elevating the awareness and prestige of the most successful local efforts. Moreover, there is much that can be learned from cross-national experience, and foundations can play an important role in making those lessons more accessible to efforts in the United States.

Foundations can also spur innovation and creativity in local efforts. It is often difficult for local governments to undertake potentially promising but untested strategies, and time-limited support for new initiatives can reduce the risk of innovation. Moreover, the case for innovation can be bolstered when resources are available for research and evaluation, and foundations can provide such support in instances where governments with strained budgets are unable to do so. Foundations also can play a key role in helping identify the most effective ways to communicate about the needs, challenges and approaches being undertaken.

The lessons of recent decades tell us that the United States has the capacity to cut poverty in half, and that we would be a stronger nation if we did so. Foundations can play a critical role in spurring the local, state and national efforts that can help our country adopt and reach this goal.

Mark H. Greenberg is a senior fellow at American Progress. He previously served as the executive director of American Progress' Task Force on Poverty, whose report, *From Poverty to Prosperity: A National Strategy for Cutting Poverty in Half*, was issued in 2007. Prior to joining American Progress, he was the director of policy for the Center for Law and Social Policy (CLASP). He has written extensively on issues relating to federal and state welfare reform efforts; workforce policy issues affecting low-income families; child care and early education policy; and other poverty-related issues. He frequently provides technical assistance to state and local governments regarding requirements and options under U.S. welfare, workforce and child care legislation.

Sustaining Anti-Poverty Solutions: Keep an Eye on the Prize

by Jodie Levin-Epstein

Neighborhood funders have long been in the business of ameliorating the consequences of poverty and finding solutions that reduce it. The good news is that around the United States, governments and other entities are giving increased attention to poverty and opportunity. The challenge is to build and sustain this attention at all levels of government so that poverty is cut dramatically in the next decades.

Local solutions to poverty that provide opportunity are taking hold in different ways. For example:

- In Savannah, Georgia, the Poverty Reduction Initiative is housed in the local Chamber of Commerce.

- The cities of Providence, Milwaukee and New York have established mayoral task forces.

- In San Francisco, a partnership of city departments, private foundations, nonprofits and residents called Communities of Opportunity is devising strategies to improve the lives of a pilot group of 2,600 families that will be expanded.

Numerous religious and civic organizations have also begun to mount campaigns to gain support for tackling poverty. A funder-led initiative, Spotlight on Poverty and Opportunity, for example, was launched in 2007 to get the presidential candidates to discuss the issue and how they would address it. After the campaign, Spotlight (*www.spotlightonpoverty.org*) will work to sustain public engagement and foster accountability. Already, elected officials and national figures have written commentary for Spotlight, offering their solutions and positions. Diverse ideas from Speaker of the House Nancy Pelosi and former Speaker Newt Gingrich have been posted on the Internet, and other exclusive commentaries point to common ground in such areas as expanding the Earned Income Tax Credit. These actions are important because, in recent decades, poverty has been politically "invisible."

How invisible? Former Senator Tom Daschle tells an illustrative story about the late Senator Paul Wellstone. In 1997, Wellstone decided to revisit the places Bobby Kennedy had seen on a poverty tour 30 years earlier, to assess how much progress had been made and what remained to be accomplished. When Wellstone, one of the Senate's leading progressives, informed his staff of this idea, a staffer piped up, "Senator, we don't talk about poverty." So even progressives felt that making the issue visible was politically problematic. As Daschle notes, Wellstone went forward, took the tour–and he talked.

What evidence is there that poverty has increased in visibility more recently? At least 18 states, most of them since 2006, have established a poverty commission, planned a statewide conference or created a new legislative caucus to address the issue. This trend is a dramatic signal that governors and legislatures feel a need to take stock and take action on poverty and opportunity. And, in a new initiative, The National Governors Association is providing grants to 10 Governors to host poverty summits before summer 2009.

What policy recommendations have been promoted? Most state commissions and legislative caucuses are so new that they have not yet issued their recommendations; the summits announced by governors have yet to be held. And since recommendations will be made in the context of each state's pre-existing circumstances and policies, they should be developed individually.

Where recommendations have been issued, they cover a wide range of strategies. Connecticut, the first state to establish a poverty target–to cut child poverty in half by 2014–originally identified 67 policies to pursue. Recognizing that prioritizing was essential to action, the state's commission pulled together a group of experts to identify which strategies held the most promise based on available evidence and the timeframe for anticipated impact. The 13 specific priorities that were identified included income supports such as the Earned Income Tax Credit; child-care subsidies available to all low-income families with incomes up to 200 percent of the poverty level; education investments in areas such as improving teacher quality and supporting early-childhood and postsecondary education; and family-structure supports such as programs related to teen pregnancy prevention. The few other states that have made recommendations to date also tend to take a two-generation approach to recommendations; that is, they recommend policies that address adults (e.g. job retention and advancement, and income issues such as assets and predatory lending) as well as children (e.g. early childhood education).

While each state is unique, every one should consider how to address a variety of wage and tax policies, including minimum wage, state thresholds for income tax, state earned income tax credits, grocery taxes, etc. Further, work supports such as child-care subsidies and transportation also enhance people's ability to secure and sustain employment. These steps are vital if income from a job is to have the maximum effect in lifting families out of poverty. And since housing and health care too often remain unaffordable even for people who are employed, government must step up to the plate and devise strategies that help secure these essentials.

Poverty is defined as a function of inadequate income. However, personal income is only part of the picture. Poor people often live in poor communities with inadequate institutions and systems that need strengthening. Improved schools and educational attainment, job-training services, more and better banking options and financial literacy, and improved infrastructure and transportation systems are among the many local issues that could be part of the solution that reduces poverty and increases opportunity.

The policy options are numerous and varied. There is, however, one policy tool that can help provide a common focus–a poverty reduction target. A poverty reduction target sets a numerical goal (e.g. cutting poverty in half) and a timeline for getting there (e.g. a decade). A target is agnostic about which policies should be implemented. If wielded effectively, however, a target helps keep stakeholders' eyes on the prize: cutting poverty.

A poverty reduction target has four "S" strengths. It offers a *shared* vision that establishes the intent to tackle poverty; a *simple* metric whose simplicity fosters transparency and is readily understood by both policy makers and the public; a *silo-busting* tool, since reaching the target invariably requires cross-agency work; and a *solution-building* environment, since if a proposal is rejected or a program fails to work, another solution needs to take its place. Further, since a target is typically in place for the long term–a decade or more–it can, if used effectively, contribute to sustained attention.

At least eight states have now established a poverty reduction target: Connecticut, Delaware, Illinois, Louisiana, Maine, Minnesota, Oregon and Vermont. Some targets focus on child poverty, while others aim at overall poverty or extreme poverty (those living below 50 percent of the poverty line). At the national level, the U.S. House of Representatives passed a Sense of the Congress resolution in January 2008 that calls for a national goal of cutting poverty in half over the next 10 years.

While reducing poverty by 50 percent in 10 years sounds like a simple goal, measuring poverty is not so simple. The United States has an official poverty line, but the way it is calculated is out of date. It only considers whether a family has enough earned income to purchase a minimally adequate diet, and fails to consider other expenses such as child care and other income such as tax credits. For example, the current official poverty measure does not take the Earned Income Tax Credit into account. If a city or state sought to reduce poverty by offering or increasing tax credits on earned income, it would help poor families but would not change the official measure. (New York City has developed a new measure of poverty for this reason.) Fortunately, it appears that Congress may soon address this issue seriously. Yet even though a new poverty measure is vital, its absence is not a rationale for inaction. Our current measurement tool is flawed, but it does tell us something important.

A related issue is how to measure progress in cutting poverty at the community or neighborhood level. The official poverty line–even a new and improved version–has less statistical validity when applied to smaller local populations. Thus, at the neighborhood level, it will continue to be important to use appropriate alternative indicators to measure the progress of policies and programs. Around the country, different indicators and different ways of employing them have been developed. For example, the Annie E. Casey Foundation's Making Connections initiative, which involves 10 cities and multiple neighborhood sites, uses a set of indicators to measure the impact of employment and asset-building strategies, and of efforts to ensure that young children are healthy and prepared to succeed in school.

Make no mistake: We have a lot of poverty for a rich nation. More than 37 million Americans–one of every eight–live below the poverty line. For a family of four that translates into living on $1,770 a month or less, and many do in fact live on less. About 15.6 million of us subsist at or below half the poverty line, currently pegged at $885 a month for a family of four.

Yet a dramatic cut in poverty is doable. Perhaps the greatest challenge facing any community, state or national anti-poverty campaign is overcoming the impression that the problem is insoluble. That impression is based on a myth–that "we fought a war on poverty and poverty won." In truth, the U.S. has been witness to substantial declines in poverty in the past. For example, because of the War on Poverty and the strong economy of the 1960s, our poverty rate dropped more than half between 1959 and 1973, from 22.4 percent to 11.1 percent.

With the nation's financial institutions in an upheaval and massive federal expenditures directed at addressing that problem, it is even more challenging to address the needs of those struggling to make ends meet. For neighborhood funders, the recent trend of making poverty visible among governments and politicians provides a rare opportunity to foster a vision, build partnerships, adapt existing solutions and create new ones. There is a legitimate attention to our financial institutions and righting them; this action, however, should not crowd out the need to ensure families are out of poverty and contributing to our national engine. The process can start by setting specific state and national targets for reducing poverty. A target is a tool that can help unify and sustain the mission. It can help motivate a movement. One example comes from Catholic Charities USA, whose campaign to reduce poverty in America has a simple goal that anyone can understand and support: Cut poverty in half by the year 2020, and help make our nation whole.

Jodie Levin-Epstein is Deputy Director of CLASP. Her focus is on working conditions—issues such as paid leave and workplace flexibility, particularly as they impact on low income workers. She has established CLASP's Project on Reproductive Health, Adolescents and Welfare, a project that explores the intersection of welfare and other low-income social programs with fertility and health. She is also involved in organizational capacity issues.

Community Organizing, Public Policy and Building a Vibrant Democracy

by Spence Limbocker

Anyone who reads the newspaper or watches the evening news can tell you that a sense of change is in the air. Both major political parties are using the word "change" to describe their campaigns and what they see as a vision for the future in America. We have not seen this type of interest or energy around a campaign for President in this country since the 1960s. This is particularly true in the Obama campaign with its heavy emphasis on community organizing as a way to expand voter rolls and energize voters. Whether or not Obama is elected, it is clear that the country is moving away from the anti-government, pro-corporate policies that we have seen over the past eight years. I am hopeful that we are going to see an openness to public policies that address issues of lower- and middle-income people in this country at the local, state and national level. With this change in the national psyche occurring, now is the perfect time for a greater emphasis on organizing people in low- and moderate-income communities to take a more active role in shaping their lives. The two issues that I want to briefly explore in this paper are:

- What are the changes in community organizing that are increasing the capacity of low- and moderate-income people to become effectively engaged in public policy?

- How can foundations support policy initiatives and organizations that grow out of these grassroots efforts?

These are large questions and in a short paper it is not possible to delve deeply into all the aspects of how public policy is developed, debated and moved through the various levels of government. But I will touch on a few points that I think are important.

The process of engaging low- and moderate-income people in public policy is beginning to change. The major networks of community organizations across the United States along with many local community-based organizations have expanded significantly in the past 10 years and many of them have begun to take on regional, state and even national public-policy issues. Many have the capacity to engage thousands of organized people in discussions where they can take an active role in developing public policy and are able to influence decisions at different levels. But even more importantly, because they are building strong permanent organizations they have the capacity to hold decision-makers accountable for policy decisions that have been collectively agreed upon.

In a recent study for the Charles Stewart Mott Foundation that I participated in, we found that the organizing networks we surveyed had grown substantially over the last decade or so by adding new affiliates and continuing to deepen their bases. The growth has been dramatic in both the national and regional networks that we studied. Collectively, they have engaged tens of thousands of new activists and leaders. Some examples of this growth include:

- PICO has grown from 22 groups in 1997 to 53 in 2007.

- Gamaliel has doubled in size and is now in 22 states and 50 metro areas.

- DART has grown from 12 affiliates in 1997 to 21 in 2007.

- ACORN has more than doubled its size and now has organizations in 110 cities.

- The InterValley Project in the Northeast has expanded into Maine and developed new chapters in other states.

- The Virginia Organizing Project (VOP) has doubled in size and grown to 15 chapters in Virginia.

The community organizers in these and other community-based organizations specialize in helping people develop the skills and knowledge they need to become active participants in our democracy. The organizers' goal is to help people become effective and engaged leaders so they can influence the democratic process where policy decisions are made. By working collectively across often divisive lines, they learn how to exert power to change the policies and practices of government and other major institutions whose decisions have a major impact on their communities and lives.

While organizing has always been about building power and developing leaders, there has been a notable change in recent years as community-organizing groups and networks have dramatically expanded their involvement in big-issue campaigns across geographic boundaries. In the process they have won significant victories and brought public and private dollars into their communities. There is strong evidence that they have been able to increase their constitutents' clout on issues affecting poor and moderate-income families across state and regional boundaries. Some examples of significant wins by some of these groups are:

- ACORN estimates the monetary impact of its campaigns across the United States to be more than $15 billion. Included in this amount were:

  o $2 billion in living- and minimum-wage increases

  o $6 billion in victories over predatory lenders

  o $6 billion in loan counseling and Community Reinvestment Act agreements

  o $33 million in housing development

  o $350 million in local infrastructure and public services

  o $226 million in budget cutbacks averted/restored

- The InterValley Project won an increase of $2 million per year in federal funding for job training, passage of a cap on transportation fees for 70,000 temporary workers, and $36 million for the Neighborhood Opportunities Program, resulting in 966 affordable housing units.

- The Virginia Organizing Project won $339 million to finance low-income home ownership and rental construction loans, and an increase of $1.5 billion in new state support to public schools.

- Gamaliel affiliates have won such victories as an agreement with 16 banks to lend $700 million to 7,000 homeowners, reversal of a decision to close a major hospital in a working class neighborhood, and increased funds for drug rehab programs as a result of a "treatment instead of prison" campaign.

- PICO has won expansion of the Children's Health Insurance Program in California and expanded access to health insurance for uninsured people. It has convinced the State of California to invest $50 million in after-school programs in poor districts, provide $15 million for parent/teacher home visitation, and invest $42 million in improving the infrastructure of health clinics.

- Metro IAF has built 150 new townhouses in Washington D.C., won agreement for hundreds of new living-wage construction apprenticeship jobs, and worked to create a $100 million Neighborhood Investment Fund. It recently won funding for 400 units of supportive housing for homeless families.

- In Miami in 2002, PACT doubled the county's bus fleet and won a transportation referendum that will bring $17 billion over 20 years to the public rail and bus systems.

In recent years we also have seen community-organizing groups and networks dramatically expand their involvement in voter registration, voter education, get-out-the-vote campaigns and other efforts to expand participation by low-income people and people of color in the democratic process. The networks are careful to avoid stepping over the line into electoral political activity, but have clearly succeeded in energizing increasing numbers of voters, especially in 2008.

Most networks have adopted voter-participation work to demonstrate their power to politicians and others. Over the years these voter-engagement strategies have grown and become more sophisticated inside many organizing groups. ACORN, for example, has used these strategies to register hundreds of thousands of new voters.

Many organizing groups have already had real impact at the state and regional level. PICO has strong statewide affiliates in California and Louisiana. Other organizing networks with strong statewide affiliates include IAF in Texas, ACORN in several states, the Northwest Federation of Community Organizations in Washington, Oregon and Idaho, and the Virginia Organizing Project in Virginia. In addition, the Valley Projects have organized multi-state North East Joint Action and Gamaliel has organizations covering several metro regions. They have all won significant policy victories over the past several years.

This is a major change from earlier decades when most groups shied away from such activities. There is clear evidence that these efforts are increasing their constituents' clout on issues affecting poor and moderate-income families.

The other critical asset that strong organizing networks and other organizing groups offer is their capacity and commitment after elections to keep elected officials and others connected and accountable in positive ways to the local communities they represent.

But as community organizing has moved to influence decisions at higher levels, there often has been a significant internal cost to the groups. It is a tremendous stretch for a local group to begin devoting substantial time to working on statewide issues while also maintaining its local work. Most organizations have internal constraints on staff-time, a limited number of skilled leaders and small budgets. They also know how difficult and time-consuming it is to take on larger issues. In many cases, some leaders and staff are much more interested in staying focused on local communities and neighborhoods. It takes significant time and effort to work through these tensions and engage a broad range of leaders in the decision to expand the group's work.

Despite these constraints, there are significant reasons why many community groups and networks are deciding to tackle state, regional or federal policy. Quite simply, many of the most important issues that these groups are working on are decided at those higher levels—not by local governments. For example, the main resources needed for providing affordable health insurance, supplementing urban budgets, subsidizing housing or addressing immigrant issues are at the state and national levels. The leaders of strong, sophisticated groups are therefore often anxious to join network affiliates and other allies in joint campaigns to influence state and federal policies.

Several networks now have a new perspective on this dilemma and see their local organization-building as a first step toward the goal of building regional or statewide power. This is leading to substantial changes in their strategies.

2009 may well provide opportunities for the networks and other community-organizing groups, which have quietly built increased power and sophistication over the last decade. It may give them a chance to have a major impact at the federal level on issues of poverty, race, opportunity and community revitalization.

This convergence of growth, engagement in local, state and national voter engagement, and focus on larger public-policy issues creates a valuable opportunity for foundations to expand their support for these groups or begin supporting community organizing as a strategy for carrying out their own missions. Every foundation should carefully consider how to capitalize on these opportunities to support broad-based community organizing and networks, so even greater gains can be made at all levels of public policy.

Some things that all foundations should consider in their public-policy and issue-funding strategies:

1. How might community organizing fit into your foundation's mission? How might it strengthen or contribute to your present funding efforts? Review current grantmaking priorities to determine how a community organizing strategy might fit.

2. Are the groups you are supporting engaging their members in public-policy discussions and activities, and building the power necessary to effectively engage decision-makers over a long period of time?

3. How might your funding help your grantees develop the capacities they need to effectively engage in public-policy activities?

4. You can educate yourself to the options of supporting community organizing by talking with colleagues who already do.

5. Keep in mind that community-organizing entities need basic operating support to carry out their efforts.

6. Be aware that funding from foundations can help community organizations work through the internal tensions that often result when they become involved in larger public-policy activities.

Organizing and civic engagement have played essential roles in keeping American democracy vibrant and responsive to the needs of low- and moderate-income people. Many of the major movements in the past have grown out of efforts by organized groups. A few creative and forward-looking foundations have been there to support these efforts in the past, and it is now time for more funders to join them if we are going to truly build a more just society.

Spence Limbocker has worked as a community organizer, ran a training center for organizers and leaders and managed a 400 unit housing cooperative in San Francisco. In 1984, he moved to Washington, D.C. where he worked with the Catholic Campaign for Human Development, providing funding to community organizations. In 1996, he was hired as the director of the Neighborhood Funders Group where he worked until his retirement in 2008.

PART IV Conclusion: Toward a Just Society, the Role of Social Workers

Overview

As we noted in the Introductory chapter of this text one of the key characteristics of this profession is its emphasis on social justice. The definition of social justice focuses on reducing our society's basic inequities in the distribution of basic resource- e.g. education, income, housing, health care, and child care. How does social work accomplish this task? And how is the task pursued in these initial years of the 21st century, with a changing economy, political system, with the emergence of a global interconnected world, with the key role now played by technology? How can this goal be pursued in light of the fact that the profession itself has had a lessening involvement with political and social advocacy? In this Overview, we explore the key factors that are now shaping the profession and explore the opportunities and challenges for social work to promote social justice and advocacy in general. Although the profession's interest in advocacy has been prominent in selected historical periods and less in others, it still remains a key obligation of the profession. Yet, if we are intent on pursuing political advocacy we must be aware of how our world/society has changed. It is important to understands these changes. The key changes which have occurred include the following: (1) globalization and the change in our economic system (2) the use of technology (3) the devolution of government (4) the privatization of social services and health services.

With respect to globalization and changes in the economic system, Haskett writes, "the economic system has undergone the most performed changes. Many of which have direct implications on the social welfare system. These include globalization, decentralization and the use of the knowledge worker and of knowledge as a store of wealth "... The latter," Haskett notes: "This is a central issue in the transition from an industrial to an information economy" (Haskett, 2002, p. 174). A second major area of change relates to

the welfare of government and is marked by devolution and decentralization. Devolution

refers to the moving of control not only to lower levels of government but also to the private

section. In the United States greater controls over policy and program are being exercised

not at the national or federal level but at the state and local- county/city levels. Further, the

private sector is increasingly a key player in policy and program delivery.

Technology is, also, increasingly demonstrating its important potential to promote

change. McNutt (2002) writes: "The development of new tools and more important, new

perspectives means that technology will be a part of social change in the future.

Technology will facilitate a vast number of processes and enhance communication across

a variety of distance and dividing lines . . . The use of government and e-democracy may

also affect advocacy practice. In creating new ways to control government and to

participate in policy deliberations the architects of these new technologies will change

the nature of this ascent (McNutt, 2002, P.8).

This chapter is divided into four sections. In Section A - a comprehensive guide

to advocacy is presented. The document entitled Speak Out! was prepared by Michael

Friedman, Director of the Center for Policy and Advocacy of the Mental Health

Associates of New York City and Westchester County. In Section B we review, briefly,

the emerging role of advocacy through the Internet. In Section C we discuss actions to

change agencies and in Section D, we discuss the needs of the profession and the schools

of social work to promote the development of advocacy.

The social work profession has recently celebrated its 100th birthday. A key role

for the profession, especially through its roots in the settlement house movement, has

always been advocacy and social justice and we need to explore how it's best

accomplished in this initial decade of the 21st century.

SECTION A

THE GERIATRIC MENTAL HEALTH ALLIANCE OF NEW YORK

50 Broadway, 19th Floor, New York, NY 10004   212-614-5753   center@mhaofnyc.org
www.mhawestchester.org/advocates/geriatrichome.asp

The Geriatric Mental Health Alliance of New York: An Overview

The Mental Health Associations of New York City and Westchester established The Geriatric Mental Health Alliance in January 2004. The Alliance was formed to confront the mental health challenges of the elder boom and to promote critical changes in practice and policy.

Since its inception the Alliance – made up of mental health, health, and aging service professionals and providers, researchers, academic leaders, consumers, older adults, advocates, family members, and public officials – has grown from about 100 members to over 3000. The Alliance has active workgroups in NYC and Albany. There are local spin-offs of the Alliance in Suffolk, Nassau, Westchester, Rockland, Orange, Ulster, and Monroe Counties.

The long-term goal of The Alliance is to promote improved geriatric mental health practice by identifying best and innovative practices, identifying barriers to their use, developing policy proposals to overcome these barriers, and advocating for policy and practice changes. To this end, The Alliance conducted over 30 focus and discussion groups during its first year. These groups resulted in several papers on geriatric mental health needs, best practices, and barriers to using best practices. In addition the Alliance sponsors consensus building workgroups on topics related to geriatric mental health. To date the Alliance has written policy papers on the needs of aging people with serious and persistent mental illness, the housing needs of older adults with serious mental illness, mental health and long-term care, workforce development, Asian geriatric mental health needs, and Latino mental health needs.

Alliance Advocacy

The initial short-term goals of The Alliance were (1) to persuade the state to develop a long-term plan regarding geriatric mental health and (2) to raise consciousness about the importance of geriatric mental health among local, state, and federal governments; providers; trade associations; and advocacy organizations about the importance of geriatric mental health. These we saw as essential leverage for long-term, comprehensive change.

With government our strategy was (1) to focus mainly on the state level with some advocacy at the local level and (2) to target both the executive and legislative branches.

Our first thrust towards building awareness about the importance of geriatric mental health came shortly after the inception of the Alliance. That month the NYS Office of Mental Health released its first population-based five year plan, and to our great surprise and dismay it contained only a single footnote about geriatric mental health. That spring we organized our new Alliance members to testify at the hearing on the Plan, and as a result over 50% of the presentations regarding any and all aspects of the plan contained, or were solely focused on, geriatric mental health. After the hearing we met with leadership in both The NYS Office of Mental Health and the Office of the Aging. Within a year both offices made geriatric mental health a priority.

During that same period, we formed a capitol-based workgroup made up of 25 key statewide advocacy organizations that focus on mental health, health and/or aging in order to give legitimacy and power to our state-based advocacy work, particularly with the Legislature.

Our work with the Legislature, which began in the summer of 2004, involved working with the chairs of the mental health and aging committees in both the Senate and the Assembly as well as with other legislative leaders. We did not organize a grassroots effort because we did not have enough staff or funding and because we believed that we could achieve our initial goals by working only with leadership. These goals were quite modest—to hold hearings and pass a study bill, but we were prepared with an outline of a Comprehensive Geriatric Mental Health Act just in case. We found that the legislative leaders wanted to move fast, and we worked with them to draft identical bills in both houses. We also lined up support from 110 organizations. This required a lot of telephoning and follow ups as well as contact via E-mail. We also helped the legislative staff to organize a bicameral/bipartisan press conference. By that time we were lucky enough to get a grant to hire lobbyists to press the bill forward both in the Legislature and in the Governor's office, which had threatened a veto. Once the bill was poised to be passed in both houses, The Governor's office proposed a compromise; and we accepted. In August 2005, the Geriatric Mental Health Act (not "comprehensive") was signed into law.

The Act established an Interagency Geriatric Mental Health Planning Council, which is co-chaired by the Commissioner of the Office of Mental Health and the Director of the State Office for the Aging with appointments from seven other state departments and six political appointments. The Council is charged with making recommendations regarding a long-term plan to address the mental health needs of older adults in NYS; the Commissioners of Mental Health and of Aging are charged with creating a plan. The Act also established a services demonstrations grants program contingent on an appropriation. The Governor included initial funding of $2 million in his 2006-7 executive budget request. There were 68 applications in response to the request for proposals (RFP). This is the largest response to an RFP in OMH history. Only nine programs were funded – five to integrate mental health into primary care and four to establish a community gatekeeper program. We have been advocating for additional funding for service demonstration grants, especially since there are so many organizations that are ready and willing to mount services but need the support to get started. The first year we asked for additional support, all the powers-that-be were reluctant because no grants had yet been made. The second year the Legislature was on the verge of adding another $1.5 million, but the upper leadership of the Assembly decided to put the funding into mental retardation instead. That, of course, was a big disappointment, but the 2008-9 budget includes a number of other items for which we and other groups have been advocating which, we believe, will open the door for much greater expansion.

Although most of The Alliance's efforts are devoted to the state, The Alliance has also been active at the local level, especially in NYC, where the City Council now provides $2.7 million for geriatric mental health programs to expand their services in non-traditional settings such as the home or senior centers. In addition, we have been actively involved in NYC's effort to "modernize" aging services and in the City Council's "age-friendly city" initiative.

Alliance leaders have also provided consultation in other states and linked with national efforts to address the mental health needs of older adults.

The Alliance's Educational Activities

The Alliance has also become a major source of information, training, and technical assistance regarding geriatric mental health practice and policy. This includes an annual lecture series on best practices with national experts, organization of an annual statewide conference, co-sponsorship of numerous local and state conferences, clinical training, technical assistance regarding service models and funding, frequent presentations at conferences, advocacy events, trade association meetings, etc., a website, a bi-weekly newsletter, numerous reports, and more.

These educational events are of significant value to our constituency in themselves. They have been a major source of building our membership and of getting support for our advocacy goals from those who attend the events and/or read our newsletter and/or website.

Chapter One

What is Mental Health Advocacy?
Who Is This Handbook For?

■   This handbook is designed for people who care about mental health and about people who have mental illnesses or psychiatric disabilities, including children, adolescents, and adults of all ages.

■   I will use a number of different terms to refer to this population—most often "people with mental illnesses", "people with psychiatric disabilities", and "children and adolescents with serious emotional disturbances", but also "people with mental health problems", "consumers", "recipients", "people with serious and persistent mental illnesses", "person diagnosed with mental illness", etc. Some of the language I use may be controversial. I apologize in advance to anyone who is insulted by my choice of language.

The Value of Speaking Out

■   People who care about mental health can be and have been powerful forces in moving the mental health system in progressive directions.

■   This includes people with histories in the mental health system—both people with mental illnesses and their families.

■   It includes concerned citizens.

■   It includes mental health professionals.

■   It includes professional mental health advocates.

■   All people who care about mental health have important stories to tell and information to provide to policy makers.

■   Public officials—especially elected officials—like to hear directly from the people their decisions will affect.

Advocacy Regarding Mental Health Policy

■ This handbook is about advocacy for changes in the mental health system. This handbook is not about how to advocate for individuals on a case-by-case basis.

■ Advocacy for individuals is very important work, but is an art of its own. It focuses on helping people get what they need and want from systems as they are currently structured.

■ Systems advocacy is based on the realization that some people cannot get what they need from systems as they are currently structured and that helping them therefore requires working for changes in public policy.

■ You and the organizations you are part of need to decide what changes you think are important. Better access to better treatment, better places to live, more opportunities to work, more peer-run programs, greater respect for people's rights, equal health insurance coverage for mental health, etc. Mental health advocates have identified many needed changes in the mental health system.

■ Trying to persuade government or the private sector to make changes in mental health policy so as to help achieve these goals is the kind of advocacy that this handbook is about.

What Is Mental Health Policy?

■ Mental health policy consists of laws, regulations, plans, program models, licensing standards, budgets, financing models, organizational policies and procedures, etc.

■ These elements of policy are derived from broad visions of the role of society in helping people with mental health problems. For example until the mid-20th century, public mental health policy was institution-based. For the past 50 years, it has been based on a vision of people with mental illnesses leading free and satisfying lives in the community.

Who Makes Mental Health Policy?

■ Public mental health policy is made by legislatures, by elected chief executives such as the President, governors, and mayors, by their appointees such as commissioners, and by the courts.

■ Some mental health policy is made by the private sector. For example, in the U.S., most people's health benefits are provided by their employers, who decide whether and to what extent to provide mental health coverage.

Why Change Mental Health Policy?

■ Most people who are familiar with the mental health system believe that it is inadequate in some important ways. Even people who believe that NYS's mental health system is one of the best in the United States realize that it could be better. In recent years the greatest concerns have related to (1) the failure to reach people diagnosed with mental illnesses who reject traditional treatment, (2) inadequate services for children and adolescents with serious emotional disturbances, (3) lack of readiness for the elder boom, (4) lack of adequate housing, (5) obstacles to work, (6) issues of coercion, (7) access to treatment and medication, and (8) mental health insurance coverage. There are, of course, many other issues.

How To Change Mental Health Policy: The Framework for This Handbook

■ You need to **work in advocacy groups to be effective.**

■ Effective **advocacy requires planning**.

- A sound advocacy plan rests on **a good assessment** of need, policy, history, cost, and politics.

- A sound advocacy plan has three parts: an **agenda**, a **strategy**, and **tactics**.

- The **agenda** consists of your advocacy goals. Perhaps what you think is important is better access to better treatment, decent housing, family support, access to work for people with psychiatric disabilities, and adequate insurance coverage for mental health treatment. Your "agenda" would include those goals. These are just examples, of course. You may think that other goals are equally important or more important.

- The **strategy** identifies what private or public organizations and officials you are going to try to reach in order to bring about the changes that you want to achieve. It is based on an analysis of who has the power to achieve your goals, of who can influence those with power, and of what will persuade them to do what you want them to. Usually there is more than one person or organization with the power to do what you want. Your strategy is your selection of which point(s) of power to focus your efforts on, your sense of what will motivate them to change policy, and your selection of advocacy partners.

- **Tactics** are the methods that you use to carry out your strategy and to achieve your goals. Once you know what you want to achieve and decide which powers-that-be you want to reach and what you think will motivate them, you need to develop a detailed plan about how to carry out your strategy. Will you organize a letter writing campaign? Will you seek a face-to-face meeting? Will you demonstrate? Will you try to get headlines? These specific actions constitute your "tactics."

Planning must lead to action, and sometimes action cannot wait for a refined plan.

ADVOCACY IS ACTION

WHAT CAN YOU DO?

Register to vote and vote.

Contact your elected and appointed public officials.

Join an advocacy or an advisory group.

Make a financial contribution to an advocacy group.

Participate in actions organized by an advocacy group

such as letter writing or attending lobby days.

Work and provide leadership for an advocacy group.

ADVOCACY PLANNING

ASSESSMENT:

What is the need? The problem?
What is the current policy?
What is the history of the policy and of advocacy to change it?
What is the political context?
How much will the desired change cost?

AGENDA:

What are your goals?

STRATEGY:

Who has power?
Who has influence?
What will motivate them to change policy?
Who can be good advocacy partners?

TACTICS:

How will you persuade the powers-that-be to change policy?
Lobbying?
Public education?
Demonstrations?
Social Defiance?

Chapter Two

Advocacy Groups

ADVOCACY IS MOST EFFECTIVE IN GROUPS

Why Advocacy Depends on Working in Groups

■ On rare occasions, individuals working alone have been able to capture public attention and persuade public officials to make changes in policy. But for the most part, advocacy must take place through groups because (1) in a democracy change only takes place when there are many voters who support change, (2) advocacy takes a lot of work, (3) working in groups helps to test ideas, and (4) groups can capture public and media interest better than individuals working alone.

Join An Advocacy Group

■ Advocacy groups need members. Join one.

What you can do as a member

■ All advocacy groups need money to do their work. Making a financial contribution is very important.

■ If you join an advocacy group, you will get mail or E-mail from time to time asking you to write to or telephone certain people. Your letter or call helps to show that many people care about the issue.

■ You will also be asked to attend events where it is important that large numbers of people turn out. For example many organizations have lobby days in Albany or Washington, and from time to time there are demonstrations about mental health issues.

■ Of course, you can also choose to do much more.

- Advocacy requires a lot of work. You will make yourself very popular and important in your group by volunteering to do anything that needs to be done.

- When you have the opportunity to attend a meeting to discuss an advocacy plan, you should feel free to speak up. But remember that if you are new, listening may be more valuable than speaking. As in all groups, it takes a while to be a fully accepted member whose opinions are welcome and respected.

- Keep in mind that the purpose of discussion is not just for everyone to voice his or her opinion. It is to help the group make a decision about what it will do.

- **ADVOCACY IS ULTIMATELY ABOUT ACTION NOT ABOUT TALK.**

- Once a decision is made, everyone in the group must back it. Differences of opinion are fine in the privacy of the group, but are very damaging if aired in public.

- Effective action requires that people stand together. **"United we stand; divided we fall."**

Leadership functions in advocacy groups

- **Chairing a meeting**: Good meetings allow participants to feel like valued members and enable them to join forces on some plan of action. Most meetings allow for differences of opinions to be expressed, but good meetings also have a sense of order and move to a meaningful conclusion.

- **Building consensus**: To be effective, groups must reach agreement and take action together. There are no general rules about how to build consensus. It is a skill that varies from person to person.

Communication and Advocacy Materials: One of the most important functions in an advocacy group is preparing written materials both for advocacy and for communication within the group.

- Advocacy materials include letters to public officials, position papers, press releases, etc.

- Communications materials include letters to members, newsletters, minutes of meetings, etc. Many groups now use E-mail as the major mechanism for communication within their group.

- **Being out front with public officials and the media**: Many people find this frightening. But advocacy groups need people who are able to speak out publicly even if they are nervous about it.

- **Follow through**: If you get the work done that you agree to do, you will be perceived as a leader.

Forming New Groups

If you find that none of the many mental health advocacy groups adequately represents your interests and beliefs, you may decide to form a new advocacy group. What does this take?

- Identify people or organizations with mutual interests.

- Talk with some of them individually before you convene the first meeting of a group.

- Negotiate some issues about goals, and sometimes about leadership roles, with key players before the first meeting.

- Convene an exploratory or planning meeting. At this meeting you should:

  - Identify mutual interests

  - Begin to develop shared positions

- Begin to develop an agreeable division of labor

- Develop an action plan

■ Follow up on the action plan.

■ Convene subsequent meetings consistent with the action plan. But do not have

  meetings before the actions agreed to at the prior meeting have been undertaken.

■ WORK CONSTANTLY AT BUILDING A CONSTITUENCY

Constituency Building

■ Both existing and newly formed groups need to work constantly to maintain

  and increase their membership and to build a cadre of people who support

  their cause.

■ This is called "constituency building."

■ To build a constituency, a group needs to reach out to people and to try to

  engage them.

■ It is important to identify which people you want to involve in your group. For

  example if your group represents families of adults with serious mental illnesses, do

  you want to limit membership to family members or be more inclusive?

  - Bigger groups generally have more impact, but the more diverse the membership

    the less focused the message.

  - There's no right choice. It's your decision.

■ You can reach people through direct contact, through mailings—including e-mail—

  and through public education activities such as speeches, conferences, websites, and

  written material.

■ From these outreach efforts you need to develop a mailing list.

■ Remember that most people do not have time to be active participants in your group, but many will send letters, make calls, or even appear at advocacy events if they know about them.

■ Communication is critical. Newsletters, issues alerts, calls for action must go out routinely to give your constituency a sense that your group is active and that they are involved.

ADVOCACY DEPENDS ON WORKING IN GROUPS

■ **JOIN A GROUP**

■ **MAKE A FINANCIAL CONTRIBUTION**

■ **SEND LETTERS AND MAKE CALLS ON BEHALF OF THE GROUP**

■ **ATTEND PUBLIC EVENTS ORGANIZED BY THE GROUP**

■ **PARTICIPATE IN CREATING THE ADVOCACY PLAN**

AND DOING THE WORK FOR A GROUP

■ **BECOME A LEADER OF YOUR GROUP**

■ **CREATE A NEW GROUP IF NEEDED**

Chapter Three

Creating An Agenda: Selecting Goals
It's Not As Easy As It Sounds

■ Since an advocacy agenda is fundamentally a list of your advocacy goals, it sounds like a pretty simple thing to do. It turns out, however, that it's not as simple as it sounds.

The Eight P's

■ In general goals need to be carefully thought through and formulated in terms which are clear to potential members of your group, to people who have the power to change policy, and to those who can influence the powers-that-be, such as the press.

■ To develop a thoughtful agenda I find it useful to consider each of the following "eight P's".

■ **Population**

Which population do you want to help? Suppose that your goal is to improve the quality of life for people with mental illnesses. While this is a noble goal, it is vague. Do you mean all people with mental illnesses? Children, adults, and geriatrics? In New York, in the United States, in the world? All diagnostic categories or only those that suggest a serious illness and ongoing disability?

Suppose that your concern is adults in New York State with long-term psychiatric disabilities. In current policy jargon this population is known as "people with psychiatric disabilities". Your goal then would be to improve the quality of life *for people with psychiatric disabilities in New York State.

■ **Problem**

This is still a nebulous goal. What's wrong with the quality of life of people with psychiatric disabilities? What's the problem? There are many possible answers.

One is that people with psychiatric disabilities are too frequently homeless or live in housing which is shabby and dangerous. Another is that they cannot get jobs. Another is that they frequently get no treatment or inadequate treatment. Another is that they are forced to stay in hospitals too long. Or they are forced to leave hospitals before they are ready. Different people have different views.

Suppose you think the major problems are lack of safe and decent housing, lack of access to high quality treatment, and lack of access to work. Your goals then would be to make more safe and decent housing available for people with psychiatric disabilities in New York State, to assure access to high quality treatment, and to create greater access to work for them. Such goals begin to be specific enough to mount a meaningful advocacy effort.

The Choice of Language in Describing the Population and the Problem

Some people might find the use of the expression "people with psychiatric disabilities" objectionable. They might want to overcome the same problems for the same people but would use other expressions such as "people with severe and recurrent mental illnesses," "people with brain disorders," or "psychiatric survivors." Terminology is very important in formulating your goals. You need to choose terminology that is acceptable to the people in your advocacy group. But you also need to gear your language to the people who have the power to make changes in public policy.

■ **Proposed Solution**

In addition to specifying the population and describing the problem, it is useful to give some idea of how the problem can be overcome. For example, you may believe that the best way to make decent housing available is for The New York State Office of Mental Health to build and fund community residences. Or you may think that rent subsidies are the answer. With regard to work, you may think that it is important to provide job coaches or that Medical insurance must be available. Again these are just examples.

You will also need to be more specific. For example, if you want more housing for people with mental illnesses, you will need to say how much more.

■ Policy

In addition to proposing a solution to the problem you have identified, it is very helpful if you can specify how to change policy. What is the current policy? How should it be changed? How much will it cost?

The amount of knowledge it takes to do this is daunting to many would-be advocates. Don't hesitate to go to the powers-that-be just because you don't know everything you need to know. They can help you learn, and they can actually help you refine your agenda in ways that will make it more feasible. Besides, it is really the people in government who have the responsibility to take your concerns and shape them into public policy.

You can also recruit or hire policy experts.

Possibility

Another consideration in developing an agenda is how idealistic or realistic you want it to be. **Politics is the art of the possible.** Ultimately it takes compromise to get policy changes that approximate your ideal goals. But advocates who insist on achieving certain ideals serve a very useful function on the stage of advocacy. Players at the extreme edges of an issue are necessary to define an acceptable middle ground. Some advocates, therefore, must be stubborn extremists while others are more realistic negotiators. Whether to tilt your agenda towards the extreme or the middle is up to you.

■ **Preservation and Development of Your Advocacy Group**

In order to achieve your advocacy goals, you need a strong group. What will it take to keep your group together and active? What will it take to make it stronger and more effective? In addition to desired systems changes, your advocacy agenda may need to include specific goals related to preserving the group, enlarging the group, or improving the group's public image and visibility.

■ **Priorities**

How many issues should be on your advocacy agenda? Some advocates insist that it must be a very few. Others argue that you should address the issues that are very important to the population you are trying to help even if there are a great many issues.

There is no correct answer. The scope of your advocacy agenda should depend on:

■ How much work can your organization take on? Don't bite off more than you can chew.

■ How many issues will the powers-that-be pay attention to at any given time?

■ How many issues have to be on the agenda to hold the advocacy group together?

■ **The Process of Selecting Goals**

A group's agenda usually arises from a group discussion and debate. The passions of the members of the group and their relationships with each other will have a great impact on the group process, whether agreement is achieved, and what is on the agenda. A good chairperson is essential.

Some groups end up with long agendas to hold the group together. This is a perfectly good reason to have a long agenda, though it sometimes leads to struggles about priorities later in the process.

Some Current Policy Issues

In New York State, mental health policy issues which are most mental health advocacy agendas include:

- Funding for community-based services for adults with serious and persistent mental illnesses, especially housing, case management, employment, and "assertive" community services.

- Funding for community-based services for children and adolescents with serious emotional disturbances.

- A long-term plan to meet the mental health challenges of the elder boom.

- Improved quality of care and treatment, using state-of-the-art methods.

- Mental health insurance coverage equal to health insurance coverage ("parity").

- Access to psychiatric medications.

Obviously this way of describing the issues does not meet the test of clarity which I have emphasized. It is meant just to give you a taste of prominent mental health policy issues at the moment.

THE 8 P'S OF SETTING AN AGENDA

Population

Who Needs Help?

Problem

What's Wrong?

Proposed Solution

How Do You Think The Problem Can Best Be Overcome?

Policy

What Policies Need To Change?
How Should They Be Changed?
How Much Will It Cost?

Possibility

What's Achievable?
Are You Willing To Compromise?

Preservation and Development of Your Advocacy Group

What Is Needed To Preserve Your Group?
What Is Needed To Make Your Group Stronger?

Priorities

What's Most Important?

Process

Who Needs To Agree?
How Will You Get Agreement?

Chapter Four

Strategy: Which Powers-That-be to Influence and how Power

- It takes power to make change. You must sort out whether the power to bring about change is in the public or the private sector or both. And you must identify specifically which organizations, parts of organizations, offices, and people have power to bring about the changes that you want to achieve.

- If this is a governmental issue, is it a federal, a state, county, or municipal issue? (In NYC, city government provides county and municipal levels of government.)

- Is your issue a legislative, executive, or judicial issue?

- It is likely that more than one level and branch of government have power regarding your goals.

  - Because the Chief Executive usually must sign a law, making law requires cooperation of legislative and executive branches.

  - Governmental budgets are key to carrying out mental health policy and are also joint products of the legislative and executive branches.

  - Determining who has power and which of the people or organizations with power to try to persuade to make changes is the first element of developing a strategy.

Influence

- Some people have "influence" rather than power.

- Powerful people can produce change through their own decision-making, either alone or with others.

- People with influence have access to people with power and may be able to persuade them how to act.

- The chairman of the political party to which the Governor belongs probably has influence. A friend or relative of the Governor may have influence, as may a recognized and trusted expert in mental health policy. A large contributor probably has influence. The news media certainly have influence.

- Determining who has influence is the second element of formulating an advocacy strategy.

Know Your Elected Officials

- Elected officials represent you in the federal, the state, and city governments. The most basic step of advocacy is to know who your elected officials are.

  - To find out who your elected officials are and where you can reach them call:

The League of Women Voters at 212-213-5286

- Next you need to sort out which of the elected officials have power, which have influence, and which have neither.

Know The Appointed Officials

- There are public officials in the administrative branch of government who are responsible for mental health services. They include:

  - The NYC Commissioner of Health and Mental Hygiene and The Executive Deputy Commissioner for Mental Hygiene

  - The Commissioner of Mental Health of NYS.

- At the federal level the Secretary of Health and Human Services (HHS) has the highest level of authority for mental health.

  - There are a number of agencies within HHS which deal directly with mental health issues including the National Institute of Mental Health (NIMH), The Center for Mental Health Services (CMHS), and The Centers for Medicare and Medicaid among others.

Motivation

- Once you have identified the people with power and influence, you need to figure out what will persuade them to help you.

- Like all of us, people with power or influence have mixed motivations.

- What mix of ideals, values, emotions, self-interest, and politics will help you win over the people you need on your side?

  - Better lives for people with mental illnesses

  - Having a family member or a friend with mental illness

  - The impact a change will have on voters or contributors

  - Building a political reputation of kindness and concern

  - Avoiding bad publicity

  - Doing what the boss wants

Form Strategic Partnerships

- In advocacy greater numbers generally mean greater power, and some advocates and advocacy groups have greater access to power than others.

- For this reason, it often makes sense to work jointly with other advocacy organizations.

- Keep in mind that some people and groups simply cannot work together and that it sometimes takes a very long time to form strategic partnerships.

- Don't lose opportunities for action because you hope for a partnership.

- But don't give up too easily on forming partnerships. Remember "United we stand, divided we fall!"

EFFECTIVE ADVOCACY DEPENDS ON GOOD RELATIONSHIPS

■ To be effective at advocacy, you must form good working relationships with people who have power, people who have influence, and people who can be partners in action.

An Example of Advocacy Strategy: The Reinvestment Act of 1993

Towards the end of the 1980's a number of mental health advocacy organizations in New York State became concerned that they were weakening each other's advocacy efforts by advocating for different goals. They decided to formulate a common agenda and to advocate for it together. They formed The Mental Health Action Network of New York State.

After a couple of years of mixed success, they decided to focus on a single theme, which they called "reinvestment." The notion was simple. The state was closing beds in state hospitals and was not providing adequate services for people in the community. Their position was that savings from closing state hospital beds should be reinvested in new services in the community.

In order to move this agenda, they had to choose an advocacy strategy. Achieving a mandate for reinvestment through the courts was clearly not feasible. The policy either could be adopted voluntarily by The Governor and the Office of Mental Health or it could be set in law by the state legislature. The advocates decided reinvestment policy would be more stable as state law than merely as the policy of the current state administration. So they chose a legislative strategy.

They knew that a legislative strategy would require that they get support from the chairs of the mental health committees of the Assembly and the Senate. So they turned to them to sponsor the legislation. Both were impressed with the idea and with the coalition of advocates and agreed to sponsor a bill.

The Governor proved to be more difficult, and his reservations affected not only the likelihood that legislation would be signed but also made it less likely that the legislative house controlled by his party would ultimately support the legislation.

The Mental Health Action Network decided that it needed a media strategy and developed a basic story about the mental health system, stressing the irrationality of closing hospital beds without developing services and supports in the community. The story drew heavily on the fact of homelessness and the widespread belief that there was a clear relationship between homelessness and mental illness. The story stressed that reinvestment could result in community-based services to prevent homelessness at no additional cost to the state. It would simply redirect money from state psychiatric centers to community-based services. The Mental Health Action Network carried the message to newspapers throughout New York State and ultimately got support for reinvestment from virtually every newspaper.

The message was also carried through vigils, rallies, and letter writing campaigns on which people with psychiatric disabilities, their families, and mental health professionals worked closely together.

The idea of addressing a major social problem at no additional cost to the state was politically irresistible. Local state legislators wanted to move ahead, and their desire to pass the law as well as consensus among the media created more and more pressure on the Governor. Eventually he conceded, after negotiating changes to the bill that focused the bill more clearly on people who were homeless.

This, of course, is a vastly oversimplified telling of the story. But what can we learn from it?

Lessons of the Campaign for Reinvestment

- Strategy begins with identifying who has the power to make a policy change and deciding which of the powers-that-be to target. The Mental Health Action Network decided on a legislative strategy.

- Carrying out a legislative strategy entails getting support from the chairs of the mental health committees in each house, from the leadership of each house, and from The Governor.

- It is important for the most influential members of the entire mental health community—including people with psychiatric disabilities, their families, and mental health professionals—to join forces.

- A persuasive advocacy story has to be formulated which has widespread ideological appeal.

- Media support ultimately carried the day.

STRATEGY

Public or Private Sector?

What Level of Government Has The Power To Change Policy?

Federal? State? County? Municipal?

What Branch of Government Has The Power To Change Policy?

Legislative? Executive? Judicial?

Which Specific Offices and People Have The Power to Change Policy?

Which elected officials?
Which appointed officials?
Which court?

Who Has Influence?

Respected Experts?
Colleagues?
Party Officials and Contributors?
Friends and Family?
The Press?

What Will Motivate Them To Help?

Ideology?
Relationships?
Politics?
A Good Story?
Pressure?

Should You Form A Strategic Partnership?

With whom?
Is It Feasible?
What Compromises Are Required?
Will It Result In Delay?

Have You Developed Good Working Relationships?

Chapter Five

Tactics: Methods to Bring About Change

Tactics are specific methods to bring about change. There are four primary ways to bring about change—**lobbying, public education, demonstrations,** and **social defiance**.

TECHNIQUES OF LOBBYING

- "Lobbying" is any effort to **directly influence** elected or appointed public officials. (Legal definitions of "lobbying" vary from state to state. Check lobbying laws to find out whether you have to register as a lobbyist and make reports.)

- Unfortunately "lobbying" has a negative connotation in our society.

- The image of lobbying as a form of political corruption neglects the fact that lobbying is an essential function in a representative democracy.

Meetings

- The term "lobbying" comes from discussions with legislators which used to take place in lobbies outside legislative chambers.

- As the term implies, direct meetings with public officials are a very effective way to lobby.

- Such meetings usually take place in the public official's office, but sometimes you can arrange for the public official to come to a meeting of your group.

- Direct telephone conversations with public officials can also be very useful.

- You should prepare carefully for a meeting with a public official. A written agenda helps.

- Think carefully about what you want to say. Try to formulate your ideas clearly and briefly. Keep in mind that most public officials—especially elected officials—will not be familiar with the issue that concerns you. They have too many issues to deal with to be able to know more than a very few in depth.

- At the beginning of the meeting you should always thank the public official for taking the time to meet with you. These are people who deserve your respect, and you should be sure to show it.

- You should give the public official **a one-page statement** of your positions at the beginning of the meeting with copies for any staff members who are also at the meeting. Written material is important as a reminder of your views after you leave. But it must be brief.

- It is not unusual in meetings with public officials not to cover your full agenda or even to drift to topics you hadn't planned to talk about. Don't worry about it as long as the meeting has been engaging for the public official. That will help you develop a relationship which will make it possible for you to work with the public official over time.

- *Working with staff*

  - Sometimes it is not possible to get a meeting directly with a public official. Usually you will be able to meet with someone on the public official's staff.

  - Don't be disappointed. Meeting with staff can be very effective. Sometimes it is more effective than meeting with the elected official because the staff member may know more and be the person who will actually develop the official's position.

- *Written Material*

  - It can be very helpful when you are working with public officials and their staffs to prepare written background information and drafts of desired changes.

Mail, E-Mail, and Phone Campaigns

- Letters in large quantities have a significant impact on public officials.

- Some advocates believe that only personal letters have an impact. It's hard to get people to write personal letters. Since volume counts, I favor form letters or postcards as well as personal letters.

- Generally letters to public officials should be no more than one page. The first sentence should tell the public official what to do. For example "Please vote for S. 1234, a bill that would provide more housing for people with mental illnesses."

- You can also fax the letter or send it by E-mail. I believe that a piece of paper received at the official's office has more impact than E-mail.

- Or you can telephone the official's office and leave a message such as "I am calling to ask the Senator to vote for S. 1234, which would provide more housing."

- Mail and phone campaigns require a great deal of organization—including compilation of a mailing list of people who will write or call, compilation of a mailing list of people to be lobbied, writing sample letters or scripts of telephone messages, communication with your fellow "lobbyists", etc.

Lobby Days

- A popular form of lobbying is a "lobby day"—i.e. a day of events at the city where the legislature meets.

■ A lobby day generally includes a large assemblage of all the people who have come to lobby. Legislators and other relevant public officials are invited.

■ At some events of this kind, representatives of the advocacy group give short speeches, hoping to capture the attention of public officials who attend. At others, public officials speak to the advocates on topics which the advocacy group has asked them to address.

■ Public officials tend to wander in and out of these events. For this reason, I believe that it is more effective to ask the public officials to speak than to lecture at them.

■ A major purpose of a legislative event is to make an impression, especially to convey a sense of numbers.

■ It also may be an opportunity to reach the press.

■ One form of lobby day includes a legislative "meal" such as a legislative breakfast, luncheon, or cocktail party.

■ A legislative "meal" creates an opportunity for advocates to talk informally with public officials as well as for formal presentations of the advocacy group's agenda.

■ Lobby days require tremendous organization and are expensive. You need to have a list of organizers who will bring groups to lobby, have a method of communicating with them rapidly, prepare materials including a handout for legislators, schedule (and confirm and reschedule) meetings, arrange for transportation, reserve a meeting room, arrange for refreshments, schedule speakers, etc.

Giving awards and recognition

■ Another effective device in wooing support from public officials is giving them awards and recognition, usually a plaque or some sort of symbolic sculpture similar to an Oscar.

Use of the Internet

- E-mail has made it relatively easy to communicate with people who may join you in advocacy by writing letters, making phone calls, or attending lobby days or demonstrations.

- You can post "action alerts" on a web site, and/or you can create a group E-mail list and notify people when action is needed.

- Some E-mail systems are constructed so as to permit people to send a communication directly. Others require people to cut and paste letters. There is dispute about the effectiveness of E-mailed advocacy communications. I favor asking people via E-mail to send advocacy letters via snail mail.

Testifying at Hearings

- From time to time public officials convene public hearings.

- There are several purposes to hearings—to hear from experts; to gather the public's opinions, whether expert or not; to publicize an issue of concern; and to get media attention.

- A public hearing is quite formal. To speak, you need to call in advance to schedule your testimony, which will be time-limited.

  - Prepare written testimony which you can read in the time that you've been given. It takes two minutes to read one page effectively.

- Say what you have to say briefly, clearly, and forcefully but not with disrespectful anger.

Campaign Contributions

- Elected officials value contributions to their campaign, both tangible and intangible.

- It is illegal for tax-exempt not-for-profit organizations to make political contributions or even to support candidates for office. For-profit organizations and not-for-profit political organizations, which are not tax exempt, are permitted to make contributions and to provide public support.

- Advocates from tax-exempt, non-profit organizations can give support personally. Financial contributions must be from your personal funds and cannot be reimbursed as business expenses or claimed as tax deductions. Work that you do on behalf of a candidate must be on your own time, not on time that is paid for by a tax-exempt organization. You can attend fundraising events, but on personal time and not as a representative of your organization. Any public statement of support must be clearly on your own behalf and not on behalf of your organization.

- There are, of course, ways for organizations to be helpful to political candidates without violating the law. Inviting them to speak at conferences gives them exposure. Putting their pictures in your newsletter or writing an article that features actions they have taken on behalf of mental health can be helpful to a candidate and are legitimate—up to a point.

Using professional lobbyists

- Many organizations that lobby on health, mental health, and social services issues use professional lobbyists, which enables them to have a regular presence with elected officials during the legislative session and saves a great deal of time which otherwise would have to be devoted to building relationships.

TECHNIQUES OF PUBLIC EDUCATION

■ Public education is any effort to influence public policy decisions by shaping public opinion or by reaching public officials indirectly.

■ The goal of public education is to swing public opinion to support your advocacy goals and to develop a cadre of supporters committed to your cause, i.e. to build a constituency. (See Chap. 2)

Analytic reports and publications

■ Studies and analytic reports which document problems that need to be addressed by government can be very effective in shaping public opinion.

■ The reports have to be credible and based on professional research and/or expert opinion.

■ In addition reports have to be readable. They require professional quality writing.

■ Reports must have wide distribution and substantial publicity.

■ There must be a follow-up plan to press for the recommendations included in the report.

Conferences

■ Another technique of public education is holding a conference to which critical audiences are invited and which hopefully attracts press attention.

■ Even conferences designed to educate professionals and others in the mental health community can serve an effective advocacy function.

■ In addition to changing public opinion, conferences can be very useful devices to build coalitions of advocates.

■ Conferences can also be very effective ways to engage public officials who attend or participate.

Written Material and Internet Web Sites

■ People in the general public who have an interest in mental health issues frequently have little access to information. Advocacy organizations typically develop and distribute printed material.

■ The Internet has created a wonderful new opportunity to make materials available.

Advertising

■ Advertising can be a very effective way to reach both the general public and public officials.

■ Ads in newspapers, on radio, and on TV can have a major impact, but of course are very expensive.

■ It is sometimes possible to get free help to develop and to place advertising, but free advertising usually ends up being run where or when no one is likely to see it.

Using the Media

■ The news media can be a great force in helping to move your agenda.

■ The media are a two-edged sword, to be treated with great caution. Historically the media have helped to move the cause of mental health with exposés of horrors in state institutions and of the terrible conditions people lived in after deinstitutionalization. But historically the media have also hurt the cause of mental health with lurid coverage of rare episodes of violence by people with mental illnesses, which have reinforced the fear of people with mental illness that pervades our society.

■ The media are motivated by factors which are not as simple as concern about the well-being of people, let alone people with mental illnesses. They need to sell papers or get TV viewers and they are more likely to try to catch people's interests with fear than human interest. Their professional values stress political neutrality. However, journalists often tell stories with a political slant; and, of course, they also write editorials to support one political view or another. But it is hard to get journalists to be advocates for your views.

- There are several basic ways to get coverage:

  - Send out a *press release*, a short informational piece designed to attract media interest.

  - Call a *press conference*.

    - Send invitations and **interesting** written material out in advance.

    - New York City is a very tough place to get coverage because there are so many competing stories. In Albany and other places outside NYC, it is frequently easier to get the press to attend a press conference and to write a story.

  - *Develop a story* and find a reporter who will write it, but remember

    - An advocate's idea of a good story is frequently not a reporter's idea of a good story.

    - Reporters like controversy, scandals, and stories of abuse. They love exposés.

    - On occasion reporters will pursue human-interest stories, more often those that are sad rather than those that show success.

- Stage a *media event*. Demonstrations with large crowds generally attract attention. Acts of civil disobedience sometimes attract attention. Celebrities attract attention.

- Be prominently involved in an event which will attract press coverage. For example, speaking at public hearings can attract coverage. You need to be provocative to get coverage.

- **Bottom line, dealing with the press is about crafting "soundbites", brief statements which take no more than ten seconds to say and which either are provocative or which seem to sum up a position perfectly.**

- *Dealing with reporters*

  - Getting your message out through reporters requires experience and skill.

  - The reporter's job is not to convey your beliefs in the way you would want them conveyed. Their job is to tell a story that will catch the interest of their readers, listeners, or viewers. It is usually pointless to try to persuade a reporter to take your side. The reporter will probably be more interested in trying to get you to state your position in a provocative way so as to contrast it with someone else's equally provocative statement of the opposite point of view.

  - Your job is to say over and over again to the reporter what you want to have appear in their story. Do not answer their questions if they do not enable you to say what you want to say.

  - You need to be very careful talking with reporters "on the record", but good reporters are trustworthy if you ask to talk "off the record" or give them "background." "Off the record" means that nothing you say will be quoted. Reporters are willing to go off the record because they can get leads that they could not get on the record. Reporters also like to get background information from knowledgeable people whom they trust even though they cannot quote it.

- *Letters to the Editor and OP-ED Essays*

  - One great opportunity newspapers provide is to express your opinion publicly and unfiltered by a reporter in a letter to the editor or an OP-ED essay.

- A letter to the editor sometimes is a response to something that has appeared in the newspaper, but sometimes it is simply a statement someone wants to make.

- Elected officials all read letters to the editor. It is an excellent way to reach them.

- A letter to the editor should be no more than 150–250 words. (Different papers have different requirements). It should be very easy to understand.

- Like letters to the editor, OP-ED essays are an excellent way to get the attention of elected officials. They also make good handouts and mailings. The fact that they have been published by a reputable newspaper lends a certain credibility to them that you can't get by sending out a statement on your own stationary.

- An OP-ED piece is a short essay (about 750 words) which states your opinion about a timely or interesting topic.

DEMONSTRATIONS

- The purpose of a demonstration is to attract attention and sympathy to your cause. It does no good to get attention which turns the public against your cause. You need the public's support.

- A good demonstration has four key characteristics.

  - First, people must attend. There is nothing sadder and more counter-productive than announcing a demonstration of thousands which is attended by fifty people. Therefore a major part of the effort to hold a demonstration is getting people there. Logistics are as important as your message.

  - Second, the news media have to attend. A demonstration has no meaning without coverage. That means that groundwork has to be done to get reporters interested in covering the event.

- Third, you need to craft a message that appeals to a constituency whose support you need to move your agenda.

- Fourth, your message must be communicated clearly, repeatedly, and briefly. The soundbite is the message.

SOCIAL DEFIANCE

- Defiance of normal social order can sometimes be a very effective form of advocacy.

- For example, economic boycotts were used very effectively to advance civil rights.

- Similarly, strikes have been effective both to help workers and to highlight injustices.

- Acts of civil disobedience can also be effective, both at gaining attention from the media and at winning public support.

- However, all acts of defiance are risky, both personally and in terms of public response.

  - You must decide if you are prepared to be gassed, arrested, or sent to jail.

  - You must assess carefully whether your act of social defiance will win or lose support.

TACTICS CHECKLIST

Lobbying

Mail
Petitions
Meetings
Relationships
Hearing Testimony
Written Material
Special Events
Awards
Campaign Contributions

Public Education

Reports
Conferences
Written Material
Web Page
Advertising
Media

Demonstrations

Attendance
Press Coverage

Social Defiance

Boycotts, Strikes, Etc.
Civil Disobedience
Risk Assessment

Advocacy Style

Confront Aggressively
Negotiate
Be At The Table
Provide Expert Advice
Work in Coalitions

ADVOCACY STYLE

■ **How to present yourself** is a major decision you need to make as an advocate. Do you want to appear to be tough, principled, and uncompromising, prepared to fight it out? Do you want to be friendly and willing to work together to find a solution that will satisfy most of the players? Do you want to come across as extremely knowledgeable and able to provide expert assistance? Do you want to be "at the table" where decisions are made so that you can influence decisions directly? Do you prefer to be outside the decision-making process so that you can stick to your guns?

- Whether **to work in coalitions** is also a very important choice. Coalitions are usually more effective than advocating alone because there is strength in numbers, but being part of a coalition requires compromise.

- **Your choice will depend primarily on who you are**. If you are confrontational by nature, you will probably work well as an outspoken, critical, demanding advocate. If you are uncomfortable with confrontation, you will probably work best as an advocate who helps to shape compromises. If you have credibility as an expert, you may want to present yourself as a source of information and counsel rather than as an advocate with a strong personal opinion. If you are not usually willing to make compromises, you should not join coalitions.

- Your choice will also depend on your relationships with people in positions of power or influence. If you have good working relationships, you will probably decide to be careful not to jeopardize those relationships by taking harsh positions in public.

- However, **you must be able to adapt your fundamental style for the needs of the moment**. Even a good confrontational advocate must graciously accept a good compromise. And even a congenial, let's-not-fight advocate needs to stick stubbornly to his or her position when a compromise would interfere with achieving the goal. And sometimes you have to take the risk of losing good relationships because the issue is too important and the compromise offered is inadequate.

Chapter Six
Persistence: The Key to Effective Advocacy

- Advocacy for changes in public policy is inherently frustrating. Changes usually take place slowly. Occasionally there are dramatic successes, but usually you win some and lose some. Sometimes it seems that you are not getting anyplace.

- It is critical to be persistent despite feeling frustrated.

- Remember that mental health policy has improved a great deal since the mid-20th century.

- For example, I originally became a mental health advocate in 1978, when I was working in a rehabilitation program for people who had been in psychiatric hospitals for long periods of time. They generally lived in shabby and dangerous places. There were virtually no community residences or supported housing programs. Few people had access to high quality mental health treatment. Most went to State aftercare clinics, which had poor psychiatric staff and outrageously high caseloads. There were only a handful of community-based rehabilitation programs. When people were in crisis, usually they were either hospitalized in poor hospitals for excessively long periods or they were turned away without the services they needed. Many State hospitals at that time were dangerous. People with mental illnesses also had very limited access to health care. They generally did not have enough money to get through a month with enough to eat. Frequently they had only worn out, dirty clothing to wear. Often they had nothing better to do during the day than to wander the streets or to sit on park benches.

- In order to change these conditions, many people fought for specialized housing and community-based treatment and supports.

- Advocacy worked. In 1978, NYS introduced the community residence program and the community support system program. Now there are about 27,500 housing units in New York State. And there has been great growth of rehabilitation programs, outpatient services, local hospital programs, crisis services, and peer support programs. In addition the quality of care in state hospital in-patient and outpatient programs is vastly improved. The mental health system is far better today than it was twenty-five years ago.

- This success reflects the work of coalitions of providers, of family members, and of recipients of services, all of whom consistently spoke to the need for more and better community services.

- Obviously much more needs to be done to create a comprehensive and responsive mental health system. And each year that passes without great improvement creates a sense of disappointment and frustration.

- But, over time, persistent and aggressive advocacy in coalitions works.

- You have a critical role to play. Your experiences, insights, and hard work are vital to effective mental health advocacy in the future. Hang in!

BASIC RULES OF ADVOCACY

Work in Groups

Plan Carefully

Take Action

Build Relationships

Be Persistent

SECTION B

Electronic Advocacy

As we noted earlier, electronic advocacy represents a crucial direction for now and the future. Hicks and McNutt have edited an important book- *Advocacy, Altruism and the Internet* (2002) that serves as a major resource for our explorations in this area. In an article in that book they note: "The development of information and communications technology (ICT) has vastly transformed the capacity of human service organizations to build coalitions and network and to advocate for their clients causes and principles . . . Activism in cyberspace really does not differ from activism everywhere else. E-mail, newsgroups, discussion, lists, web sites, chat, virtual communication, computer conferencing and online publishing are a few of the new methods that the internet enables They all, in many ways, either replace or augment activities that were previously done by other means. For example, e-mail action alerts are the electronic version of the flyers that grassroots organizes handout on street corners or at rallies. The difference is that e-mail alerts reach more people instantly, and cost nothing (Hicks and McNutt, 2002 P.167).

Current electronic strategies include:

- E-mail to coordinate efforts at policy change

- Web-based public education and awareness campaigns

- Databases

- Mapping and targeting programs

- Online Fund raising

- Blast faxing

- Intranets and extranets for policy communication

- E-mail to decision makers

- Online communities

- Internet- only advocacy groups

- Video streaming of speeches and educational resources

Since this section provides an overview and does not seek to serve as a detailed technical guide, we will limit ourselves to presenting a few key points and then provide more in depth reference information for the reader.

Online Communities

Hick and Reich (2002) note these important facts- "community involvement be it online or off, seems to be an essential part of political activism. Social movements need roots in communities, and at least to some extent, these roots can be achieved online. It remains to be seen just how effective. It will be interesting to se whether involvement in online activism takes the place of or inspires more real world involvement" (Hick and Reich, 2002).

Technology should not make us lose sight of the goals of a grassroots organization of social movement. The technology is only a tool- a means one may hope to further the ends, but not the be- all and end- all of the group or of an activity. Further, "These authors suggest that it is important to remember that, despite the fact that we cannot (for the most part and for the time being) see or touch the other people. . . . The freedom we may feel when we go online- freedom to be more ourselves or to try out entirely different selves- should not depersonalize others. It is very empowering for people who do not feel that their voices can be heard to feel that they are heard on the internet (Hick and Reich, 2002 p. 39-40).

Thus, computer skills are not a substitute for people skills and effective use of online technology involve people and computer skills.

Schwartz (2002) emphasizes the importance of e-mail for political activism. He writes "e-mail continues to be the most widely used activist tool . . . it is e- mail that we use to communicate with one another, and it is communication that makes collective action- the essence of advocacy- more possible." The author notes that" (Schwartz, 2002, p-).

E-mail has become an essential instrument of our work. Whatever digital divide may exist among American citizens at different economic levels, e-mail is now as important to our offices as phones and fax machines have been in the past. This is almost as true now for grassroots organizations as it has been for large corporations. Once an organization purchase a computer today, e-mail is not far behind. Indeed, a primary reason for groups to buy computers today is to be able to access the internet; the more organizations go online, the more pressure is placed on every other group to join them" (Schwartz 2002).

Schwartz then discusses three key uses of the e-mail for activism. The first is flash campaigns "which are online campaigns around specific issues or targets- a proposed piece of legislation. The second is "online petitions" by which specific legislature representatives are contacted either about a general issue or a specific bill. The third key issue is that of generating periodic update reports on the projection of advocacy efforts.

Resources

To the interested reader to pursue knowledge in this area the attached websites and publications are provided.

Nonprofit Informatics

    Association for Community Networking
    Bayer Center for Nonprofit Management, Robert Morris College
    Camp Yahoo
    Center for Non-Profit Technology
    CNET
    CompuMentor
    Coyote Communications
    CUSSNET Computer Users in the Social Services
    Desktop Assistance
    E-Base
    New Technology in the Human Services
    Non- Profit Matrix
    Non Profit Technology
    Non-Profit Info Tech
    NonProfit Technology Enterprise Network
    Non-Profit Zone
    Npotech
    N-Power
    OMB- Watch Nonprofit and Technology Project
    Social Informatics Home Page
    Software Tutorials from Indiana University
    Technical Resources for Non-Profits
    TechFoundation
    Tech Soup
    Technology Insights Newsletter for Nonprofits
    Technologies
    Technology Resources Catalog
    Tutorial Finder
    Wired for Good
    Bob Wood's Site on the Sociology of the Internet

References

Agre, P. (1999), Designing effective action alerts for the internet. Retrieved from the World Wide Web from http://dlis.gseis.ucla.edu/people/pagre/alerts.html

Bennett, D. & Fielding, P. (1999). The net effect: how cyberspace-advocacy is changing the political landscape. Merrifield, VA: E-Advocates Press.

Boland, K.M. (1998). Electronic advocacy: an introduction to the use of electronic techniques for social change. Boxboro, MA: New England Network for Child, Youth and Family Services. Available at http://www.nenetwork.org/infopolicy/ElecAdvo/index.html

Brainard, L.A. (2003). Citizen organizing in cyberspace: Illustration from health care and implications for public administration. American review of public administration. 33 (4) 384- 406.

Brainard, L.A. & Siplon, P.D. (2004). Toward nonprofit organization reform in the voluntary spirit: Lessons from the Internet. Nonprofit and Voluntary sector quarterly. 33 (3), 435-457.

Cornfield, M. (2004). Politics moves online. Washington, DC; Brookings.

Cyriac, J. (2000). Nonprofits use Internet as advocacy tool in cyber space. Public Interest Law Reporter 5 (3), 15-18.

Davis, S. Elin, L. & Reeher, G. (2002). Click on democracy: the internet's power to change political apathy into civic action. Boulder: Westview.

Grefe, E. (2003). E-campaigning: what it is and how to do it. Journal of Public Affairs 3 (2), 21- 27.

Hick, S. & McNutt, J. (Eds.). (2002). Advocacy and activism on the Internet: perspectives from community organization and social policy. Chicago; Lyceum Press.

John, S. & Thompson, S. (2003). Lobbying in the 21st century. Journal of Public Affairs 3 (2), 9-14.

Kaye, B.K. & Johnson, T.J. (2004). Web for all reasons: Uses and gratifications of internet components for political information. Telematics and informatics. 21, 197-223.

Levine, P. & Lopez, M.H. (2004). Young people and political campaigning on the internet. CIRCLE Fact Sheet available at http://www.circle.orgThe supportive studies are also available at this site.

McCaughey, M. & Ayers, M.D. (Eds.). (2003). Cyberactivism: on-line activism in theory and practice. New York: Routledge.

McNutt, J.G. & Appenzeller, G. (2004). The Three Ages of Cyberadvocacy: Prospects for the Future of Advocacy in Cyberspace. Paper Presented at Communication & Democracy: Technology & Citizen Engagement Colloquium, August 4-6, 2004, Freericton, New Brunswick.

McNutt, J.G. & Boland, K.M. (2003). Levels of electronic government development and citizen use of the internet for public policy change. Paper at the 32nd annual meeting of the Association of Voluntary Action Schoalrs, Denver, CO November, 20-22 [Juried].

SECTION C

Promoting Change within Social Service Organizations

Most organizations suffer from a varying degree of inefficiencies and problems. However, in organizations where the problems have a significant negative impact on meeting the intended goals of the program, it may be necessary for major or minor changes to take place in order to remedy the situation. Individuals can do a great deal to promote and effect helpful agency change.

Why promote change? Agencies fail partially or substantially in their missions to serve clients, families and/or communities. These short falls may reflect the problem of:

- *Ineffective agencies*- which could result from a number of causes, e.g. staff who are unable to deliver the intended interventions, weak program practices, insufficient funds, too large caseloads, lack of training.
- *Inappropriate/ineffective*- workers- this maybe be due to multiple reasons including lack of needed credentials or experience, lack of cultural sensitivity, and/or unprofessional behavior.
- *Ineffective interventions*- that can be attributed to numerous factors, e.g. failure to base interventions on research proven methods, outdated approaches, lack of cultural sensitive interventions, incorrect goal setting.
- *Failure to coordinate (with other providers)*- most social work clients need comprehensive services beyond the scope of a single agency; yet, agencies often don't link with other providers or do not adequately identify all the needs of clients.
- *Inaccessibility*- these barriers can include hours of operation, location, costs, lack of childcare, and lack of necessary language skills.
- *Inadequate outreach and community education*- some agencies do not provide outreach to clients who may have difficulties coming to central location; others fail to educate the community about its services.
- *Program implementation inconsistent with purposes*- occasionally, programs are not implemented in ways consistent with legislative or funding intent and may have represented a different direction than intended.
- *Plans to scale back or eliminate programs*- agencies often may scale back or eliminate programs; these may be related to budget issues or internal agency issues. Yet clients and the community may need these services.
- *Need for new programs or services*- frequently in providing services an agency may not in fact identify the need for new services or programs.

❖ *Lack of accountability-* the agency may not adequetly collect data on programs including usage and effectiveness and ineffective programs continue.

(Ezell, 2001, pgs. 54–59)

There are numbers of approaches to actually promoting change within the agency. There are several examples of texts that discuss agency change in great detail (Brager and Holloway, Changing Human Service Organization Policies and Practices. (1978); Ezell, Advocacy in Human Services (2000) and these are excellent resources for students. Based upon these texts and other writings, it is possible to articulate a framework for the promotion of agency change.

This framework articulates the following tasks:

(a)   Identifying the Change Goal

(b)   Analyzing the Forces Within the Agency that Support or Oppose the change.

(c)   Developing an Action Plan Including Strategies and Tactics

(d)   Implementing the Action Plan

(e)   Assessing/Evaluating the Impact of Actions; if changes occur then monitor implantation of changes or if changes do not occur develop revised strategies and/or tactics.

The tasks are discussed in greater detail below using the framework provided by Brager and Holloway in a classic social work text on change.

(a) Identifying the Change Goal

An analysis is necessary to identify a problem in current practice. In developing the specific goal, various alternatives are reviewed and some that may be discussed are impractical or not achievable. Further, in choosing a goal, we need to understand the difficulties in trying to achieve this objective. Questions such as: how complex is it? is a variation from agency norms and values? need to be analyzed. Goals may have to be "partialized" to make them achievable.

(b) Analyzing Forces In the Agency Either in favor or Opposed to the Goal

Our next step is to analyzing supporting and opposing forces in the agency to the goal. Who will be opposed to the goal? Who will favor the goal? How much power do people in opposition have? How much power will people in favor of the goal have? Understanding these factors and the political structure of the agency is crucial in building an action plan.

(c) Developing The Action Plan

The development of the action plan is part of the advocate's "homework" and is a continuation of the assessment in identifying the change goal and analyzing forces within the agency. Ezell notes "advocates should select their strategies and tactics based upon the specific change they wish effect as well as relevant circumstances both internal and external to the agency, including the history of advocacy" (Ezell. P. 61). He further suggests that the ultimate success of or even the opportunity of success rests on the advocates' monitoring of agency activities including it's planning and decision- making, budget preparation. In developing the action plan it is noted we should" expect the unexpected" (Brager and Holloway, p.128). Our action plan must include the potential impact of the proposal and the attitude of key actors) board, administration, staff towards the change? Our plan must take account of the degree to which it is possible to build collective support, e.g., can the change be made a "win- win situation?" We also need to ask "what are the sources for influencing behavior?" We further must understand our

motivation and our willingness to engage in risk?

Brager and Holloway define 3 types of tactics used in change actions;

collaborative, campaign and contest tactics. Collaborative tactics focus on open

communication, problem solving, joint action and mild persuasion. Campaign tactics fall

in between collaborative and conflict tactics and have elements of both. They include

"hard reassurance, political maneuvering, bargaining and negotiations and mild

persuasion." "Contest tactics is a greater action and pushes conflict a considerable

distance further and involves public conflict and public manifestos, the violation of

normative behaviors (e.g., moving out of bounds of demonstrations) and, in the extreme,

the violation of legal norm (e.g., disrupt operation by sitting in)."

(Brager and Holloway, pgs. 131–133)

(d) Implementing the Action Plan

Brager and Holloway suggest that the action activities have actually four phases:

"preinitiation, initiation, implementation and institutionalization." In each there is a

function or set of tasks that must be accomplished if the process is to move on to the

next phase. When their tasks are not completed, the process runs down. Viewing the

phases in terms of their intrinsic functions and tasks provides the practitioner with an

agenda or an approximate guide to issues in practice as the change process unfolds.

Preinitiation begins with the first act. It sets the stage for the introduction of the change-

creating the climate for organization. Initiation begins with the change is formally

introduced. The intent is to ensure a favorable introduction and win over actors to the

change. Coalitions are organized and seek to nullify opposition. This is the key phase of the process. Implementation is the stage of moving the organization of a formal

acceptance of change into it's normal operating procedures, e.g. a new program or rule.

Effective implementation is necessary to insure that the change is real.

Institutionalization is that phase of the process where the change is anchored in the

system so it becomes an outgoing component of organization life.

(e) Assessing and Evaluating the Impact of Change

The concluding step of this process is the assessment and the evaluation of the

change process: has the change been accomplished? Has it been accomplished as

intended? Has it been accomplished to reach the identifiable goal to be of benefit to the

client, community and the worker? This assessment requires the objective and subjective

assessment of the advocates his/her position. If the change is judged complete, this

advocacy activity can be deemed successful. If the change is only partially effective, the

advocate must decide: should we continue our work and how? If the change has not

occurred, the advocates must review the outcome and decide- should we continue? How?

What is needed? Do we need to change tactics? Is the goal unachievable? All their

questions are crucial to the process.

Example 1

Diane K. works in the adult outpatient clinic of a mental health agency. Most of the agency clients are enrolled in a single HMO. During the past six months relationships with the HMO have become more problematic.

Diane K, based upon skills she learned through her engagement in "change projects" in her MSW experience feels compelled to act. She approaches her supervisor, reviews the situation and requests her permission to survey other clinicians in the agency to document issues and concerns they confront with the managed care company. Diane not only asks her fellow clinicians for quantifiable information but asks them for case details. With persistence she collects the information from the 12 other clinicians in the adult clinic. Diane then tabulates and analyzes the data and drafts a 6-page report. With the permission of the supervisor a meeting is set with the clinicians and she reviews her report. In the course of the meeting the clinicians recognize that all share a range of common problems with this single HMO. A small task group (3 people) of the attendees agree to work with Diane. After several meetings the group finalizes a report that compiles the information, highlights key problems and make recommendations. The group then requests a meeting with the agency's Executive Director and Administrator and the Clinic Supervisor to review the report. The meeting with top administration and the staff goes very well and they decide they (the top administration) need to meet with the HMO to start negotiations to take corrective actions. Ultimately the negotiations lead to increased flexibility and a reduction of bureaucratic tape by the HMO.

Example 2

This second example is based on an actual change project conducted by a first year MSW student at New York University's Silver School of Social Work. The project was conducted at an emergency shelter for homeless adults. This shelter, in addition to housing provides food, showers, weekly medical and legal consultations and mental health and substance abuse counseling. The specific idea grew out of the student's analysis of the agency and gaps in services to clients. One of her observations was that women who are a minority of the clients at the agency, had less access to selected services than men. Her idea was to establish a women's support group. She commenced her work on developing the project by sharing her initial idea with agency staff. They were very supportive and offered useful suggestions. As part of the project she began by surveying adult female clients at the agencies as to their needs. Based upon the responses from these women she designed the content and structure of the support group. The group began as an 8- week pilot program and was evaluated by feedback provided by group members. The response to the group was overwhelmingly positive. As a result of the positive feedback about the project and the process used by the student involving the agency staff including the Executive Director, the agency has enthusiastically adopted the group. The agency has made an ongoing commitment to continue the group.

Issues for Students, the Profession and Schools of Social Work

Pursuing an advocacy agenda is not a simple task for the student. Neither the profession, schools of social work and our present society provide substantial encouragement. Yet, students as students, have important options. Frequently, student collectives/organizations can play an important role in (a) advocating with the school, e.g. to enhance/change curriculum, (b) in joining student groups/coalitions from other parts of a university to pursue social justice agendas (c) with a local professional group, e.g. NASW on lobbying, voter registration and (d) with local community coalitions on key issues. Finally, students individually and collectively can link with local, state or national groups to pursue social justice issues.

Although, we are in a period that seems not to value those within society that are most in need we can not lose our faith and energy.

SECTION D

Advocacy for Agency Changes

Agencies, regardless of the specific services they offer, have as their defined purpose to be responsive to the needs of individuals, families and groups in its community. Further, agencies should be culturally sensitive, offer services at days and times that are convenient to clients. Also, the opinions of consumers and the community should be solicited and their input sought into developing new programs and services. Yet, some social agencies don't implement their missions well and frequently, the needs of the clients and the community are not solicited. Further, community populations and needs may change and agencies, therefore, need to change. Thus, it is crucial for social workers to be advocates for change within their own agencies.

Social workers and social work students should have a basic understanding and teachings to promote change. This is not necessarily easy and requires substantial thought and planning. George Brager and Stephen Holloway in their classic 1978 text

Changing Human Service Organizations: Politics and Practice offer excellent

observations on these agency change activities. These observations are highlighted

below:

> Planned organizational change begins when an individual experiences a
> tension between the things as they are and things as he would like them to be.
> The actor considers a range of issues relating to the problem and subsequently
> judges it either unsolvable or amenable to change. Possible solutions are
> sounded out with trusted others, and a change idea is launched. The idea is
> debated and revised as various forces impinge on it until the organization is
> committed to a course of action. Once adopted, the change idea is actualized
> and, following a trail period, becomes an integral part of the organization's
> functioning. Planned organizational change is thus a series of events flowing
> through time – in other words, a process.

> We have selected five phases to characterize the process: (1) initial assessment,
> (2) preinitiation, (3) initiation, (4) implementation, and (5) institutionalization.

> Initial assessment, in our definition, is that phase of the change process in
> which the discrepancy between the actual and the desired state of affairs is
> recognized and some notions of what can be done about it are formulated.
> Relevant data are collected and organized, disciplined consideration is given to
> whether a change is feasible (and if so, *what* change), and a decision is made
> about attempting a remedy. If the decision is positive, further appraisal is
> necessary regarding specific courses of action. The worker must consider the
> tactics he will use to advance the change, along with the role to be played by
> both clients and himself.

> (Brager & Holloway, 1978, p.405)

The approaches they define include collecting dat.a on the problem or issue,

defining the change goal, identifying the critical factors and their possible roles in

advocating or opposing change. Brager & Holloway also urge exploring the tactics to

be utilized in promoting change. This thoroughly discusses how practitioners can

maximize their potential influence and their "positioning" themselves to be catalysts.

Further, they describe in great detail actions and directions needed to pursue the

change plan.

Gibelman, building on the pioneering works of Braga and Holloway,

highlights in Navigating Human Service Organization (2003) an overview of the

change process.

Elements of the Change Process

- Define the problem (one outcome of the needs assessment).

- Define the desired future state – How things should look when the change process is

  completed.

- Identify the level and degree of change required to move from the current state to the

  desired state.

- Identify the supporters of change and their influence and those who have a stake in

  maintaining the status quo.

- Consider the organization's culture and how culture supports or inhibits change.

- Define the people, financial, programmatic, and the procedural resources of the

  organization that must be garnered to achieve change.

- Plan and implement the action steps necessary to achieve change.

- Manage the transition.

- Monitor, evaluate, and stabilize the change.

(Gibelman, 2005 p.196)

In the sections that follow several examples of promoting agency changes are

given.

Example 1

A multi service agency was located in changing neighborhoods of a large urban setting. Among the services it provided were early childhood services e.g. nursery, early head start. The children and families served were usually working and middle class primarily white. Many of these families had parents and grandparents who had lived in this community. Yet, the nature of the population was changing. Young Mexican and other Central American families, some legal and some undocumented, were moving into the area. Two of the social workers in the agency who provided outreach services began noticing the change. They realized that the agency was not serving the population and that the agencies had no Spanish speaking staff. These two staff felt it would be important that the agency should serve these families and especially the young children.

With this in mind, they gather population data from the local planning department, spoke to a few of the families, and representatives of the school. To get support from the agency, they met with the Director of the Early Childhood division and together worked out a plan for expanding services to the new population and for hiring bilingual staff. They also built in ways to finance the new services. The Division Director went to the Agency Director and after he approved the idea, it was taken to the Board of Aging who also approved it. The program is in the process of outreach to the community and in hiring the first Spanish speaking social worker.

Example 2

Often as a result of declining budget, agencies often retrench funding for training programs and for conference attendance by the staff. An AIDS/HIV community operated agency, as a result of some budget declines, was forced to cut back and conference attendance. At the same time, agency staff were experiencing a sharp rise in the number of seriously mentally ill with drug and alcohol problems and who had HIV coming in for service. The staff felt they lacked the basic knowledge to help them address their mental health issues. A social work student placed in the agency had a very creative idea. She realized that there was a mental health center several blocks away and wondered if their staff had the knowledge and ability to educate seriously mentally ill about protective steps they could take to avoid becoming HIV infected. She called the Director of the Mental Health Center and discussed the issue with him. He indicated that work with population in HIV prevention education was important but not addressed. The student went back to the Director of the HIV program and suggested perhaps that agency and the Mental Health Center could develop a collaborative program in which the HIV/AIDS staff could train the Mental Health Center staff on HIV prevention and the Mental Health Center staff could train the HIV program staff on the basics of working with the seriously mentally ill. After 3 months of discussions, the collaborative program was established.

Example 3

A first year student had her internship in a new urban high school located in a primarily poor black and Latino community. As a new school one aspect that the students noted was missing was health education classes. This was of concern because based upon research for another class she recognized that younger students (9th graders) were very unlikely to use condoms and were at high risk for sexually transmitted infection and pregnancy. Undertaking research she identified a model health education that was appropriate for this age group and which relied heavily on open group discussion. With the approval of the Principal and key staff the program was implemented. The evaluation of the prospect showed positive results.

Concluding Observations

In this section we have reviewed numerous strategies for advocacy. Advocacy for change must be a key part of the social work agenda. It is imperative for students to understand the crucial role of promoting social justice as a part of social work. Incorporating this value into your identity as a professional social worker you will take a major step in serving the society, the community and your clients.